Seattle & Portland For Dummies, 1st Edition

BESTSELLING BOOK SERIES

D0281373

Sea...

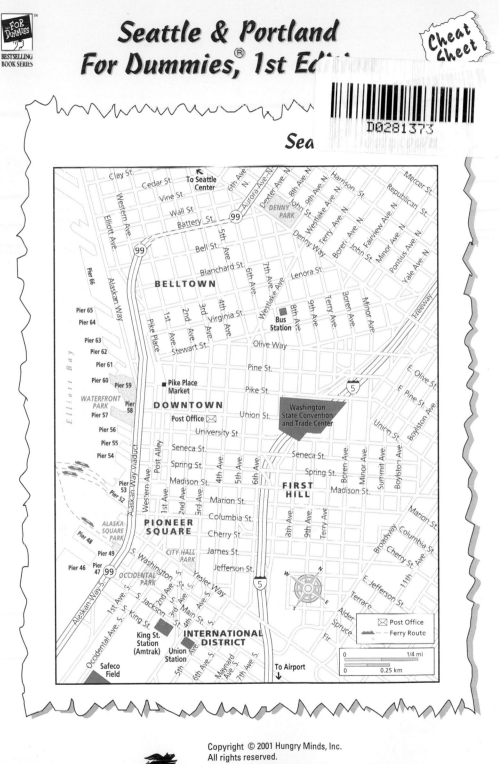

Hungry Minds™

For more information about Hungry Minds,
call 1-800-762-2974.

For Dummies: Bestselling Book Series for Beginners

Portland Neighborhoods

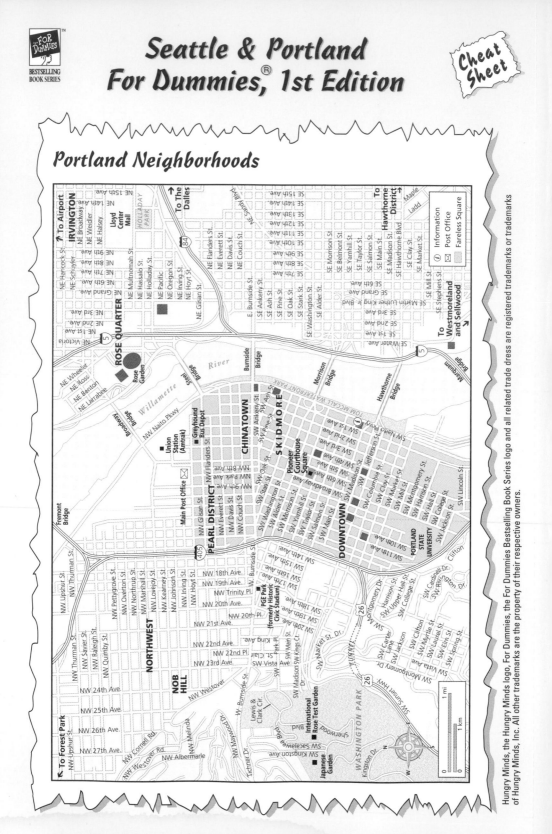

TM

References for the Rest of Us!™

Seattle & Portland

FOR

DUMMIES®

1ST EDITION

by Jim Gullo

Hungry Minds™

Best-Selling Books • Digital Downloads • e-Books • Answer Networks
e-Newsletters • Branded Web Sites • e-Learning

New York, NY ◆ Cleveland, OH ◆ Indianapolis, IN

Seattle & Portland For Dummies,® 1st Edition

Published by:
Hungry Minds, Inc.
909 Third Avenue
New York, NY 10022
www.hungryminds.com
www.dummies.com

Library of Congress Control Number: 2001092733

ISBN: 0-7645-5382-8

ISSN: 1535-7457

Printed in the United States of America

10 9 8 7 6 5 4 3 2 1

1B/RV/QY/QR/IN

Distributed in the United States by Hungry Minds, Inc.

Distributed by CDG Books Canada Inc. for Canada; by Transworld Publishers Limited in the United Kingdom; by IDG Norge Books for Norway; by IDG Sweden Books for Sweden; by IDG Books Australia Publishing Corporation Pty. Ltd. for Australia and New Zealand; by TransQuest Publishers Pte Ltd. for Singapore, Malaysia, Thailand, Indonesia, and Hong Kong; by Gotop Information Inc. for Taiwan; by ICG Muse, Inc. for Japan; by Intersoft for South Africa; by Eyrolles for France; by International Thomson Publishing for Germany, Austria and Switzerland; by Distribuidora Cuspide for Argentina; by LR International for Brazil; by Galileo Libros for Chile; by Ediciones ZETA S.C.R. Ltda. for Peru; by WS Computer Publishing Corporation, Inc., for the Philippines; by Contemporanea de Ediciones for Venezuela; by Express Computer Distributors for the Caribbean and West Indies; by Micronesia Media Distributor, Inc. for Micronesia; by Chips Computadoras S.A. de C.V. for Mexico; by Editorial Norma de Panama S.A. for Panama; by American Bookshops for Finland.

For general information on Hungry Minds' products and services please contact our Customer Care department; within the U.S. at 800-762-2974, outside the U.S. at 317-572-3993 or fax 317-572-4002.

For sales inquiries and resellers information, including discounts, premium and bulk quantity sales and foreign language translations please contact our Customer Care department at 800-434-3422, fax 317-572-4002 or write to Hungry Minds, Inc., Attn: Customer Care department, 10475 Crosspoint Boulevard, Indianapolis, IN 46256.

For information on licensing foreign or domestic rights, please contact our Sub-Rights Customer Care department at 212-884-5000.

For information on using Hungry Minds' products and services in the classroom or for ordering examination copies, please contact our Educational Sales department at 800-434-2086 or fax 317-572-4005.

Please contact our Public Relations department at 212-884-5163 for press review copies or 212-884-5000 for author interviews and other publicity information or fax 212-884-5400.

For authorization to photocopy items for corporate, personal, or educational use, please contact Copyright Clearance Center, 222 Rosewood Drive, Danvers, MA 01923, or fax 978-750-4470.

Hungry Minds™ is a trademark of Hungry Minds, Inc.

About the Author

When not swilling frequent cups of coffee or mowing his way through the Pike Place Market's food stalls, Seattle-based writer **Jim Gullo** travels the world on assignment for magazines that include *Islands, Diversion,* and the *Alaska Airlines Magazine.* He is also the author of *Just Let Me Play,* the autobiography of golfer Charlie Sifford, and a three-act comedy entitled *Held Over in Pottstown.* You can find him on various playgrounds hoisting jump shots or challenging all comers to games of two-on-two with his 12-year-old son, Mike.

Dedication

To Kris, Mike, and Joe, my favorite urban dwellers.

Author's Acknowledgments

Many thanks to all of the restaurateurs, hoteliers, tour operators, and public relations mavens who so generously provided information and access for this book. A special thanks to Gretchen Heilshorn and Deborah Wakefield of the Portland Oregon Visitors Association, as well as Bette Sinclair, for their excellent assistance on Portland matters, Titian-haired Alexis Lipsitz Flippin for her fine editorial hand, and, in Seattle, David Blandford of the Seattle King County Convention & Visitors Bureau, Norma Rosenthal, Tamara Wilson, and the inestimable Lorne Richmond, whose puny backhands are so easily smashed across the ping-pong tables of western Washington.

Publisher's Acknowledgments

We're proud of this book; please send us your comments through our Online Registration Form located at www.dummies.com.

Some of the people who helped bring this book to market include the following:

Editorial

Editors: Alexis Lipsitz Flippin, Development Editor; Mary Goodwin, Project Editor

Copy Editor: Mary Goodwin

Cartographer: Elizabeth Puhl

Editorial Manager: Jennifer Ehrlich

Editorial Administrator: Michelle Hacker

Editorial Assistant: Jennifer Young

Senior Photo Editor: Richard Fox

Assistant Photo Editor: Michael Ross

Cover Photos:
Front Cover:
© Hollenbeck Productions
Back Cover:
© Craig Tuttle/The Stock Market

Production

Project Coordinator: Jennifer Bingham, Maridee Ennis

Layout and Graphics: Amy Adrian, Joyce Haughey, Jacque Schneider, Julie Trippetti

Proofreaders: David Faust, Marianne Santy, Charles Spencer, TECHBOOKS Production Services

Indexer:
TECHBOOKS Production Services

General and Administrative

Hungry Minds, Inc.: John Kilcullen, CEO; Bill Barry, President and COO; John Ball, Executive VP, Operations & Administration; John Harris, CFO

Hungry Minds Consumer Reference Group

Business: Kathleen Nebenhaus, Vice President and Publisher; Kevin Thornton, Acquisitions Manager

Cooking/Gardening: Jennifer Feldman, Associate Vice President and Publisher; Anne Ficklen, Executive Editor; Kristi Hart, Managing Editor

Education/Reference: Diane Graves Steele, Vice President and Publisher

Lifestyles: Kathleen Nebenhaus, Vice President and Publisher; Tracy Boggier, Managing Editor

Pets: Dominique De Vito, Associate Vice President and Publisher; Tracy Boggier, Managing Editor

Travel: Michael Spring, Vice President and Publisher; Brice Gosnell, Publishing Director; Suzanne Jannetta, Editorial Director

Hungry Minds Consumer Editorial Services: Kathleen Nebenhaus, Vice President and Publisher; Kristin A. Cocks, Editorial Director; Cindy Kitchel, Editorial Director

Hungry Minds Consumer Production: Debbie Stailey, Production Director

◆

The publisher would like to give special thanks to Patrick J. McGovern, without whom this book would not have been possible.

◆

Contents at a Glance

Maps at a Glance

Table of Contents

Introduction

What do you know about Seattle and Portland, the two urban anchors of that mountainous, forested region tucked away in the farthest corner of the United States, an area collectively known as the Pacific Northwest? Maybe you've visited here once or twice; maybe you've passed through on your way to Canada or Alaska; or maybe you've simply been intrigued by what you've heard and read. For a long time, both cities made all of those "Best Places to Live" lists, and media stories extolled the beautiful views, the clean air, and the forward-thinking urban planning. That caused about a million Californians to move here — only to leave a year or two later because it rained too much in the winter. Then for some reason, the winter rains detoured south, and for several years the Pacific Northwest enjoyed near-perfect weather while Los Angeles flooded.

Seattle went on to make more news: downtown demonstrations, riots in the streets, and *boom!*, a major earthquake, the biggest in these parts in more than 50 years. The high-tech and Internet industries created another kind of boom here, and then almost as quickly began to shake out. The picture, it appeared, was not nearly as rosy as it had been only ten years ago. So what, you might ask, is really going on in the Pacific Northwest?

The short answer is that everything is just fine. The streets are safe, the earthquake damage has been swept away, and the weather continues to be just lovely, as far as I'm concerned. Those of us who have chosen to make it our home are very, very fond of the place and eager to show it off at a moment's (or a relative's) notice. Hence, I've written this guidebook, which attempts to steer you toward the places I know and love about Seattle and Portland.

You're coming at a good time, whether it's your first visit or you're returning for another slice of the Northwest pie. If you haven't been to Seattle since the early-1990s, you won't recognize the place — the city has undergone major renovations and renewal in the last five years. The high-tech boom was very generously shared by all of those Microsoft millionaires who invested in the community and helped fund, among other things, a new symphony hall, a sparkling new ballpark, and new museums, and helped transform whole neighborhoods like Belltown. Portland, too, has enjoyed a prosperity that has the city bustling and building. With the exception of traffic, which continues to be lousy, both places have managed to hang on to a quality of life that is cherished by its proud residents. This book is the first step toward helping you discover the best of the Pacific Northwest in general, and Seattle and Portland in particular.

About This Book

This book is designed to get you quickly acclimated to Seattle and Portland and to provide you with the best, most essential ingredients for a great vacation. As a travel writer who's been in the business for several years, I find that traditional guidebooks often drown the reader in too much information — leaving the reader high and dry, trying to make sense of it all. Here, I've done the legwork for you, offering my expertise and not-so-humble opinions to help you make savvy, informed decisions in planning your trip. What you *won't* find here is a numbing phone-book-style directory of every single place to eat, sleep, and do your laundry in Seattle and Portland or statistics of people who have registered satisfaction with a particular restaurant or attraction. Frankly, those kinds of guidebooks make my eyes glaze over. In *Seattle & Portland For Dummies,* 1st Edition, I cut to the chase. I've chosen my favorites in many categories and put them into a form you can easily access to make your own decisions, whether it's from your living room couch while you're watching *Frasier* (which is set in Seattle), or wandering the Pike Place Market looking for Frasier (he doesn't actually live here, I'm sorry to tell you). I also want to give you a good idea of where to go to find things on your own, because I feel that a major part of travel is the discovery of your own favorite places and experiences along the way.

This book is designed for you to flip to the exact parts you want at any given moment. Dog-ear the pages, make notes in the margins, attack it with a highlight pen, spill mustard on the parts you don't need, or tear them out and throw them to the winds (but if you want to act like a Northwesterner, you'll recycle them). You can even find pages in the back to use for notes, along with worksheets to help you plan your budget and other facets of your trip.

Our esteemed legal team (the highly annoying Fractious, Soomee, and Torte) wishes to add that the travel industry changes rapidly, especially in terms of prices. In other words, if things cost a tad more (or less) by the time you use this book, don't blame me. Rates are always subject to change, and you should call, surf the Web, or fax ahead of time to make sure that places are still open, restaurants are still seating, ballgames are still being played, and kids are still welcome before you embark on your trip to the great Northwest. And if you find that a certain coconut-cream pie I've highly recommend is less than scrumptious, I'm sorry about that, too. (But I'm betting you'll love it.) Finally, if you're nose-deep in my brilliant analysis of the Pearl District and you trip over a Dungeness crab on the sidewalk, it's not my fault. Fractious, Soomee, and Torte have spoken.

Foolish Assumptions

In writing this book, I made some of the following assumptions about you, the reader:

- ✔ You may be an inexperienced traveler who is interested in Seattle and Portland and wants to know when to go and how to arrange your trip. Maybe you're a little nervous about traveling to such a distant corner of the country, and you want to know exactly what to expect.

- ✔ You may be an experienced traveler who has visited the region before, but you want an informed opinion to help you plan your latest vacation; you want to know what's new, and you want to quickly access information.

- ✔ If you live practically anywhere in the United States, Seattle and Portland are a heck of a long way away, and making the trek to the Northwest may involve a significant portion of your vacation time and budget — so you want to be sure you do it right and plan the best vacation possible.

- ✔ You're not alone, and you realize that hundreds of thousands of visitors come to the Northwest every year. I want to give you the tools to make your own, unique choices in Seattle and Portland so that you aren't simply following the crowds from place to place.

If any of these assumptions ring a bell with you, then *Seattle & Portland For Dummies,* 1st Edition, is your guidebook of choice.

How This Book Is Organized

This book is divided into seven parts, which cover all of the major aspects of your planning and your trip. Since I cover two cities here, I combine some of the up-front information (such as how to plan your budget), but then break Seattle and Portland out separately in their own specific parts. Within each of the seven major parts, you find a number of chapters that help you quickly find the specific information you want and need. The Table of Contents at a Glance and the complete Table of Contents that preceded this introduction are perfect tools for finding general and specific information. At the back of the book you find worksheets and quick listings of helpful service information and phone numbers.

Part 1: Getting Started

Here's where that old proverbial ball gets rolling with some information on when to plan a trip to the Northwest, some events to keep in mind, and a framework for establishing your budget, as well as a preliminary list of good reasons why Seattle and Portland are so much fun to visit.

Part II: Ironing Out the Details

Details, details. Should you look into a package tour? What kind of lodging is right for you? How can you get the best bang for your buck? Should you buy travel insurance? Do you need traveler's checks? After you read this part, the suitcase is pretty much on the bed and ready to be packed!

Part III: Settling in to Seattle

Arriving in a new city and getting acclimated is one of the great joys of travel, and this part makes it easy. Here's where you really get to know the Emerald City and address those two very basic human needs: food and shelter. You find out where things are located in the city, get reviews of hotels, figure out how to get around town, and (after you've worked up a good appetite) read about the best places to eat.

Part IV: Exploring Seattle

The Space Needle beckons, the Experience Music Project invites you inside, and the Pike Place Market reserves a flying fish in your name in this part, which offers maximum information on the best things to do and see in and around Seattle, with special sections for exploring the city with kids and teens. You also find invaluable tips on organizing your time in order to explore the city more efficiently.

Part V: Settling in to Portland

Now you move down I-5 and over the Oregon border to Portland, the Rose City, and quickly get acclimated to the layout. You see how to get around the city, how to find your hotel, and how to decide which place is just right for you. By the end, you'll be figuratively tucking in to a fine Portland meal of sturgeon and pinot noir wine from an Oregon winery after a discussion of the city's lively food and restaurant scene.

Part VI: Exploring Portland

Here you discover Portland's marvelous gardens and attractions, beginning with the International Rose Test Garden, which gives the Rose City its nickname. If you're a runner or hiker, you may find the section on great places for jogging and Portland's enormous urban park invaluable. Parents can discover the best places to bring the kids and teens, and book and art lovers are steered to fantastic bookstores and galleries. Here too are tips on day trips you can easily make from Portland into the rugged Oregon countryside and be back in time for dinner.

Part VII: The Part of Tens

I offer some tips on pronouncing place names correctly so you won't sound like such a tourist when you come, as well as suggestions on the right clothing to pack so that you not only learn the Northwest lingo, but dress the part as well. I also tell you about some not-to-miss food sensations to be found in the area

Conventions and Icons Used in This Book

I list the hotels, restaurants, and attractions in this book alphabetically. I use the following series of abbreviations for credit cards in the hotel and restaurant reviews:

AE: American Express

DISC: Discover Card

DC: Diners Club

MC: MasterCard

V: Visa

For most of you, cost is a factor in choosing hotels and restaurants. To cut out the hassle of closely reading to find out the exact prices of places, I denote the relative cost of things with dollar signs. My scale ranges from one dollar sign ($) to four ($$$$) for restaurants and accommodations. To see the chart for each individual city's different price scales, go to the Seattle and Portland hotel and dining chapters.

I also include several icons scattered around the book to alert you to special cases or particularly useful information.

The Tip icon delivers some inside information and advice on things to do or ways to best handle a specific situation that can save you time or money.

The Heads Up icon tells you when you should be especially aware of a situation that may be potentially dangerous, a tourist trap, or, more likely, a rip-off. In other words, Heads Up!, and be especially alert.

Families with kids in tow may appreciate the Kid Friendly icon, which identifies places and attractions that are welcoming or particularly suited to kids.

Bargain! Bargain! The Bargain Alert icon tells you when you're about to save a bundle, or suggests ways that you can cut costs.

Especially created for this book is the Northwest icon, which points to attractions or things that you shouldn't miss that are unique to Seattle, Portland, or the Pacific Northwest.

Where to Go from Here

Huh? I thought that was obvious. Get on a bus, plane, train, or car and head to Seattle or Portland as fast as you can and have a blast. You may find, as so many other people have, that this is your favorite place in the whole country to visit, and you'll be reaching for this book again soon to plot your return.

Part I
Getting Started

The 5th Wave — By Rich Tennant

"Don't worry son. By the looks of it I imagine that cloud's headed straight for Seattle."

In this part . . .

The two preeminent cities of the Pacific Northwest are primed for visitors, each boasting stellar sights and attractions in a majestic setting. Here in Part I, I help you plan your trip soup to nuts, with loads of helpful insider information and advice. I've done all the planning legwork for you, taking you through every aspect of trip preparation — from budgeting your vacation to finding the best value in airfares to working with travel agents. Want to know the best season to come? Are discounts available for seniors or children? Can tacked-on taxes tip a tight budget? Look no further; the answers are here. You get a calendar of events, money-saving tips, and special advice for seniors, gay and lesbian travelers, and travelers with disabilities. All the major planning bases are covered here, so that once you get to Seattle and Portland, all you have to do is sit back and enjoy.

Chapter 1

Discovering the Best of Seattle and Portland

In This Chapter

▶ Views you only see in the Northwest

▶ A palette of new flavors to explore

▶ Gorgeous gardens and fine wines

▶ Mr. Gates's neighborhood

▶ Outerwear makes the Northwesterner

. . . .

*O*utside my window, as I write this, a floatplane is flying across the city on its way home from the San Juan Islands. It is superimposed against a tall, craggy range of mountains in the distance that is covered in snow, and below it are glimpses of a blue waterway. Spread out before me are hills blanketed with trees and houses. It's no exaggeration to say that my favorite view of Seattle is the one from my office window.

I'm not alone. Plenty of people who call Seattle or Portland their home enjoy sensational vistas from their own front doors. You, too, will come away from Seattle and Portland with your own favorite moments and scenes. Maybe it will be the view at sunrise of **Mount Rainier** or **Mount Hood,** or the sight of a solitary ferry crossing **Puget Sound** from your hotel window. Maybe it will be a tour of a gorgeous garden, or the fun your family has together on a perfect summer day. You'll also come to understand the differences between the two cities, because in the minds of many people who've never actually spent time here or just passed through, the two cities are virtually indistinguishable. Both share gorgeous Northwest scenery and climate, but you'll find that the character of each is very different.

In the following pages, I offer up a few images for you to savor as you contemplate your trip, a kind of appetizer to the fully-laden buffet that follows. With all of the attention to details that a big trip or vacation requires — from budgeting, to buying tickets, to packing, to making sure the cat's fed while you're gone — it's good to remember the payoff you'll receive when you finally arrive. Come back to this chapter whenever you need to remember *why* you're taking a visit to the Northwest, and the planning and plotting will only get easier.

Of Mountains and Water

The landscapes of the Pacific Northwest, surrounding Seattle and Portland, truly are unlike anything you've ever seen. Seattle is flanked by high mountain ranges on two sides: the **Cascades** to the east and the **Olympics** to the west. Both ranges are dusted with snow almost all year long and offer great vistas from nearly every corner of the city. To the south of the city lies magnificent **Mount Rainier,** one of the tallest peaks in the continental United States, which looms overhead like a giant sentinel. Portland has **Mount Hood** to the east, another high Cascades peak, and old flat-top, **Mount St. Helens,** to the north, which blew its lid nearly 30 years ago. Then there are the waterways that snake through both cities, offering peaceful landscapes and great recreation. In Seattle, there is **Puget Sound** and its many bays that lap up against the city's western edge, and two big urban lakes that are connected to the sound by a placid canal. Portland is cut in half by the broad **Willamette River** and rimmed to the north by the **Columbia River,** which forms the border between Washington and Oregon. Mountains, water, and trees are the defining physical features of this area, and you will not want for splendid photo opportunities.

A Palette of Northwest Flavors

Oysters and clams are grown in the bays and estuaries of Puget Sound. Dungeness crabs are piled high on fishmongers' tables. Salmon and halibut are flown in fresh from Alaska. Washington grows more apples than any other state, as well as peaches and cherries, and in Oregon you can buy hazelnuts or forage for wild mushrooms. It all adds up to a culinary feast and a distinctive cuisine that local restaurants ply with vigor and finesse. Add to that the myriad Asian influences that have permeated Pacific Northwest cooking, as well as a broad selection of excellent French, Italian, and Continental-style restaurants. Many people are content to graze their way through the **Pike Place Market,** with its lunch-counter-style restaurants and food sellers, to gain an instant appreciation for the diversity of foods that the region offers. Finish it off with a slice of huckleberry pie and, of course, a cup of caffe latte for the full Northwest experience.

Days of Wine and Roses, Portland Style

Portland is known for its distinctive gardens and urban parks full of trees and hiking trails. The **International Rose Test Garden** blooms with hundreds of varieties of roses during the summer months, when the whole city gets into the spirit and celebrates the monthlong **Rose Festival.** Other magnificent gardens offer the serenity of Japanese and Chinese influences. The wine part? It comes from the plethora of Oregon wineries, many of which are located within an hour's drive of the city, busily producing first-rate pinot noirs, among other fine wines.

Because Bill Gates Lives Here

Seattle is in the midst of a renaissance, a fine symbol of which is the presence of Bill Gates, the world's richest man, who continues to live and work here. Although you may not see Bill or his equally affluent sidekick Paul Allen, their influence is spread across the region. Seattle has become known for its philanthropies: The Gates Foundation is the largest charitable organization in the world and donates millions to health and computer-literacy programs. Allen is very active in preserving forests and funding medical research. You can see the benefits of local philanthropy when you visit the new symphony hall, football and baseball stadiums, and museums like **Allen's Experience Music Project.** You can also drive out to the suburb of Redmond to see the campus of Microsoft or take a boat tour that passes by the waterfront estate that Gates built a few years ago.

Provisioning for the Gold Rush

Seattle, and to a lesser extent, Portland, have been centers of commerce since the days when gold-rushers stopped here to buy provisions for their expeditions north. The cities are known for producing fine outerwear, and they share a casual, comfortable, active-living approach to fashion. You'll find plenty of stores that can outfit your own personal expedition into the Northwest-casual lifestyle of jeans, flannels, comfortable shoes, and outerwear.

Chapter 2

Deciding When to Go

● ●

● ●

*R*ain or shine, Seattle and Portland are year-round destinations, pulsing with events and activities spring, summer, fall, and winter. So no matter when you come, you're guaranteed to experience the best that the Pacific Northwest has to offer.

The Secret of the Seasons

It's a myth! It's a fantasy! It's a vicious lie perpetuated by disgruntled Californians! No, it doesn't rain *all* the time in the Pacific Northwest; it only rains when you come to visit (just kidding). Yes, Seattle and Portland are known the world over for their soggy climates, but if you come expecting constant, steady deluges of rain, you may be in for a surprise.

As the tourism boards of both cities are quick to point out, in terms of annual rainfall, the areas receive less than New York and Boston. But it usually rains more than 200 days a year here, with periods of steady drizzle interspersed with sun breaks. On the plus side, however, it rarely freezes or snows in this neck of the woods — particularly in Seattle, where one snowfall per year is about the norm, and it rarely sticks around for more than a day. Portland is prone to cold snaps that fly down the Columbia River Valley and ice the city for a few days at a time every winter. In both cities, winter high temperatures generally hover around a mild 50 degrees. Locals will take that and a little rain over blizzards and bone-chilling lows anytime.

Spring

Spring is great in Seattle and Portland for the following reasons:

- ✔ The crocuses and daffodils begin to bloom as early as late February, and the trees of the Pacific Northwest begin to bud and flower.
- ✔ Safeco Field opens up again for a new season with the Seattle Mariners baseball club, and the NBA playoffs get under way with (usually, at least) appearances by the Seattle SuperSonics and Portland TrailBlazers.

But keep in mind that the weather can be maddeningly cool and damp this time of year, with the same gray, 50-degree days in February continuing right up to the first of July.

If you plan to spend the day outdoors, you may need to wear layers — a turtleneck under a fleece jacket under an overcoat, for example — that you can peel away as the day warms up . . . or keep on if it doesn't.

Summer

Summer is great in Seattle and Portland for the following reasons:

- ✔ From the 5th of July to the end of September, the weather is typically gorgeous and sunny, averaging 75 to 80 degrees nearly every day. Thanks to daylight savings time and northern latitudes, summer sunlight can extend well past 8:30 p.m.
- ✔ Opportunities to participate in the Northwest's range of outdoor activities — hiking, boating, paddling, and bicycling — are unlimited.
- ✔ Seattle and Portland put on their biggest and best annual festivals, drawing hundreds of thousands of residents and visitors alike for food, music, and entertainment.

But keep the following things in mind if you visit during this time:

- ✔ Summer is the peak season for visitors. The hotels are all packed and charging top dollar, and you can have plenty of competition for space in restaurants, ferries, and downtown parking.
- ✔ June is typically the most disappointing month, weather-wise — you keep expecting summer to unfold, and the gray dampness lingers; July and August are the best if you can schedule yourself accordingly.

Fall

Fall is great in Seattle and Portland for the following reasons:

- Most tourists clear out after Labor Day, but the September weather is clear and gorgeous, leaving you to enjoy summer-style activities with far fewer crowds.

- Northwest produce is at its peak, and along with berries, apples, and mushrooms, you have access to the freshest crabs, oysters, and salmon from Northwest waters.

- The leaves begin to turn color in October, with beautiful, New England-like landscapes to explore in many parts of the Northwest.

But keep in mind that the end of daylight savings time means that darkness descends on the Northwest before 6 p.m., and gray, cloudy weather begins to move in for days at a time by mid-October.

Winter

Winter in Seattle and Portland is great for the following reasons:

- Seattle and Portland hotels compete like crazy to offer discounted rates, with programs available through and sponsored by the local tourist boards.

- The cultural seasons of each city are in full swing, with new exhibitions opening at art museums, plays premiering, and opera, ballet, and symphony available nearly every night.

- The downtown areas are spruced up and alive with holiday shoppers, and Oregon's no-sales-tax policy provides instant discounts.

But keep in mind that the parks will be mushy and wet, colors are muted, and days can be gray and dark from dawn to early dusk. You'll need your raincoat, waterproof shoes, and a hat (but not an umbrella, which marks you as a tourist).

Seattle Calendar of Events

In this section I list a select few of Seattle's nonstop annual festivals and events. Please check the Web sites or call the numbers I give to confirm dates and times before you plan your vacation; events are subject to change.

Some of Seattle's finest events include the following:

- **January:** Seattle kicks the year off with the **Seattle International Boat Show,** a huge exhibition of sailboats, yachts, kayaks, and canoes for the boating-crazy Northwest at the Stadium Exhibition Center. Call ☎ **206-634-0911;** Internet: www.seattleboatshow.com. Late January.

✔ **May:** The Seattle Center is the site for the **Northwest Folklife Festival,** a weekend of international folk entertainment that draws thousands of people to Seattle Center for dance, music, crafts, and food. Call ☎ 206-684-7300; Internet: www.nwfolklife.org. Memorial Day weekend.

Also happening in May is the **Seattle International Film Festival,** which holds premieres and international screenings at theaters around the city. Call ☎ 206-464-5830; Internet: www.seattlefilm.com. Late May to mid-June.

✔ **July:** During the **Bite of Seattle,** the city's top restaurants set up booths for zillions of starving visitors who stroll around Seattle Center, forks in hand, sampling small dishes from several of their favorite eateries. Go early and bring an appetite. Call ☎ 206-684-7200; Internet: www.seattlecenter.com. Third weekend in July.

Seafair is Seattle's biggest festival of the year, with parades downtown, foot races, hydroplane boat races on Lake Washington, and appearances by the Blue Angels aerobatic team. Call ☎ 206-728-0123; Internet: www.seafair.com. Early July to early August.

✔ **September: Bumbershoot,** the Seattle Arts Festival, is a delirious weekend of entertainment, with every venue at Seattle Center open and jammed with patrons taking in popular music, dance, literary readings — the works. Save yourself a long wait in line by buying advance tickets at a participating retailer (usually Starbucks). Call ☎ 206-281-1111; Internet: www.bumbershoot.com. Labor Day weekend.

✔ **December:** Don't miss **New Year's Eve at the Space Needle,** when Seattle's favorite landmark ushers in the new year with a grand fireworks show at midnight. Call ☎ 206-443-2111; Internet: www.seattlecenter.com.

Portland Calendar of Events

In this section I list a select few of Portland's nonstop annual festivals and events. Please check the Web sites or call the numbers I give to confirm dates and times before you plan your vacation; events are subject to change.

You can look forward to the following events in Portland:

✔ **February:** The **Portland International Film Festival** imports three weeks worth of artful films from around the world, shown in several downtown venues. Call ☎ 503-221-1156; Internet: www.nwfilm.org. Generally the second weekend in February through the last weekend.

✔ **May:** Help celebrate the **Cinco de Mayo Festival,** one of the largest Hispanic fests in the country, held at Tom McCall Waterfront Park. Call ☎ **503-222-9807;** Internet: www.cincodemayo.org.

✔ **June:** The **Portland Rose Festival** is the city's major blowout, with events throughout the entire month that include parades, the crowning of a Rose Queen, and lots of beautiful floral displays around the city. Hotel rooms can be very tough to come by, so book well ahead. Call ☎ **503-227-2681;** Internet: www.rosefestival.org. Month of June.

✔ **July:** The **Oregon Brewers Festival** brings one of the city's favorite libations, craft-brewed beer, to center stage at Tom McCall Waterfront Park. Call ☎ **503-778-5917;** Internet: www.teleport.com.

✔ **August: The Bite: A Taste of Portland** is the Rose City's eating extravaganza, with dozens of booths set up in Tom McCall Waterfront Park, offering some of the best dishes from local restaurants. Go early; it's packed. Call ☎ **503-248-0600;** Internet: www.biteofportland.com. Mid-August.

✔ **November:** The Christmas **Festival of Lights,** at The Grotto, offers a holiday light show at a lovely, serene religious site, with live choral music. Call ☎ **503-254-7371;** Internet: www.thegrotto.org. Late-November to Christmas.

✔ **December:** During the **Christmas Ship Parade**, the boats of Portland don lights and parade on the Willamette and Columbia Rivers. Internet: www.christmasships.org. Two weeks in December.

Chapter 3

Planning Your Budget

● ●

In This Chapter

▶ Building a budget for your trip to Seattle or Portland

▶ Uncovering any hidden expenses

▶ Traveler's checks, cash, credit cards: Planning what to bring

▶ Discovering cost-cutting tips for the savvy traveler

● ●

*A*nybody remember John D. Hackensacker III? He was a wealthy rube played by Rudy Vallee in Preston Sturges's great comedy *The Palm Beach Story*. John D. was rich beyond compare, but he had a niggling little habit: He loved to whip out a notebook and record every single expense he incurred, to the last nickel, all the while wooing Claudette Colbert on a journey to Palm Beach. Claudette was not amused by this Uncle Scrooge–like behavior, and in the end, it was someone other than poor John D. who got the girl.

I'm not saying that budgeting your trip isn't important. It is. You can get a good idea of the expenses you can expect to pay on your visit to Seattle and/or Portland by utilizing the "Making Dollars and Sense of It" worksheet in the back of this book. This worksheet breaks down the approximate hotel, transportation, food, and entertainment expenses from the minute you leave home until the moment you return. But don't let a budget rule your life: Think of it as a framework that gives you an approximate idea of your financial limitations. Having to pass up a great Northwest meal of Dungeness crab or fresh salmon, having to miss an opportunity to see a TrailBlazers or Mariners game, or having to forgo a production of the Seattle Opera's vaunted *Ring* trilogy (if you're lucky enough to get tickets) would truly be a pity.

Build a good 20 percent cushion into your budget so that you won't feel deprived when opportunities present themselves during your trip. And they will. But don't worry: Seattle and Portland are very reasonably priced places to visit, with few or none of the stratospheric temptations that are regularly available in New York or San Francisco. You can find plenty of ways to cut corners and get back on budget, and I offer suggestions on how to do so in this chapter. Just promise me that you won't have your nose stuck in an accounting notebook when a pod of killer whales swims by the ferryboat in Puget Sound or fireworks light up the Willamette River. Take heed from the sorry tale of John D. Hackensacker.

Adding Up the Elements

Your vacation budget consists of the following main elements. Depending on your preferences (and your appetite), where you lay your head at night should run about equally with food as your major expenses in Seattle and Portland, but beware of those pesky hidden expenses. Here, I list what you should expect to pay, on average, for lodging, transportation, dining, attractions, and shopping and entertainment in Seattle and Portland.

Lodging

Both cities provide a wide range of lodging opportunities, and you don't have to head to the outskirts of town in order to save money on hotels. Aside from the big, downtown luxury hotels, where rooms set you back $250 per night and up, you have several options for cheaper accommodations that are located centrally. Midsize hotels and the plethora of boutique hotels that are unique to Seattle and Portland offer rooms for around $150, and budget places can be had for $100 or less a night. Hostelers who don't mind sharing bathrooms can find beds for under $20 in great downtown locations. Each city also has several B&B options for rooms in the $75 to $90 range, and many new hotels built out of restored apartment houses offer rooms with furnished kitchenettes.

Many inns include breakfast in the tariff, which can save you a few more bucks every day. See Chapters 6 and 7 for a more thorough breakdown of money-saving lodging opportunities.

Transportation

Use of public transportation and cabs can cut your transportation costs down dramatically in Seattle and Portland, particularly if you're staying in the downtown areas and don't need a rental car for most of your visit (see Chapter 11 and 21). Renting cars from downtown agencies can fill in your needs for getting out of town on day trips.

Costs can jack up dramatically if you have to park a car downtown (most Seattle hotels charge $18 per day for parking), but parking on neighborhood streets is usually free — and you can take a handy bus ride to and from your parking place.

Dining

Food is such a huge part of the Northwest experience that budgeting yourself out of the chance to eat well in Seattle and Portland would be a shame. Sure, both cities have fast-food joints and the same family-style chain restaurants that you can find in every burg from Missoula, Montana, to West Orange, New Jersey. But where else can you get fresh king salmon and Northwest oysters; hazelnuts, blackberries, and Rainier cherries; clams, mussels, and Dungeness crabs; fresh apples and asparagus; and those ubiquitous cups of caffe latte? And while you're in the neighborhood, shouldn't you try an award-winning bottle of Oregon pinot noir, Washington merlot or chardonnay, or one of the dozens of excellent microbrew beers so renowned in the Pacific Northwest? Of course you should!

You can eat very well indeed at the many upscale restaurants springing up in Seattle's **Belltown** and Portland's **Pearl District** for $40 to $80 per person, not including wine. I say make room in your budget for at least one of these splurges, and then cut costs by eating inexpensively, but well, at places like the **Pike Place Market** in Seattle, diners, or local family restaurants. Portland, especially, offers tons of places that serve great pizza and burgers where an entire family can eat quite well and soak up some local atmosphere for under $30. This is one corner of the country where you can easily avoid fast-food chain places altogether without compromising your budget.

Attractions

The sightseeing attractions in Seattle and Portland may end up being the biggest bargains on your trip. Plenty of attractions and things to do are free, and the area museums, tours, and other attractions (with the exception of the wildly-overpriced **Experience Music Project** in Seattle, at $20 per adult and $15 per child) are very reasonable. It costs very little to hike at **Mount Rainier** or **Mount Hood,** visit the spooky remains of **Mount St. Helens,** or watch your kids play in the big, computerized fountain at **Seattle Center.**

You can easily balance your activities budget by mixing expensive outings or big events with cheap fun like going to **parks,** watching the salmon and boats run through the **Ballard Locks,** visiting the excellent **zoos** in Portland and Seattle, or just taking a **ferryboat ride** for $3.50. Lingering at a **sidewalk cafe** with a glass of microbrew beer or caffe latte and watching the parade of Northwesterners pass by is an awfully inexpensive way to enjoy a nice morning or afternoon.

Shopping and entertainment

With half of the people in Seattle (and three-quarters of those in Portland) dressed casually in jeans and flannel shirts, you probably won't feel a huge, overwhelming urge to blow a fortune shopping for new clothes while you're here. You certainly can do so if you like, and then you can break the rest of the bank on cool housewares and gifts. But shopping isn't an overwhelming part of the local scene.

As far as activities go, it's up to you and your lifestyle when it comes to the importance of going out every night and spending money on music, beer, and entertainment. Both Seattle and Portland have plenty of bars and clubs where microbrews run $3 and $4, and cover charges are usually a modest $5 or so. Even fairly pricey activities have bargain opportunities. Cheap theater, music, and symphony tickets, for example, can be purchased at half-price ticket windows at two locations in Seattle.

If you're interested in seeing the **Seattle SuperSonics** basketball team, family tickets are offered every month for just $9 a ticket (including a hot dog and soft drink), which you can only buy from the Key Arena box office with all family members in tow.

Keep an eye peeled for inexpensive concerts in parks and public places, such as Portland's **Pioneer Courthouse Square,** particularly in the summer months when the weather is nice enough for outdoor concerts.

Watch Out for Hidden Expenses!

Oh, those hidden charges — they can blow up a budget faster than you can say "Have you seen my wallet, honey?"

Oregon has no sales tax, but in Washington the sales tax is 8.8 percent. Both places charge additional taxes on hotel rooms, and rental car taxes are nearly through the roof. (That's why you should make a point of enjoying **Safeco Field** when you visit Seattle; you and a zillion other tourists paid for it through special taxes.)

If your budget is tight, inquire about all of the added taxes when you make your hotel or car reservation, because the added tax can really make a difference in how many days you decide to rent or stay. Keep in mind that when you buy tickets to concerts, ballgames, or special events from TicketMaster, you pay a surcharge. Try to buy tickets directly from each event's box office to get the best price.

Traveler's Checks, Credit Cards, ATMs, or Cash?

I don't want to suggest that you forgo bringing traveler's checks — they're still the safest way of carrying money — but you may not need them here in the Northwest as much as you would in other parts of the country or abroad. Seattle and Portland are very safe cities, and incidences of street crimes, like mugging or pickpocketing, are few and far between. On top of that, many small businesses and restaurants are reluctant to cash traveler's checks, especially in amounts over $20. You just may find that traveler's checks are more trouble than they're worth.

Both Seattle and Portland have a zillion ATM machines, not only at banks throughout the downtown areas and the neighborhoods, but in convenience stores, grocery stores, and public places like **Seattle Center, Safeco Field,** and the **Rose Garden.**

You can use an ATM to get a cash advance from your credit card (if necessary, carry the PIN number for your card with you). You may well find that your ATM card and a credit card (preferably MasterCard or Visa) are the only methods of payment you need. See Chapters 12 and 22 for specifics on getting to your money in Seattle and Portland, respectively.

Hot Tips for Cutting Costs

Even people with the biggest pockets don't like to throw money away for no good reason. There's a little cost-cutter in everyone, I say. Here are some savvy money-saving tips for chipping away at your vacation budget:

- ✔ **Take advantage of seasonal rates.** Hotel rates are generally lower in the slower seasons. The time of year you decide to visit may affect your bargaining power more than anything else. During the peak season — basically summer — when a hotel is booked up, management is less likely to extend discount rates or value-added package deals. In the slower season — winter — when capacity is down, they're often willing to negotiate.

  Both cities have great winter promotional deals. Seattle's Super Saver promotion lists some three dozen hotels, most of which are in the downtown core, that cut prices dramatically between November and March (call the reservations line directly at ☎ **800-535-7071** or book online at www.seattlesupersaver.com). Portland's winter promotion is the Portland Big Deal (☎ **87-PORT-LAND**), which includes attractions, performances, and restaurants in the package, with the rates in effect from October 1 to May 31.

- ✔ **Make use of membership discounts.** Membership in AAA, AARP, or frequent flier/traveler programs often qualifies you for discounted rates. You may also qualify for corporate, student, or senior discounts even if you're not an AARP member, although I highly recommend joining (see Chapter 4 for details). Members of the military or those with government jobs may also qualify for price breaks.

- ✔ **Ask about package deals.** Even if you're not traveling on an all-inclusive package, you may be able to take advantage of packages offered by hotels and condos directly. See Chapter 5 for more details on package tours.

✔ **Call the hotel direct in addition to going through central reservations.** See which one gives you the better deal. Sometimes the local reservationist knows about packages or special rates, but the hotel may neglect to tell the central booking line.

✔ **Surf the Web to save.** A surprising number of hotels advertise great value packages via their Web sites, and some even offer Internet-only special rates (see Chapter 7 for more on Internet booking services).

✔ **Consult a reliable travel agent.** A travel agent can sometimes negotiate a better price with certain hotels and assemble a better-value complete travel package than you can get on your own. Even if you book your own airfare, you may want to contact a travel agent to price out your hotel. On the other hand, hotels, condos, and even B&Bs sometimes discount your rate as much as 30 percent — the amount they'd otherwise pay an agent in commissions — if you book direct. For more advice on the pros and cons of using a professional go-between, see Chapter 5.

✔ **Book your rental car at weekly rates when possible.** If you simply must have a car, keep in mind that weekly rates are generally considerably lower than daily rates. See Chapters 11 and 21 for details.

✔ **Reserve a hotel room with a kitchenette or a condo with a full kitchen, and do your own cooking.** You may miss the pampering that room service provides, but you can save lots of money. Even if you only prepare breakfast and an occasional picnic lunch in the kitchen, you still save significantly in the long run.

✔ **Ask whether the kids can stay in your room.** A room with two double beds usually doesn't cost any more than one with a king-size bed, and most hotels don't charge an extra-person rate when the additional person is your kid.

✔ **Enjoy a takeout lunch in a picnic setting.** Get something to go from **Pike Place Market** in Seattle, for example, and take it to **Myrtle Edwards Park** or **Discovery Point.** In Portland, enjoy a midday picnic in **Washington Park.** See Chapters 13 and 23 for more tips on cutting food costs.

Chapter 4

Planning Ahead for Special Travel Needs

. . . .

In This Chapter

▶ Planning a no-fuss family vacation

▶ Discovering special deals for seniors

▶ Enabling the disabled

▶ Finding gay-friendly communities and resources

. . . .

*V*isitors of all sizes, stripes, and ages flock to Seattle and Portland, and the cities respond in kind, happy to put out the welcome mat for any and all. Here are some travel tips and invaluable resource information for travelers with special needs or preferences.

Advice for Families

Seattle and Portland are both kid-friendly cities, with plenty of activities to keep the little ones amused and loads of outdoor spaces to let them blow off excess energy. Keep in mind that not all hotels have swimming pools, and the few that have outdoor pools only keep them open for a few months of the year. By the same token, don't expect to catch much swimming time on a Puget Sound or Columbia River beach: The water is freezing, even during the hottest part of the summer. If in your kids' estimation it just isn't a proper vacation if the lodging doesn't have a pool, then make sure that your hotel choice has one — preferably indoors. I point out in my hotel recommendations which places have pools and which have in-room Nintendo.

You'll do a fair amount of walking in either city, and a good stroller is an absolute necessity if you're traveling with toddlers, especially when tackling Seattle's steep hills. When museums and sightseeing get to be too much for the young ones, head to the wonderful neighborhood parks, many of which have swings and slides. Ask your hotel's front desk for the nearest one, or look in the Yellow Pages under Parks and Recreation for a list. Kids will also love a visit to the amusement park rides in **Seattle Center** and at **Oaks Bottom** park in Portland.

When it comes to food, you needn't forgo a great Northwest meal if your child's idea of eating seafood is fish sticks. Most restaurants offer kids' menus or offer kid-friendly burgers or pastas. You could also let them pick and choose their own meals from the familiar options at the food court at **Westlake Center** or the stalls at **Pike Place Market,** which sell everything from noodles to fresh doughnuts.

For those moms and dads who crave a night on the town or a grown-up dinner without children in tow, many hotels offer baby-sitting services. If your hotel does not have such a service, try **Best Sitters** (☎ **206-682-2556**) in Seattle and **Wee Ba-Bee Child Care** (☎ **503-786-3837**) in Portland.

If you get to the point where you're all sick and tired of sightseeing or it's pouring buckets outside, keep in mind that both Seattle and Portland are a cinemaphile's dream, and you're likely to find a movie theater within a few blocks of where you're staying.

Advice for Seniors

People over the age of 60 are traveling more than ever before. And why not? Being a senior citizen entitles you to some terrific travel bargains. If you're not a member of **AARP,** the **American Association of Retired Persons,** 601 E St. NW, Washington, DC 20049 (☎ **800-424-3410** or 202-434-AARP; Internet: www.aarp.org), do yourself a favor and join. You'll get discounts on car rentals and hotels.

Mature Outlook, P.O. Box 9390, Des Moines, IA 50322 (☎ **800-336-6330**), is a similar organization, offering discounts on car rentals and hotel stays at many Holiday Inns, Howard Johnsons, and Best Westerns. The $19.95 annual membership fee also gets you $200 in Sears coupons and a bimonthly magazine. Membership is open to all Sears customers 18 and over, but the organization's primary focus is on the 50-and-over market.

In addition, most of the major domestic airlines, including American, United, Continental, US Airways, and TWA offer discount programs for senior travelers — be sure to ask whenever you book a flight. In most cities, people over the age of 60 get reduced admission at theaters, museums, and other attractions, and they can often get discount fares on public transportation. Carrying identification with proof of age can pay off in all these situations.

The Mature Traveler, a monthly newsletter on senior-citizen travel, is a valuable resource. It is available by subscription ($30 a year); for a free sample send a postcard with your name and address to GEM Publishing Group, Box 50400, Reno, NV 89513 (E-mail: maturetrav@aol.com). GEM also publishes **The Book of Deals,** a collection of more than 1,000 senior discounts on airlines, lodging, tours, and attractions around the country;

it's available for $9.95 by calling ☎ **800-460-6676.** Another helpful publication is **101 Tips for the Mature Traveler,** available from Grand Circle Travel, 347 Congress St., Suite 3A, Boston, MA 02210 (☎ **800-221-2610;** Internet: www.gct.com).

Grand Circle Travel is also one of the literally hundreds of travel agencies that specialize in vacations for seniors, but beware: Many of them are of the tour-bus variety, with free trips thrown in for those who organize groups of 20 or more. Seniors seeking more independent travel should probably consult a regular travel agent. **SAGA International Holidays,** 222 Berkeley St., Boston, MA 02116 (☎ **800-343-0273**), offers inclusive tours and cruises for those 50 and older.

Advice for Travelers with Disabilities

A disability shouldn't stop anybody from traveling. There are more options and resources out there than ever before. For the most part, Seattle and Portland are both well-equipped for disabled or handicapped travelers. Most of Seattle's city buses have wheelchair lifts, and drivers will help a wheelchair traveler get to a secure space on the bus. The city's hills can be awfully difficult to negotiate, but picking your spots and planning excursions carefully can help flatten the journey. With its packed sidewalks and cobblestone streets, the **Pike Place Market** in Seattle can be tough to negotiate by wheelchair, but the Market has elevators that can lift you to or from Western Avenue and the waterfront. **Experience Music Project** has an elevator on Fifth Avenue that can lift you to the level of its main entrance.

Portland is flatter and more manageable than Seattle. All MAX trains have wheelchair lifts and dedicated wheelchair spaces, as do many of **Tri-Met's** buses. Tri-Met may also be able to offer special door-to-door service to visitors; call ☎ **503-238-4952** for information.

Disabled travelers can get more general information from **A World of Options,** a 658-page book of resources for disabled travelers around the world, which covers everything from biking trips to scuba outfitters. It costs $35 and is available from **Mobility International USA,** P.O. Box 10767, Eugene, OR, 97440 (☎ **541-343-1284,** voice and TYY; Internet: www.miusa.org). Another place to try is **Access-Able Travel Source** (Internet: www.access-able.com), a comprehensive database of travel agents who specialize in disabled travel; it's also a clearinghouse for information about accessible destinations around the world.

Many of the major car rental companies now offer hand-controlled cars for disabled drivers. Avis can provide such a vehicle at any of its locations in the U.S. with 48-hour advance notice; Hertz requires between 24 and 72 hours of advance reservation at most of its locations.

Wheelchair Getaways (☎ **800-536-5518** or 606/873-4973; Internet: www.wheelchair-getaways.com) rents specialized vans with wheelchair lifts and other features for the disabled in more than 35 states, plus the District of Columbia and Puerto Rico.

Travelers with disabilities may also want to consider joining a tour that caters specifically to them. One of the best operators is **Flying Wheels Travel,** P.O. Box 382, Owatonna, MN 55060 (☎ **800-535-6790;** Fax: 507-451-1685). They offer various escorted tours and cruises, as well as private tours in minivans with lifts. Another good company is **FEDCAP Rehabilitation Services,** 211 West 14th St., New York, NY 10011. Call ☎ **212-727-4200** or fax 212-727-4373 for information about membership and summer tours.

Vision-impaired travelers should contact the **American Foundation for the Blind,** 11 Penn Plaza, Suite 300, New York, NY 10001 (☎ **800-232-5463**), for information on traveling with seeing eye dogs.

Advice for Gay and Lesbian Travelers

Seattle and Portland are both welcoming and tolerant of gay lifestyles, but keep in mind that when you leave either city and venture out into parts of rural Washington and Oregon, the acceptance levels can go south in a hurry. Seattle's most gay-friendly neighborhood is **Capitol Hill,** where a popular Gay Pride March is conducted down Broadway every year in June. The **Seattle Gay News** (☎ **206-324-4297**) is a free community newspaper that you can find in most Capitol Hill bars and restaurants. The **Pink Pages** (☎ **206-238-5850**) is a directory of gay-friendly businesses. Find both at the **Beyond the Closet Bookstore** (☎ **206-322-4609;** 518 East Pike St.), which also has a great deal of resource information and a bulletin board. There is also a **Lesbian Resource Center** (☎ **206-322-3965;** 2214 South Jackson St.) for all types of referrals.

In Portland, **Just Out** (☎ **503-236-1252**), generally found at **Powells** bookstore, is a monthly newspaper for the gay community. They also publish a gay and lesbian business directory. Powells will also have copies of Portland's Gay and Lesbian Community Yellow Pages.

Part II
Ironing Out the Details

THE HARRISONS PREPARE FOR THEIR MOUNTAIN BIKING VACATION IN SEATTLE'S OLYMPIC NATIONAL PARK.

Awesome move, Mom.

In this part . . .

In Part I, I lay out the groundwork for your trip to Seattle and Portland. In this part, I get down to the nitty-gritty: offering hard-working advice on the best ways to get around once you're there, how to avoid driving in rush-hour traffic, how to book tickets and reservations online, and the pros and cons of package tours. I provide invaluable tips on packing and what kind of clothes to bring, what to do if you get sick away from home, and advice on when to make advance reservations for events or special meals — all the last-minute details to help make your trip a smooth and safe one!

Chapter 5

Getting to Seattle and Portland

· ·

In This Chapter

▶ Using a travel agent

▶ Comparing escorted tours and package tours

▶ Making your own travel arrangements

▶ Finding the best airfare

▶ Getting to Seattle and Portland by car, train, or bus

· ·

*Y*ou've read about all the great attractions Seattle and Portland have to offer. You're sold on the notion that either would make a great vacation destination, and you're rarin' to go. Now it's simply a matter of figuring out the best way to get there.

Travel Agent: Friend or Foe?

A good travel agent is like a good mechanic or a good plumber: hard to find, but invaluable once you've got the right person. And the best way to find a good travel agent is the same way you found that good plumber or mechanic — by word of mouth. Any travel agent can help you find a bargain airfare, hotel, or rental car. But a good travel agent stops you from ruining your vacation simply trying to save a few dollars. The best travel agents can tell you how much time you should budget for each destination, find a cheap flight that doesn't require that you change planes three times, get you a hotel room with a view for the same price as a lesser room, arrange for a competitively priced rental car, and even give recommendations on restaurants.

Travel agents work on commission. The good news is that *you* don't pay the commission — the airlines, accommodations, and tour companies do. The bad news is that unscrupulous travel agents often try to persuade you to book the vacations that land them the most money in commissions.

In the past few years, some airlines and resorts have begun limiting or eliminating travel agent commissions altogether. The immediate result has been that travel agents don't bother booking these services unless the customer specifically requests them. But some travel industry analysts predict that if other airlines and accommodations follow suit, travel agents may have to start charging customers for their services.

Here are a few hints for tracking down the travel agent of your dreams:

- ✔ **Ask friends.** Your best bet, of course, is a personal referral. If you have friends or relatives who have a travel agent they're happy with, start there. Not only is this agent a relatively proven commodity already, but she's extra-likely to treat you well, knowing she'll lose two customers — not just one — if she screws up your vacation.

- ✔ **Go with what you know.** If you're pleased with the service you get from the agency that books business travel at your workplace, ask if it also books personal travel. Again, here's another relatively proven commodity — one that has a vested interest in not screwing up. Also, because business travel tends to be booked in volume, a lot of the agencies that specialize in this kind of business act as consolidators for certain airlines or have access to other discounts that they can extend to you for your personal travel.

- ✔ **Go to the travel agent source.** If you can't get a good personal or business referral, contact the **American Society of Travel Agents (ASTA)** (Internet: www.astanet.com), the world's largest association of travel professionals, which can refer you to one of its local member agents. ASTA asks that all its member agents uphold a code of ethics and has its own consumer affairs department to handle complaints and help travelers mediate disputes with ASTA member agencies. This doesn't guarantee that you'll get an agent you're thrilled with, but it's a giant step in the right direction and offers you a measure of consumer protection in case something goes wrong.

Once you have referrals and the names of recommended travel agents, it's time to refine your search and look for an agent whose qualifications match your needs. Here are some tips for choosing the right travel agent for you:

- ✔ Look for an agent that specializes in planning vacations to your destination.

- ✔ Choose an agent who's been in business a while and has an established client base.

- ✔ Consider everything about the agent, from the appearance of his or her office to the agent's willingness to listen and answer questions.

Remember: The best agents want to establish a long-term relationship with a client, not just make one sale.

Escorted Tours: Sit Back and Enjoy the Ride

Many people prefer to experience a destination on escorted tours, whether by bus, motor coach, train, or boat. Escorted tours let travelers sit back and enjoy their trip without having to spend lots of time behind the wheel. All the little details are taken care of for you; you know your costs up front; and there are few surprises. Escorted tours can take you to the maximum number of sights in the minimum amount of time with the least amount of hassle — and you don't have to sweat over the planning and plotting of a vacation schedule. It's no wonder that many people derive a certain ease and security from an escorted tour.

What you *give up* when you choose to take an escorted tour is a certain freedom of movement and spontaneity — the opportunity to discover a destination on your own, find a gem of a restaurant, or stumble upon a charming back road. That's why you may want to select an escorted tour with some flexibility in the schedule to allow you time to explore on your own.

Ask before you buy

If you do decide to take an escorted tour, ask a few simple questions before you buy:

- **What's the cancellation policy?** Do I have to put a deposit down? Can they cancel the trip if they don't get enough people? How late can I cancel if I'm unable to go? When do I pay? Do I get a refund if I cancel? If they cancel?

- **How jam-packed is the schedule?** Do they try to fit 25 hours into a 24-hour day, or is there ample time for relaxing, shopping, or hitting the pubs? If you don't like getting up at 7 a.m. every day and returning to the hotel at 6 or 7 p.m. at night, certain escorted tours may not be for you.

- **How big is the group?** The smaller the group, the more flexible the tour and the less time you'll spend waiting for people to get on and off the bus. Tour operators may be evasive about this because they may not know the exact size of the group until everybody has made their reservations, but they should be able to give you a rough estimate. In fact, some tour companies have a minimum group size, and they may cancel the tour if they don't book enough people.

✔ **What's included?** Don't assume anything. You may have to pay to get yourself to and from the airport. Or a box lunch may be included in an excursion, but drinks might cost extra. Or beer might be included, but wine may not. Find out if you're allowed to opt out of certain activities or meals and if the tour bus schedule is flexible. Ask also about meal preferences: Can you can choose your own entree at dinner, or does everyone gets the same chicken cutlet?

Tours of the Pacific Northwest

If you want to undertake a long tour of the Pacific Northwest and wind up in either Seattle or Portland, several tour companies will be happy to put you on the bus for one of those "If this is Thursday, that must be the Space Needle" tours. **Collette Travel Service** of Rhode Island (☎ **401-728-3805;** Internet: www.collettetours.com), which started out 80 years ago providing tours of Boston, packages a nine-day trip that begins in Northern California and winds up in Seattle, with daily stops along the way in Oregon and Washington. It also offers a nine-day tour that begins and ends in Seattle and explores the San Juan Islands and north Cascades mountain range.

On a similar track is **Globus Tours** (☎ **303-797-2800;** Internet: www.globusandcosmos.com). Globus began business by rowing people across Lake Lugano in northern Italy and then transporting them by bus across Switzerland. It's now a huge international tour operator that moves more than 500,000 tourists a year and can take you to Seattle or Antarctica with equal ease. In the Northwest, they do an eight-day tour of Seattle and the San Juan Islands that visits Victoria, British Columbia, and winds up in Vancouver, Canada. The dizzying 11-day trip starts in Portland, races around the mountains of central Oregon and then the Oregon coast, dashes north to Seattle, and then heads off to scenic mountain villages in the north Cascades and the San Juan Islands. Whew!

The Ins and Outs of Package Tours

Package tours are not the same thing as escorted tours. They're simply a way to buy your airfare, accommodations, and other elements of your trip (car rentals, airport transfers, and sometimes even activities) at the same time — kind of like one-stop vacation shopping.

For popular destinations like Seattle and Portland, packages can be a smart way to go because they can save you money. In many cases, a package that includes airfare, hotel, and transportation to and from the airport costs you less than just the hotel alone if you booked it yourself. That's because packages are sold in bulk to tour operators, who resell them to the public. It's kind of like buying your vacation at Sam's

Club or Costco, except that it's the tour operator who buys the 1,000-count box of garbage bags and resells them ten at a time at a cost that undercuts what you'd pay at your average neighborhood supermarket.

What's the catch?

You almost always save money when you go the package route, but you may also have limited choices, such as a small selection of hotels to choose from or a fixed itinerary that doesn't allow for an extra day of shopping. Some packages offer a better class of hotels than their competitors while others offer the same hotels for lower prices. Some packages offer flights on scheduled airlines while others book charters. Some offers are only valid on specific travel dates while other packages have more flexible travel times. Some packages let you choose between escorted vacations and independent vacations while others allow you to add on a few guided excursions or escorted day trips (also at prices lower than if you booked them yourself) without booking an entirely escorted tour.

Which package is right for you depends entirely on what you want; the time you spend shopping around will be well rewarded.

How to tell the deals from the duds

Once you start looking at packages, the sheer number of choices may overwhelm you — but don't let them. Use these tips to help you distinguish one from the other and figure out the right package for you.

- **Read this guide.** Do a little homework. Decide what cities, towns, and attractions you want to visit, and pick the type of accommodations you think you'll like. Compare the rack rates that I list in this book against the discounted rates being offered by the packagers to see if you're actually being given a substantial savings, or if they've just gussied up the rack rates to make the full-fare offer sound like a deal. And remember: Don't just compare packagers; compare the prices that packagers are offering on similar itineraries. The amount you save depends on the deal; most packagers can offer bigger savings on some packages than others.

- **Read the fine print.** When you're looking at different packages, make sure you know exactly what's included in the price you're quoted and what's not. Don't assume anything: Some packagers include everything but the kitchen sink, including lots of extra discounts on restaurants and activities, while others don't even include airfare. Believe it or not, lots of airline packages don't include airfare in the prices — these packagers know better than anybody how fares can fluctuate, and they don't want to get locked into a yearlong airfare promise.

✔ **Know what you're getting yourself into — and if you can get yourself out of it.** Before you commit to a package, make sure you know how much flexibility you have. Some packagers require ironclad commitments, while others go with the flow, perhaps charging minimal fees for changes or cancellations. Ask the right questions: What's the cancellation policy if my kid gets sick at the last minute and we can't go? What if the office calls me home three days into my vacation? What if we have to adjust our vacation schedule; can we do that?

✔ **Use your best judgment.** Keep your antennae up for fly-by-nights and shady packagers. If a package appears to be too good to be true, it probably is. *Go with a reputable firm with a proven track record.* This is where your travel agent can come in handy; he or she should be knowledgeable about different packagers, the deals they offer, and the general rate of satisfaction among their customers. If the agent doesn't seem savvy, take your business elsewhere.

Where to find the packager for you

The best place to start looking is the travel section of your local Sunday newspaper. Also check the ads in the back of national travel magazines like *Travel & Leisure, National Geographic Traveler,* and *Condé Nast Traveler.* Then call a few package tour companies and ask them to send you their brochures. The biggest hotel chains also offer packages. If you already know where you want to stay, call the hotel and ask if they offer land/air packages.

For one-stop shopping on the Web, go to www.vacationpackager.com, an incredibly extensive Web search engine where you can link up with hundreds of different package tour operators and custom design your very own package.

Buying packages through the airlines

Another good resource are the airlines themselves, which often package their flights together with accommodations. When you pick an airline, you can choose one that has frequent service to your hometown and/or one on which you accumulate frequent-flier miles. Buying your package through an airline is a safe bet — you can be pretty sure that the company will still be in business when your departure date arrives, and the prices are usually comparable to what you get from other packagers.

Although you can book most airline packages directly with the airline itself, your local travel agent can also do it for you. No matter who's doing the booking, you should be sure to give the airline your frequent-flier account number. Most airline packages reward you with miles based not only on the flight, but on all the dollars you're spending, which can really add up and earn you credit toward your next vacation.

Among the airline packages, your options include:

- ✔ **American Airlines Vacations** (☎ **800-321-2121**; Internet: www.aavacations.com)

- ✔ **Continental Airlines Vacations** (☎ **888-898-9255**; Internet: www.coolvacations.com)

- ✔ **Delta Vacations** (☎ **800-872-7786**; Internet: www.deltavacations.com)

- ✔ **US Airways Vacations** (☎ **800-455-0123**; Internet: www.usairwaysvacations.com)

Package tours to Seattle and Portland

For Seattle or Portland-specific tours, look to the airlines, which package vacations by combining airfare and hotel with an option for a rental car. **Horizon Airlines** (☎ **800-547-9308**; Internet: www.vacations.alaskair.com), the regional carrier of Alaska Airlines, can set you up in either city, with rooms at the Roosevelt or Paramount hotels in Seattle, or the Paramount or Benson hotels in Portland. **American Airlines Vacations** (☎ **800-433-7300**; Internet: www.aavacations.com) offers hotel packages in Seattle only, with rooms at the Westin or Madison Renaissance hotels.

Another good option is **Gray Line of Seattle** (☎ **800-426-7505**), a motorcoach tour company that offers a number of package options throughout the Northwest. Their Northwest Triangle tour is a 7-day, 6-night swing from Seattle, with a city tour and a visit to Mount Rainier, to Victoria, British Columbia, and Vancouver, Canada. Another week-long option goes from Seattle to the San Juan Islands, Vancouver, and the ski resort town of Whistler, British Columbia, before returning to Seattle via Victoria. They offer three different hotel pricing options, utilizing the Holiday Inn Express, Paramount Hotel, Warwick Hotel, and Renaissance Madison Hotel.

If you book a package tour that winds up in either Seattle or Portland, see if the tour operator offers an extension stay on your hotel room rate that allows you to stay put in either city for a few days. You may be able to get a better rate this way, but be sure to check on other offers to be sure you get the best deal possible.

The Independent Traveler: Making Your Own Arrangements

An escorted or package tour may be just the ticket for some vacationers. Others wouldn't dream of letting anyone else plan their trip. If you're a do-it-yourselfer, the following information should prove invaluable.

The airline players in the Northwest

Seattle's Sea-Tac Airport and Portland's PDX Airport are served by most of the big hitters in the airline biz. Major regional carriers, with the most arrivals and departures from and to west coast cities, are **Alaska Airlines** (☎ 800-426-0333; Internet: www.alaskaair.com) and its regional carrier, **Horizon Airlines** (☎ 800-547-9308; Internet: www. horizonair.com), which serves smaller airports in Washington, Oregon, Montana, Idaho and northern California; **Southwest** (☎ 800-435-9792; Internet: www.southwest.com), and **United** and **Shuttle by United** (☎ 800-241-6522; Internet: www.ual.com). The big boys who come into the region are **American Airlines** (☎ 800-433-7300; Internet: www.aa.com), **America West** (☎ 800-235-9292; Internet: www. americawest.com), **Continental** (☎ 800-525-0280; Internet: www. flycontinental.com), **Delta** (☎ 800-221-1212; Internet: www. delta.com), **Northwest** (☎ 800-225-2525; Internet: www.nwa.com), **TWA** (☎ 800-221-2000; Internet: www.twa.com), and **US Airways** (☎ 800-428-4322; Internet: www.usairways.com).

International carriers who fly directly into Seattle are **Air Canada** (☎ 800-776-3000; Internet: www.aircanada.ca), **British Airways** (☎ 800-247-9297; Internet: www.british-airways.com), **Asiana Airlines** (☎ 800-227-4262; Internet: www.air.asiana.co), and **Scandinavian Air** (☎ 800-221-2350; Internet: www.flysas.com). For a complete list of all carriers who use Sea-Tac, check out the airport's Web site at www.portseattle.org/seatac. Portland isn't on the route maps of international carriers; you have to change to a domestic carrier in New York, Dallas, Atlanta, or Chicago. For the carriers who serve PDX (Portland Airport), see www.portlandairportpdx.com.

Don't forget that airlines are consolidating and cross-promoting each other's frequent-flier programs like crazy these days. Alaska Airlines, for example, has co-benefits with American, Northwest, and several international carriers, and if you fly an Alaska Airlines flight, you can charge the miles to your frequent-flier account on those airlines, or vice-versa. Be sure to check with your frequent-flier program to see which regional carriers are included, and make sure they enter the appropriate frequent-flier account when you buy the ticket or check in for your flight.

Tips for getting the best airfare

The regional carriers that serve Seattle and Portland offer the best deals on the West Coast for getting to either city. These include **Alaska Airlines, Horizon Airlines, Shuttle by United,** and **Southwest.** Look to them first when you begin shopping for airfares. Shuttle by United is hooked into the enormous United route system, and Southwest has recently begun to branch out across the country, offering good fares to Seattle from cities like Baltimore, Cleveland, Detroit, and Tampa. Here are some other invaluable tips on getting the best airfare:

- ✔ **Shop around.** It's not unusual to find that the 11 people sitting in a row on a sold-out flight have paid 11 different fares; your mission is to be the one who paid the least. It's prudent to shop as much as possible for the best fare before you buy and to even check back with the airline if you bought your ticket in advance to see if a lower fare has been instituted before you travel — fares can be raised or lowered to any destination at any time. You almost never get an advertised bargain on airfares to the Pacific Northwest in the high-season summer months of July and August (remember, I said *almost*), but check anyway to see if some bean-counter at an airline decided to try to corner the market with a special sale.

- ✔ **Be flexible.** Since most airlines cater to business travelers who have to be sitting in that boardroom meeting at a specific time and date, you can have a lot of leverage if your travel dates are flexible. When you book your ticket, ask if lower rates are available on other departure or arrival dates or times.

- ✔ **Buy well in advance.** This usually secures the best price for you, but remember: Most supersaver tickets are nonrefundable, and the airlines charge stiff penalties if you want to change your travel plans.

- ✔ **Check with ticket consolidators.** Otherwise known as bucket shops, these companies buy seats from the airlines ahead of time at considerable discounts and then sell them to the public at fares that are almost always well below the airlines' listed fares. Be aware that bucket shops are utterly loath to refund your money; after you buy from them, you're stuck, with cancellation penalties that can exceed 50 percent of the ticket price. Consolidators can be a fine way to go, though, and you may be astonished by how much less they charge for the same seat that an airline lists for four times the amount. Some good consolidators are **Council Travel** (☎ **800-226-8624;** Internet: www.counciltravel.com) and **1-800-FLY-CHEAP** (Internet: www.flycheap.com). Look for the small ads in the Sunday travel sections of most big newspapers, and act fast if you see a rate that you like, because consolidators have a limited number of seats to offer.

Three scary scenarios to avoid

The following three airport horror stories can happen to the most savvy of travelers. Try to ensure that they don't happen to you on your trip to Seattle and Portland.

The late-check-in scenario

If you want to experience true horror, arrive less than an hour before your flight leaves at the busy, overworked Sea-Tac or PDX airports — with bags to check in. In peak tourist seasons, you find lines spilling out of the concourses onto the sidewalk, with more enormous lines waiting to get through the security checks. That sinking feeling you're experiencing suggests that you've just bought a one-way ticket to Missed-Your-Flights-ville. Do yourself a favor and get to the airport at least an hour and a half before your flight leaves during the busy seasons. If you're late, try to check your bags with a skycap (tip him a dollar per bag) and then race to the gate for your boarding pass.

The late-to-the-gate scenario

Want to experience more true horror? You've raced to your gate after arriving late to the airport and made it with minutes to spare. The doors are still open and they're boarding the last of the passengers, but guess what? They've given away your seat. If you don't check in ten minutes before a domestic flight (more for international flights), the airlines begin to release seats to stand-by passengers, and no amount of screaming or sobbing can get your seat back. If you're cutting it close, try to get to a ticket agent fast — any ticket agent for your airline — to secure your seat.

The missed-flight scenario

Even more horror: You miss your flight. If so, then whine, plead, and beg the gate agent to try to confirm you on the next flight out. If that one is full, get on the waiting list for standbys right away. The closer you get to the top of that list, the better your chances for averting total travel disaster. If all else fails, check with other airlines to see if they'll honor your ticket and put you on their own flight to the same destination; most of them will say that they can't, but they can, and will, if seats are available and you look pitiful enough in explaining your predicament.

Booking your ticket online

The Internet has spawned a whole new industry in researching and buying travel online. Every Internet service provider and home page worth its salt has links to travel sites that claim to get you the fastest, cheapest, most convenient airfares available. You can go to a site like **www.travelocity.com** or **www.expedia.com** and find powerful search engines that research flights and fares and book seats in an instant. Don't stop there, though; you might still find better deals with a little shopping. Check out online consolidators such as **www.airoutlet.com** (☎ **877-456-5678**) or **www.priceline.com** before you make a final purchasing decision.

Airlines have joined in the online booking phenomenon as well; nearly all airlines have Web sites that allow you to book tickets directly with them. Some even let you reserve specific seats. Frequently, they offer specials that are only available to Web purchasers as an incentive for booking your ticket online. And why not? By acting as your own travel agent, you save the airlines money on customer service agents.

How does it work? The Web sites give you complete fare and schedule information, and when you're ready to purchase, make your reservation with your credit-card number. Some sites allow you to send a check after making a reservation or allow you 24 hours to get to a ticket office and purchase your ticket, but usually, they want you to complete the transaction before you sign off. After you purchase your ticket, the airline sends you confirmation via e-mail. On the day you travel, you take your confirmation number to the airport; your ticket is then issued at the counter.

No doubt: A few minutes of Web surfing can save you a lot of bucks. But before you log on to purchase your ticket, however, keep the following information in mind:

- ✔ **You bought it; it's yours.** After you agree to purchase a ticket online, there's no turning back. Be sure that you understand the conditions of your purchase, such as cancellation policies, and make sure this is the fare and ticket that you want before you push the final "okay transaction" button.

- ✔ **Don't dally getting to the airport.** Buying a ticket online forces you to use the main ticket counter at the airport to pick up your ticket and boarding pass. If you're late or traveling during a busy time, get to the airport well in advance of your flight departure, or risk standing in a huge line just to get your ticket.

- ✔ **Some airlines make it easier than others.** Alaska and Horizon Airlines have entered the online ticket buying process in a big way. They have several electronic kiosks at Sea-Tac and other airports in their system that allow you to print out your own E-ticket based on your confirmation number that you received online. This saves lots of time if you don't have luggage to check, and it allows you to proceed directly to your departure gate with ticket and boarding pass in hand.

Spinning wheels: Getting to Seattle and Portland by car, train, or bus

Flying may be the quickest way to get to Seattle and Portland, but you can make a real adventure out of your travel time by driving, riding the rails, or hopping a bus. Here are your non-flying alternatives.

By car

Have some time on your hands and want to get a sense of how vast the American West really is? Get into your car, fill it up, and head to the Pacific Northwest. Seattle is a good, hard, two-day drive from San Francisco, and a three-day excursion from Los Angeles or Las Vegas. Chicago is a long, lonely, four- to five-day trek across the Dakotas and Montana, and Florida is farther than you even want to think about unless you happen to have a *lot* of time on your hands. It takes five hours to cross the state of Washington from Seattle to Spokane, three hours from Seattle to Portland, and a little more than two hours from Seattle to Vancouver, British Columbia.

Both Seattle and Portland are located on the I-5 corridor that stretches all the way down to Southern California. Seattle is reached from the east by I-90; Portland by I-84 is navigable by the fine **Washington State Ferries** (☎ **800-84-FERRY** or **206-464-6400**), with connections for passengers and cars to the Olympic peninsula towns of Bremerton and Southworth. Portland is connected to the Oregon coast by U.S. 26.

For information, maps, and roadside assistance, a membership in the **American Automobile Association (AAA)** can be invaluable. Call ☎ **800-222-4357**.

By train

Amtrak (☎ **800-872-7245;** Internet: www.amtrak.com) services both Seattle and Portland with several trains a day. Both cities' stations are located conveniently downtown; a one-way trip takes about three and a half hours and costs about $29. The Amtrak Cascades route connects Vancouver, British Columbia, Seattle, Portland, and Eugene, Oregon, on a route that roughly parallels I-5 but also hugs the Puget Sound coastline, with some great views along the way. The Coast Starlight route goes all the way south to Los Angeles on a long, scenic run. Heading east, Amtrak's Empire Builder connects Seattle to Spokane and points east. Check train schedules carefully if you're not going to or coming from a major city, because many Amtrak routes to the Northwest include bus service through some sections of the routes.

By bus

Greyhound (☎ **800-231-2222**) serves Seattle and Portland, with connections to other cities throughout the country. Both bus terminals are located in the heart of downtown, within walking distance of hotels and hostels.

Chapter 6

Deciding Where to Stay

· ·

In This Chapter

▶ Sorting out lodging alternatives and choosing the place that's best for you

▶ Getting your money's worth: What your dollar buys

· ·

*H*otels, motels, inns, guesthouses, and hostels: All are places where you can lay your head and feel at home during your visit to the Pacific Northwest, but the differences between these accommodations can be enormous. Lodgings in Seattle and Portland range the gamut, from a simple bed in a stark, spare room with an adjoining or shared bathroom all the way to a luxurious, top-of-the-line hotel with dazzling furnishings, 24-hour room service, and a full array of services and staff to meet your every need. The kind of place that works best for you hinges on your desires, comfort level, and budget. An understanding of the different types of places can help you separate and clarify the choices. Remember that, in general, *you get what you pay for*.

In this chapter I give you a general discussion of the different options that you face in Seattle and Portland. For specific details on individual lodgings in each city, see Chapters 10 and 20. A breakdown of prices and amenities follows at the end of this chapter to give you an idea of the types of places you can expect to find in your price range.

The Chains: Tried and True

Chain hotels and motels are the kind that you can find in virtually every city and state in the country. You recognize the names: Holiday Inn, Marriott, Comfort Inn, Embassy Suites. They make a lot of money by offering hotel rooms that are pretty much the same regardless of what part of the country you visit, with standard rooms and rates that try awfully hard to appeal to the widest range of people. The room decor and furnishings are simple and basic, with a minimum of color or style; the services are equal across-the-board; and the rates are similar from one end of the country to the other. You can find these kinds of properties in the Northwest, but I haven't listed many of them in my breakdowns of the top hotels in Seattle and Portland simply because both cities offer so many better, more stylish, and more quintessentially

Northwest options. If you dislike surprises in your choice of lodging, a chain place might be just right for you, but it's a little like going all the way across the country to eat at a fast-food burger joint: You could have had the same experience at home. I prefer to try out new and unusual places in big cities and stick to the chains in more rural areas, such as when I leave Seattle or Portland and set off across the states of Washington and Oregon.

Motels and Motor Inns: No Frills

Motels are budget havens that consist of strips of rooms, usually with an outside entrance to each one or long corridors of rooms that are stacked atop each other, and a sign out front that indicates VACANCY/ No VACANCY. These lodgings are generally the least expensive in a city, frequently located on the outskirts of town or in close proximity to the major highways — largely because their biggest distinction from hotels is that they offer parking and cater to people who are driving. They generally don't have elevators or staff available to help you carry bags, and services are limited to phone calls and cable TV, with (if you're lucky) a bar of soap in the bathroom and a coffeemaker (bring your own coffee). In the Northwest, it's rare to find a motel with a pool, but most motels offer nonsmoking rooms. Give the furniture a good sniff before you settle in to see if the previous guests stuck to the rules, and if it smells smoky, ask to be moved into another room. Motels in the Northwest range from chain brands to independent places that aren't affiliated with any particular group. Don't be shy about asking to see a room and testing the bed before you put your money down. On the plus side: If you're driving, you can save as much as $18 a day in parking charges by staying at a motel rather than a downtown hotel.

Hostels and B&Bs: Close Encounters

Hostels, also frequently known as "youth hostels," are usually the sparest of accommodations, meant for travelers on extremely low budgets. They're called youth hostels because teenagers and college kids don't mind sleeping in a same-sex dormitory room with 20 or more beds lined up in rows, with shared group bathrooms. Many hostels also have a few private rooms, which cost a few dollars more and provide a modicum of privacy. Seattle and Portland both have highly rated hostels in good locations that attract young people, backpackers, and couples on a tight budget. Families might not feel safe because of the large numbers of people who come and go. Hostels are popular with international travelers and are a good place to meet people. Most hostels have shared kitchen facilities that you can use.

Bed-and-breakfasts, or B&Bs, are generally rooms that are rented out in private homes or converted mansions, with breakfast included in the price. There may be a shared living room that you can use to sit and read or meet other guests, and guest rooms frequently won't have television sets or private phones. The breakfast may be served at a communal dining table; it might consist of cereal and toast, or it could be a full spread of bacon and eggs and freshly baked bread or coffeecake. B&Bs are a good choice in neighborhoods with few or no hotels or motels, and they're a good place to meet locals who can give you the lowdown on places to go in the city. Prices are generally lower for B&B rooms than hotel rooms, and equal to or slightly more than motels. The downside is that you may have to sacrifice some privacy.

Inns and Converted Apartment Houses: The Personal Touch

Inns used to be very basic lodgings, frequently in a converted home, where you could get a meal and a comfortable bed, usually with a shared bathroom. Now an inn can refer to anything from bed-and-breakfast places to luxurious suite hotels. For the most part, an inn is a lodging with fewer than 50 rooms and no on-premises food service, with amenities that range from the downright rustic (shared baths and no TVs or phones in the rooms) to plush and luxurious rooms with private baths and adjoining living rooms. In Seattle in particular, there are also several converted apartment houses that are now called hotels or inns (I list the better ones in the guide to the city's hotels), which have small sitting areas and kitchenette units where you can cook your own meals, thus saving a bundle on restaurant prices. Most inns include in the price of the room at least a continental breakfast of coffee, juice, and rolls or cereal.

The Big Corporate Hotels: Grand and Glitzy

Every big city has its grand, expansive hotels that cater to the convention trade and frequent business travelers, and Seattle and Portland are no exceptions. Hotel chains like Sheraton and Westin operate large hotels with hundreds of rooms, two or more restaurants, and amenities that range from doormen to valet parking, 24-hour room service, and on-premises health clubs and pools. Convention hotels are often bustling places with above-average rooms and services, but the sheer volume of people who come and go contributes to an air of informality. Club-level rooms at higher prices are generally offered; these have a private sitting area that typically offers a continental breakfast and afternoon cocktail and wine service. These hotels are typically located right in the thick of things in the most vibrant parts of the city, and they convey that vibrant, big-city feeling from the moment you enter their lobbies.

Boutique Hotels: Quiet Luxury

In recent years, European-style boutique hotels have become a popular alternative for travelers, particularly business travelers who prefer a quieter, less-bustling lodging to the usual large corporate or convention hotels. A boutique hotel is, by definition, a smaller, more intimate place, usually with fewer than 100 rooms. The rooms are tastefully decorated and often quite comfortable, with thick comforters on the beds and full bathrooms that may include hot tubs. Most boutiques also offer a warm, cheery, living-room-style lobby with a fireplace or library for guests to use. These hotels are generally adjoined to a good restaurant, and a crack staff is on hand to greet guests and attend to their needs. Boutique hotels beautifully fit the laid-back, comfortable lifestyle of the Pacific Northwest and are some of the best bets in Seattle and Portland accommodations.

The Upper-Crust Hotels: Top of the Line

These no-expense-spared, high-end hotels, the kinds of places where you'd want to have your wedding if you or your family had cash to burn, are the most elegant and expensive accommodations in a city, where the rooms are superbly appointed and staff is on hand to attend to your every need, from around-the-clock dining, to procuring theater or restaurant reservations, to ironing your shirts. Rooms are generally large, with nice views, classy furnishings, and huge bathrooms. The hotels usually have at least one very formal, very plush dining room that serves exquisite food from the hand of a talented chef, and you might find yourself rubbing elbows with a visiting celebrity or star athlete over afternoon tea in the beautifully decorated lobby.

What You Get for the Money

So how far do your lodging dollars go in Seattle and Portland? In my lists of hotels, I break down the various options with $ signs, and, as you can well guess, the more $ signs, the merrier, in terms of service, views, and space.

Keep in mind that I base prices on the hotels' listed rack rates, or the standard rates posted for a lodging's rooms. Most accommodations offer discounts on the rack rates at different times throughout the year, and tour operators and special-interest groups (such as AAA club members) may also receive discounts off the rack rate. Hotel prices also rise and fall with the seasons and can be influenced by such odd criteria as whether or not a big convention is coming to town, so don't be surprised if my quoted prices are slightly different when you call to make a reservation. Here's an idea of what the dollar signs represent, and what it buys for you.

$

($50–$80)

This low-end category covers most motels, hostels, and B&Bs in Seattle and Portland, as well as bare-bones chain hotels. You get a room with one or two queen-size beds (or a dormitory bed in a hostel), usually away from the center of the action, with either a shared bathroom or a small, private bath that may only have a shower and not a bathtub. Check the beds at the lower end of this scale to make sure they're not lumpy or damaged. Cable television and a phone are usually included at the upper end of this scale, and breakfasts consist of a light continental spread, if available. Few other amenities or services are offered.

$$

($80–$125)

This price category buys you a room at a newer, more centrally located chain hotel, or a room in an older and slightly run-down deluxe hotel. B&Bs and inns at this level are nicer and more decorated, and the breakfasts offered are often heartier. Rooms in the older deluxe hotels are on the small side, but they have views from the upper floors; the newer chain hotels in this price category may have a pool or fitness room. All have private bathrooms and some bath amenities, like shampoos and body lotions. Most lodgings have either a restaurant or coffee shop on the premises or are closely located to a number of eateries.

$$$

($125–$175)

This price range gives you the maximum number of pickings in downtown Seattle and Portland. You get quite a nice room in the top inns and boutique hotels in either town, or one of the cheaper rooms in a big, deluxe convention and/or luxury hotel. Amenities like wine tastings, fitness rooms, or access to local health clubs are offered, as well as in-room movies and games, room service, and a dedicated restaurant. Rooms are spacious and nicely decorated with art and fine furnishings, and they frequently have a separate sitting area or sofa along with the king-size beds. Each room has two or more phones with multiple lines, as well as Internet service on a fast connection. Services may include concierges to help with reservations and procuring tickets to events, bell staffs to assist with luggage, and attendants to valet park your car.

$$$$

($175–$250)

The top-of-the-line price gets you a standard room at the most deluxe hotels in town, or a suite (which consists of a bedroom and a separate sitting room) at a boutique hotel. Location is right in the thick of things near shopping, restaurants, attractions, and business. The large rooms have views of either water or the downtown area, and the bathrooms have two sinks and a separate tub and shower, and most likely are trimmed in marble. Amenities may include plush bathrobes, high-quality shampoos and lotions in the rooms, minibars stocked with sodas, beer, wine, and liquors, 24-hour room service from a high-end menu, and staff to assist with most needs. The lobby is grand and spacious, with lots of meeting rooms and ballrooms available for private functions, and two or more high-quality restaurants serve food throughout the day.

Chapter 7

Booking Your Room

● ●

In This Chapter

▶ Avoiding rack rates

▶ Getting your dream room at the best rate

▶ Discovering the Northwest's premier reservations services

▶ Using the Web as a bargain-hunter's resource

▶ Arriving without a reservation — how to find last-minute lodging

● ●

*B*oth Seattle and Portland offer a wide range of accommodations, from top-of-the-line to no-frills motel basic. You can shoot for the stars in a luxury suite or save by staying in a perfectly reliable (and perfectly priced) chain, small inn, or B&B. Here are some tips and insider advice on finding your dream accommodations when you visit the Pacific Northwest.

Uncovering the Truth about Rack Rates

The rack rate is the maximum rate that a hotel charges for a room. It's the rate you get if you walk in off the street and ask for a room for the night. You sometimes see the rate printed on the fire/emergency exit diagrams posted on the back of your hotel room door.

Hotels are more than happy to charge you the rack rate, but listen up: You don't have to pay it! Hardly anybody does. You can avoid paying the rack rate by simply asking for a cheaper or discounted rate. Try it — you may be pleasantly surprised at the result.

Tips for Getting the Best Room at the Best Rate

Summer is the high season in both Seattle and Portland (see Chapter 2 for more information), and any special offers hotels make to lure customers are lean during these months. In Portland, rooms can get very tough to come by during the **Rose Festival** month of June; be sure to book well in advance, or you may wind up staying miles out of town.

In the winter, it's a different story altogether. You can get substantial savings on accommodations in both cities, where hotels and other lodgings offer programs with discounts of up to 50 percent in the slower winter months. Seattle calls its promotion "Super Saver" and lists some three dozen hotels, most of which are in the downtown core, that cut prices dramatically between November and March. The Four Seasons Olympic, for example, offers rooms at $170 (down from peak rates of $375), and the Hotel Edgewater has rooms for $129 (down from $265). To get the special rates, you have to call the reservations line directly (☎ 800-535-7071) or book online at www.seattlesupersaver.com.

Portland's winter promotion is called the Portland Big Deal (☎ 87-PORTLAND), and it includes attractions, performances, and restaurants in the package, with the rates in effect from October 1 to May 31.

 If you deal with hotels directly during the winter season, ask if they can deepen the discount with a room rate cut, an upgrade, or an amenity such as free parking. Go on — it never hurts to ask.

Package tours might also be the way to go to get good hotel prices. Tour operators block rooms ahead of time and can offer substantial savings when they combine rooms with airfare, tours, and/or car rentals. See Chapter 5 for information on tour operators.

Reservations Services and Hotlines

Whether you do your travel planning over the phone, by mail, by fax, or online, you should have access to the best resources to get the information you need. Here are some of the top local reservations services and hotlines for finding the right accommodations in the Seattle/ Portland area.

Seattle

For help in securing a room reservation, turn to the **Seattle Hotel Hotline** (☎ 800-535-7071 or 206-461-5840), a service of the Convention & Visitors Bureau. Don't forget that they're the only source for booking reduced-rate hotel rooms under the off-season "Seattle Super Saver" package. **Pacific Northwest Journeys** (☎ 800-935-9730) is a booking service that plans whole itineraries; they charge a fee for booking you a hotel room, but they frequently know about unadvertised specials or discounted rates.

To find a room in a private home or bed-and-breakfast, contact the **Seattle Bed and Breakfast Association** (☎ 800-348-5630 or 206-547-1020; Internet: www.seattlebandbs.com). **A Pacific Reservation Service** (☎ 800-684-2932 or 206-439-7666; Internet: www.seattlebedandbreakfast.com) offers a wide variety of lodging options, from inns and yachts to cabins and condos. In greater Seattle, contact the **Northwest Bed and Breakfast Reservation Service** (☎ 503-243-7616) for rooms in outlying towns.

Portland

The **Portland Oregon Visitors Association (POVA)** (☎ 877-6785263; Internet: www.travelportland.com) offers a reservations service for the Portland metro area. If you want information on area B&Bs, not only for Portland but for all of Oregon, contact the **Oregon Bed and Breakfast Guild** (☎ 800-944-6196; Internet: www.obbg.org). Both **A Pacific Reservation Service** and the **Northwest Bed and Breakfast Reservation Service** (see contact information in the preceding section) offer a variety of lodging options in the Portland area. Don't forget about Portland's winter "Big Deal" promotion, when hotel prices are slashed to the bone, and extras like free parking, complimentary breakfasts, and savings on tickets and transportation are thrown in. It's run by **POVA.**

Surfing the Web for Hotel Deals

While the major travel booking sites (such as Travelocity, Expedia, Yahoo Travel, and Cheap Tickets) offer hotel booking, it can be best to use a site devoted primarily to lodging because you may find properties that aren't listed on more general online travel agencies. Some lodging sites specialize in a particular type of accommodations, such as bed-and-breakfasts, which you won't find on the more mainstream booking services. Others, such as TravelWeb (keep reading for contact information), offer weekend deals on major chain properties, which cater to business travelers and have more empty rooms on weekends.

Here is a sampling of lodging sites on the Internet:

✔ Although the name **All Hotels on the Web** (www.all-hotels.com) is something of a misnomer, the site *does* have tens of thousands of listings for hotels throughout the world. Bear in mind that each hotel has paid a small fee (of $25 and up) to be listed, so it's less an objective list and more like a book of online brochures.

✔ **InnSite** (www.innsite.com) has B&B listings in all 50 U.S. states and more than 50 countries around the globe. Find an inn at your destination, see pictures of the rooms, and check prices and availability. This extensive directory of bed-and-breakfasts only includes listings if the proprietor submits one (it's free to get an inn listed). The descriptions are written by the innkeepers, and many listings link to the inn's own Web sites. Try also the **Bed and Breakfast Channel** (www.bedandbreakfast.com).

✔ **Places to Stay** (www.placestostay.com) lists one-of-a-kind places in the U.S. and abroad that you might not find in other directories, with a focus on resort accommodations. Again, the listing is selective — this isn't a comprehensive directory, but it can give you a sense of what's available at different destinations.

✔ **TravelWeb** (www.travelweb.com) lists more than 26,000 hotels in 170 countries, focusing on chains such as Hyatt and Hilton, and you can book almost 90 percent of these online. TravelWeb's Click-It Weekends, updated each Monday, offers weekend deals at many leading hotel chains.

What to Do If You Arrive Without a Reservation

You're not necessarily out of luck if you come to the Northwest on the spur of the moment and without reservations, even in the height of the summer. You just have significantly reduced options. In Seattle, try calling the local **Hotel Hotline** (☎ 800-535-7071 or 206-461-5840) to see if any member hotels have rooms available. In Portland, try calling the **Portland Oregon Visitors Association** (☎ 877-678-5263 or 503-275-9750), which maintains a hotel reservations service for the metro area. Still no luck? Head north over the bridge to Vancouver, Washington, and check out the lodgings of that bedroom community. There, you are still minutes from downtown Portland, and you may land a room alongside the Columbia River. Call the **Southwest Washington Visitor & Convention Bureau** at ☎ 877-600-0800 or 360-750-1553.

If all else fails, cruise the strip of motels on **Aurora Avenue North,** just north of downtown Seattle, where vacancy signs alert you to the availability of rooms. If nothing else, you can get a bed for the night (if not by the hour) and a telephone to help you find something more desirable.

Chapter 8

Taking Care of the Remaining Details

. . . .

In This Chapter

▶ The lowdown on rental cars and insurance

▶ Steps to take if you get sick

▶ How to get the best tables and tickets to the hottest attractions before you leave home

▶ Whether to buy traveler's checks — or not

▶ Pack it up: How to dress like a local

. . . .

*Y*ou bought your plane tickets, reserved your accommodations, and plotted out where and how you want to tour the city. Now is the time to take care of the last-minute details of your vacation.

A Car-Rental Checklist

Not sure if you should rent a car in Seattle or Portland? Table 8-1 gives you a checklist to help you decide. Put a mark by the statements that are the most important to you and see if the pros outweigh the cons.

Table 8-1	The Pros and Cons of Renting a Car
PROS	**CONS**
Want ultimate freedom of movement	Downtown parking very expensive
Want to explore distant parts of the city	Street parking can be tough to find
Need to carry and store lots of gear, such as strollers, camera stuff, and bags	No excess gear
Most attractions in Seattle/Portland within walking distance of downtown hotels	Walking more than three or four blocks makes me tired and grumpy

(continued)

Table 8-1 *(continued)*

PROS	CONS
Have to get back to the airport from a place that isn't readily cab-accessible	Public transportation great in Portland; passable in Seattle
Don't want to wait for cabs or buses	Whopping 28.3 percent tax in Seattle if car rented
Kids or companions unwilling to walk from airport	Driving in urban traffic is not my idea of a vacation
I just look so good in a leather bucket seat	

Getting the Best Deal on a Car Rental

Car-rental rates vary even more than airline fares. The price depends on the size of the car, the length of time you keep it, where and when you pick it up and drop it off, where you take it, and a host of other factors.

Asking a few key questions could save you hundreds of dollars. For example, weekend rates may be lower than weekday rates. Ask if the rate is the same for pickup Friday morning as it is Thursday night. If you're keeping the car five or more days, a weekly rate is often cheaper than the daily rate. Some companies may assess a drop-off charge if you don't return the car to the same renting location; others, notably National, do not. Ask if the rate is cheaper if you pick up the car at the airport or a location in town (rates are often lower in downtown Seattle and Portland than at the airports). If you see an advertised price in your local newspaper, be sure to ask for that specific rate; otherwise you may be charged the standard (higher) rate. Don't forget to mention membership in AAA, AARP, frequent-flier programs, and trade unions. These usually entitle you to discounts ranging from 5 to 30 percent. Ask your travel agent to check any and all of these rates.

And don't forget: Most car rentals are worth at least 500 miles on your frequent-flier account!

On top of the standard rental prices, other optional charges apply to most car rentals. The Collision Damage Waiver (CDW), which requires you to pay for damage to the car in a collision, is illegal in some states, but is covered by many credit card companies. Check with your credit card company before you go so you can avoid paying this hefty fee, which can be as much as $15 per day.

The car-rental companies also offer additional liability insurance (if you harm others in an accident), personal accident insurance (if you harm yourself or your passengers), and personal effects insurance (if your luggage is stolen from your car). If you have insurance on your car at home, you are probably covered for most of these scenarios. If your own insurance doesn't cover you for rentals, or if you don't have auto insurance, you should consider the additional coverages (the car-rental companies are liable for certain base amounts, depending on the state). But weigh the likelihood of getting into an accident or losing your luggage against the cost of these coverages (as much as $20 per day combined), which can significantly add to the price of your rental.

Some companies also offer refueling packages, in which you pay for an entire tank of gas up front. The price is usually fairly competitive with local gas prices, but you don't get credit for any gas remaining in the tank. If you reject this option, you pay only for the gas you use, but you have to return it with a full tank or face charges of $3 to $4 a gallon for any shortfall. If a stop at a gas station on the way to the airport may make you miss your plane, then by all means take advantage of the fuel purchase option. Otherwise, skip it.

Playing It Safe with Travel and Medical Insurance

There are three primary kinds of travel insurance: trip cancellation insurance, medical, and lost luggage.

Trip cancellation insurance is a good idea if you have paid a large portion of your vacation expenses up front.

But the other two types of insurance — medical and lost luggage — don't make sense for most travelers. Your existing health insurance should cover you if you get sick while on vacation (though if you belong to an HMO, check to see whether you are fully covered when away from home). Homeowner's insurance should cover stolen luggage if you have off-premises theft. Check your existing policies before you buy any additional coverage. The airlines are responsible for $2,500 on domestic flights (and $9.07 per pound, up to $640, on international flights) if they lose your luggage; if you plan to carry anything more valuable than that, keep it in your carry-on bag.

Some credit cards (American Express and certain gold and platinum Visa and MasterCards, for example) offer automatic flight insurance against death or dismemberment in case of an airplane crash. If you still feel you need more insurance, try one of the companies in the following listing. But don't pay for more insurance than you need. For example, if you only need trip cancellation insurance, don't purchase coverage for lost or stolen property. Trip cancellation insurance costs approximately 6 to 8 percent of the total value of your vacation. Among the reputable issuers of travel insurance are:

- ✔ **Access America,** 6600 West Broad St., Richmond, VA 23230 (☎ **800-284-8300;** Fax: 800-346-9265; Internet: www.accessamerica.com)

- ✔ **Travelex Insurance Services,** 11717 Burt St., Suite 202, Omaha, NE 68154 (☎ **800-228-9792;** Internet: www.travelex-insurance.com)

- ✔ **Travel Guard International,** 1145 Clark St., Stevens Point, WI 54481 (☎ **800-826-1300;** Internet: www.travel-guard.com)

- ✔ **Travel Insured International, Inc.,** P.O. Box 280568, 52-S Oakland Ave., East Hartford, CT 06128-0568 (☎ **800-243-3174;** Internet: www.travelinsured.com)

Staying Healthy When You Travel

Apart from how getting sick can ruin your vacation, it can be hard to find a doctor you trust when you're away from home. Bring all your medications with you, as well as a prescription for more if you're concerned that you may run out. Bring an extra pair of contact lenses in case you lose one.

If you have health insurance, check with your provider to find out the extent of your coverage outside of your home area. Be sure to carry your identification card in your wallet. And if you worry that your existing policy won't be sufficient, purchase medical insurance (see "Playing It Safe with Travel and Medical Insurance" earlier in this chapter) for more comprehensive coverage.

If you suffer from a chronic illness, talk to your doctor before taking the trip. For such conditions as epilepsy, diabetes, or a heart condition, wearing a Medic Alert identification tag immediately alerts any doctor to your condition and gives him or her access to your medical records through Medic Alert's 24-hour hotline. Membership is $35 with a $15 renewal fee. Contact the **Medic Alert Foundation,** 2323 Colorado Ave., Turlock, CA 95382 (☎ **800-432-5378;** Internet: www.medicalert.org).

If you do get sick, ask the concierge at your hotel to recommend a local doctor — even his or her own doctor, if necessary. This is probably a better recommendation than any national consortium of doctors available through an 800 number. If you can't get a doctor to help you right away, go to the emergency room at the local hospital. Many hospital emergency rooms have walk-in-clinics for emergency cases that are not life-threatening. You may not get immediate attention, but you won't pay the high price of an emergency room visit (usually a minimum of $300 just for signing your name, on top of whatever treatment you receive). Go to Appendix A and Appendix B for the names, addresses, and phone numbers of local hospitals and medical centers.

Making Reservations and Getting Tickets in Advance for Restaurants, Events, and Sightseeing

At certain times of the year — when the sports teams are in town, when the big arenas are rocking with name acts, and when theaters and symphony halls are lit up — Seattle and Portland have an awful lot of entertainment going on. Big events always sell out quickly, so make sure you don't forget to book your Pearl Jam tickets, TrailBlazers seats, or a table at that hot new restaurant by making reservations in advance.

Seattle Center's huge arts festivals, such as **Bumbershoot** or **Northwest Folklife,** offer tickets at the gates, but you have to wait in mammoth lines to score them. You can save lots of time by buying advance tickets at a sponsoring retailer (usually Starbucks; see the events' Web sites in Chapter 2 for specific info), even on the day you want to attend.

As far as restaurants are concerned, the most popular places in town can book up fast, particularly on Friday and Saturday nights. Really special events, such as **Rover's** over-the-top Halloween feast (13 courses, and everyone in costume) sell out months in advance. In Seattle, call well ahead for a table at **Cascadia, Brasa, El Gaucho, Canlis, Rover's,** or the **Dahlia Lounge.** In Portland, you want to snag a table in advance at **Higgins, Wildwood,** the **Heathman,** and **Atwater's.**

Seattle and Portland on the Web

For listings of what's happening in each city in sports, entertainment, and the arts, check out Web sites like www.seattleinsider.com (which also offers cool cam views from atop the Space Needle and Queen Anne Hill), or the sites for the **Seattle Weekly** (www.seattleweekly.com) or **Seattle Post-Intelligencer** (www.seattle-pi.com) newspapers. **City Search** also gets into the act with Web sites for both Seattle (www.seattle.citysearch.com) and Portland (www.portland.citysearch.com), both of which have listings and feature articles on the local dining, club, and entertainment scene. Also for Portland, check out the online version of the **Willamette Weekly newspaper** (www.wweek.com). **The Seattle-King County Convention & Visitors Bureau** (☎ 206-461-5840) can be accessed through www.seattleinsider.com, and has links and calendars for all of the arts organizations and sports teams in town. The same goes for the **Portland Oregon Visitors Association (POVA)** (☎ 503-222-2223; Internet: www.pova.com).

Your hotel concierge is always a good source for obtaining tickets or hard-to-come-by restaurant reservations. If you can, contact the concierge before you come to town to get advice on good seats to a hot show or restaurant reservations. To buy directly in Seattle, call **TicketMaster** (☎ 206-622-HITS; Internet: www.ticketmaster.com) or **Pacific Northwest Ticket Service** (☎ 206-232-0150). In Portland, call **TicketMaster** (☎ 503-224-4400) or **Fastixx** (☎ 503-224-8499) for tickets to concerts, sporting events, and special events.

Getting Traveler's Checks

Traveler's checks are something of an anachronism from the days when people wrote personal checks instead of going to an ATM. Because traveler's checks could be replaced if lost or stolen, they were a sound alternative to filling your wallet with cash at the beginning of a trip.

These days, most cities have 24-hour ATMs linked to a national network that almost always includes your bank at home. **Cirrus** (☎ 800-424-7787; Internet: www.mastercard.com/atm/) and **Plus** (☎ 800-843-7587; Internet: www.visa.com/atms) are the two most popular networks; check the back of your ATM card to see which network your bank belongs to. The 800 numbers and Web sites give you specific locations of ATMs where you can withdraw money while on vacation. For specific information on money matters in Seattle and Portland, respectively, see Chapters 12 and 22.

If you prefer the security of traveler's checks, you can get them at almost any bank. **American Express** offers checks in denominations of $20, $50, $100, $500, and $1,000. You pay a service charge ranging from 1 to 4 percent, although AAA members can obtain checks without a fee at most AAA offices. You can also get American Express traveler's checks over the phone by calling ☎ 800-221-7282.

Visa (☎ 800-227-6811) also offers traveler's checks, available at Citibank locations across the country and at several other banks. The service charge ranges between 1.5 and 2 percent; checks come in denominations of $50, $100, $500, and $1,000. **MasterCard** also offers traveler's checks; call ☎ 800-223-9920 for a location near you.

Packing for the Flannel Curtain

Call it the Northwest Flannel Curtain. When you enter the states of Washington and Oregon, you leave your fine suits and designer clothes behind and slip into some comfortable blue jeans and loose flannel shirts. I can't emphasize it enough: Seattle and Portland, despite their veneers of sophistication and software wealth, are utterly, completely, resolutely casual. You'll feel as out of place walking the streets of **Belltown** or **Nob Hill** in a fine suit (Armani or Chanel) and overcoat as you would walking into a ritzy Manhattan restaurant in a sweatsuit. People simply don't dress up at night; the proof can be found in the dress codes of restaurants, where only one place in Seattle — *one place!* — even suggests that gentlemen wear a jacket to dinner (**Canlis,** and even there they won't give you much attitude if you show up without one). The same goes for wearing stylish black designer clothes, Los Angeles style, which immediately brands you as a conspicuous outsider in most neighborhoods in Seattle and Portland.

Dress for comfort

Dress for comfort and you can go just about anywhere in either town. Call it a gift or a curse, depending on your fashion awareness, but it's not unusual at any event — the opera, the symphony, or a fine restaurant — to see attorneys and executives who come straight from work in suits mingling freely with people in jeans and Topsiders. (At least folks don't wear sweatsuits in public here, as some people do in Los Angeles and Phoenix.)

Prepare for a drizzle — or two

Bring a raincoat, but leave the umbrella at home. Most people don't bother with umbrellas here; the rain clouds come and go too quickly. If you want to look like a local, wear a hat or a baseball-style cap when it starts to drizzle, or leave your head bare to enjoy the fine moisturizing. Also, keep in mind that just because it's June, it's not necessarily summer. It can still be chilly and damp right up to the 4th of July, so bring along a light sweater and jacket.

Pack lightly

As airplanes get more stuffed with passengers — as they inevitably do during peak tourism seasons — airlines have gotten tighter with restrictions on carry-on baggage. You're generally limited to one carry-on bag per person in addition to a purse or small briefcase, and that bag had better be small enough to fit under the seat in front of you if you don't want it eye-balled and gate-checked by an agent.

For men only

If you *really* want to fit in with the locals in Portland, here's another style suggestion, for men only. It may take a while, but it's worth it. Before going to Portland, grow your hair long enough to rubber-band it into a ponytail. Wear said ponytail in any establishment, along with the requisite flannel shirt and blue jeans, and you'll be a hail-fellow-well-met in the Rose City in no time!

Part III
Settling in to Seattle

The 5th Wave By Rich Tennant

"It's a little known fact that the same people who designed the Seattle Space Needle also designed pilot uniforms."

In this part . . .

Here I provide the lowdown on visiting the Emerald City, giving you all the information you need to familiarize yourself with the city's different neighborhoods, find the lodging that's just right for you, and choose among Seattle's fine assortment of restaurants. I tell you the best ways to get around the city, whether by car, train, monorail, or ferry, and where you can find delicious, inexpensive eats. In the chapter on money matters, I tell you where to get quick cash, what to do if your wallet is stolen, and what to expect in tacked-on taxes.

Chapter 9

Location, Location, Location: Seattle

In This Chapter
▶ Downtown: Where the beds are
▶ The neighborhood that's fit for a queen (Queen Anne, to be precise)
▶ Where to live like a local

*I*n your fondest hotel dreams (and come on, I know you have them), are you staying in the thick of things in a vibrant city, with the best restaurants, shopping, and nightlife just steps from your door? Or do you prefer to spend your nights in a neighborhood where the locals live in order to experience how the natives work, shop, and play? If budget is your sole consideration, are you willing (and logistically able) to bed down in the part of town that's largely known for its cheap motels?

In this chapter I discuss the location choices for lodging in Seattle. In the case of the Emerald City, this overwhelmingly means staying downtown in the heart of Seattle. But even within that rather wide chunk of the city, you find plenty of choices to help you select the downtown location that best suits your style and mood.

The pickings get slimmer if you're determined to go out among the people and live in a neighborhood like a dyed-in-the-flannel Seattleite, but it's still possible. The street life and activity of near-north neighborhoods like Ballard, Fremont, Green Lake, and Wallingford (see Chapter 11 for more information on these neighborhoods) are definitely worth experiencing, but you have to settle for far fewer lodging options. The neighborhood of Queen Anne bridges that gap by providing a variety of lodgings in a near-downtown setting that is also home to some lovely homes with astonishing views.

And, finally, if budget is your primary consideration, I can send you to a part of town with more cheap, gritty motels than you've ever seen outside of a Quentin Tarantino movie. But keep in mind that you need a car for exploring — and the ambience is just this side of dreadful.

Greater Seattle

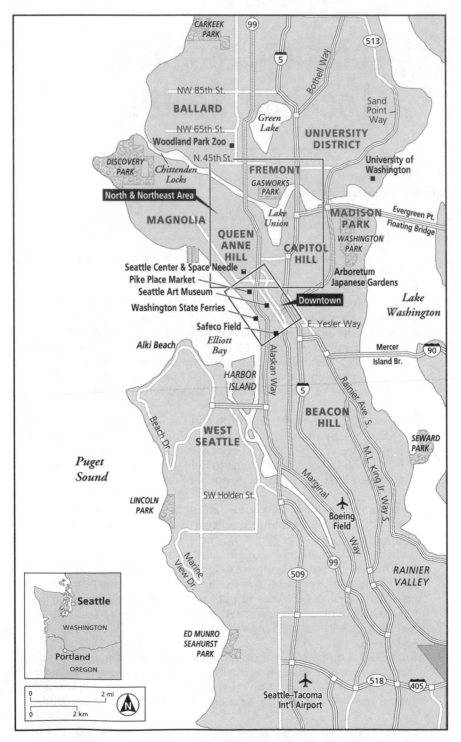

CARKEEK PARK

99

513

5

Bothell Way

NW 85th St.

BALLARD

Green Lake

Sand Point Way

NW 65th St.

UNIVERSITY DISTRICT

Woodland Park Zoo

DISCOVERY PARK

Chittenden Locks

N. 45th St.

FREMONT

University of Washington

North & Northeast Area

GASWORKS PARK

MAGNOLIA

Lake Union

Evergreen Pt. Floating Bridge

MADISON PARK

WASHINGTON PARK

QUEEN ANNE HILL

CAPITOL HILL

Seattle Center & Space Needle

Arboretum Japanese Gardens

Pike Place Market

Seattle Art Museum

Downtown

Lake Washington

Washington State Ferries

E. Yesler Way

Safeco Field

Alki Beach

Elliott Bay

HARBOR ISLAND

Mercer Island Br.

90

Alaskan Way

5

BEACON HILL

SEWARD PARK

Beach Dr.

WEST SEATTLE

Rainier Ave. S.

Puget Sound

Marginal

M.L. King Jr. Way S

LINCOLN PARK

SW Holden St.

Boeing Field

RAINIER VALLEY

Marine View Dr.

99

509

Seattle

WASHINGTON

Portland

OREGON

ED MUNRO SEAHURST PARK

Seattle–Tacoma Int'l Airport

518

405

0   2 mi

0   2 km

N

The Downtown Experience

Staying downtown, meaning roughly the large area of central Seattle between Pioneer Square and Lake Union, is where all but a few hardy travelers wind up laying their heads during their visit to Seattle. Why? To paraphrase a certain well-known bank robber, you stay in downtown Seattle because that's where the beds are. It's the home of the city's biggest and finest hotels, including the only waterfront lodging in town. It's also the location for most of the best new restaurants, much of the best shopping, and many of Seattle's top attractions and festivals. It's safe, too, and relatively easy to get around on foot (see Chapter 8 for a discussion of whether you need to rent a car).It may seem that your only choice is to reside alongside skyscrapers and shopping malls, but look closer: Downtown Seattle is separated into a number of manageable divisions, each with its own singular charm and character. **The Market** refers to the blocks on First Avenue adjacent to the lovely Pike Place Market, where open stalls sell flowers, produce, fresh fish, and delicatessen foods. Staying in the middle of the Market, with close proximity to the Seattle Art Museum, sidewalk cafes, and several fine restaurants, reminds many people of visiting Europe.

Just a few blocks north on First Avenue is **Belltown,** the neighborhood centered on Bell Street that has become the hippest part of downtown Seattle. Here, you can barely walk down the street without bumping nose-first into a chef who has just hung out his shingle on a fabulous new restaurant, or young high-tech types who have snapped up the million-dollar condos that overlook Elliott Bay. Belltown has Seattle's hottest new restaurants, bars, and nightclubs.

In the middle of things downtown, centered roughly around 5th Avenue and Pine Street, is the **Shopping District,** within a block or two of which are not only the city's largest retailers (see Chapter 16 for shopping tips) but also the city's biggest and finest hotels. Chapter 6 discusses the many options in this, the heart of downtown, but suffice it to say that in this area, your choices include both big, convention hotels and intimate boutique hostelries, all within a block or two of lots of shops and restaurants. On the fringes of the Shopping District and at the very edges of downtown are even more lodging choices. Keep in mind that this entire area, from the Market to the Shopping District, is easily walkable and convenient to just about every downtown lodging.

Queen Anne's Lace

Creating a kind of transition zone between downtown Seattle and the near-north neighborhoods is **Queen Anne,** the section of town that begins just north of Denny Way in a cluster of retail shops and apartment houses, climbs a steep hill (with Queen Anne Avenue N. the main

Downtown Seattle

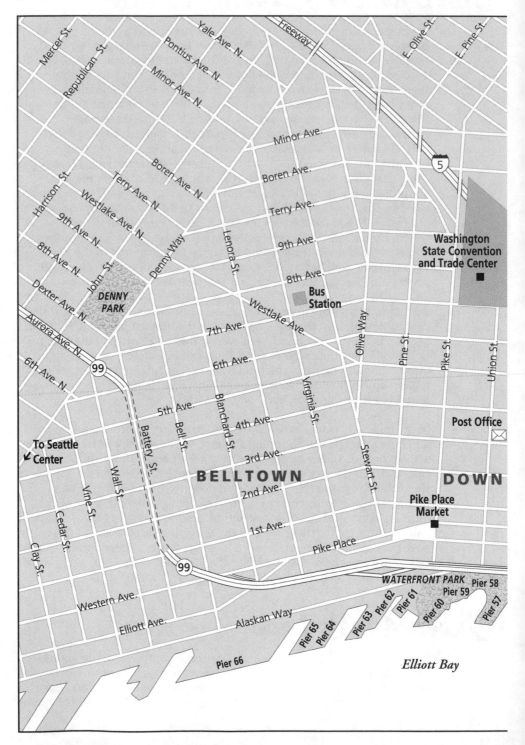

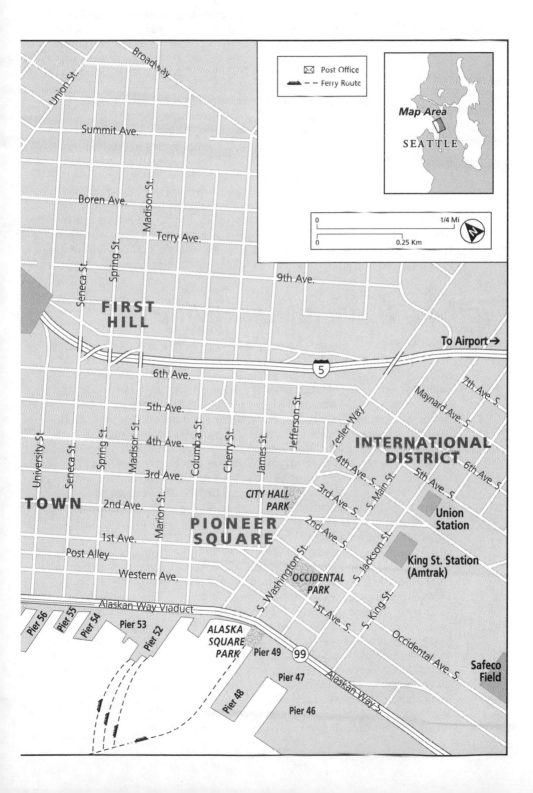

thoroughfare), and winds up in a quiet, residential neighborhood alongside the Ship Canal. Here you find residential-style hotels in converted apartment houses near the bottom of the hill and budget accommodations on the eastern edge of the neighborhood, near 5th Avenue and Roy Street.

Queen Anne is also the closest neighborhood to the **Seattle Center,** the multi-block complex where Seattle's big festivals, like Bumbershoot and A Bite of Seattle (see Chapter 2 for a calendar of events), are staged, and which houses Key Arena (the home of the SuperSonics basketball team), the Opera House, Pacific Northwest Ballet, several theaters (including the Seattle Children's Theatre), the Pacific Science Center, and the Experience Music Project. And, of course, towering over the entire complex is the **Space Needle.** Lower Queen Anne provides a good base for walking to Seattle Center events and facilities, hopping a cab or bus into downtown Seattle, or exploring the city's neighborhoods by car. Upper Queen Anne Avenue also has a retail district with great shops and restaurants and sterling views of the city and Mount Rainier on a clear day.

Bunking Down in Huskyville

If you want to live among the people, you have to cross the Ship Canal, heading north, on either the Ballard, Fremont, Montlake, or Aurora bridge. Here you find gentle hills packed with single-family houses — Seattle's bedrooms — interspersed among parks, retail corridors, and lovely views. No full-service hotels yet exist in the urban neighborhoods of Fremont, Ballard, Green Lake, or Wallingford, but you can find bed-and-breakfast accommodations. A string of cheap, budget motels (keep reading for more information) line Aurora Avenue N. in Fremont. To stay close to the **University of Washington** (known locally as "U-Dub"; "Go Huskies" is your rallying cry), you find several hotel and motel choices just off the freeway in the **University District,** or U-District, as the locals call it, that make good bases of operations.

If budget is your main consideration — meaning that you don't care where you sleep because you plan to be on the go most of the day anyway — a string of cheap motels lies on Aurora Avenue N. beginning right after the Ship Canal in Fremont and stretching roughly up to 175th Street and the outer limits of Seattle proper. The places that I list in Chapter 10 (see the section "No Room at the Inn?") are all clean and safe, but this part of town is admittedly less than desirable — if not outright seamy — for walking or sightseeing. You definitely need a car to get around, and you get virtually none of the ambience, street life, or views that make Seattle such a great place to visit. You are, however, just minutes away from many of the city's best neighborhoods for exploring, within easy reach of movie theaters at the Oak Tree and Northgate shopping centers, and just a 10-minute drive straight into downtown on Aurora Avenue N. (also called Route 99).

Chapter 10

The Best Hotels in Seattle

In This Chapter

▶ A complete breakdown of Seattle's best lodgings

▶ Accommodations by price and location

▶ Where to go and what to do if the best hotels are booked solid

*I*n this chapter I bounce on the mattresses and snoop through the closets of my favorite hotels in Seattle in order to give you all the information you need to make the right choice. The following lodging recommendations are the places I'd book if I were visiting the Emerald City. Remember that summer is high season, and if you find that your favorite hotel choices are booked solid, look to the list at the end of this chapter for some runners-up that I can also recommend.

In Chapter 9 I give you a breakdown on the neighborhoods and sub-neighborhoods of the city. Here, I place the lodgings in those parts of town and let you know which are closest to shopping, nightlife, and museums, or which just flat out have the best views. Most of Seattle's hotels are located in the downtown corridor, but even within that space there are several sub-sections that offer different flavors of the city.

Throughout the chapter, look for the Kid-Friendly icons that point out the lodgings that are especially good for families.

Feel free to use the margins of the book to check or note the hotels that seem just right for your needs, and then go to the "Sweet Dreams: Choosing Your Hotel" worksheet at the back of the book to help narrow down your choice. Happy hunting!

Seattle Hotels from A to Z

The breakdown on hotel prices is as follows. The stars accompanying every listing are based on the hotel's posted rack rates for a standard room. Suites are much more expensive. Keep in mind that rates fluctuate,

Downtown Seattle Accommodations

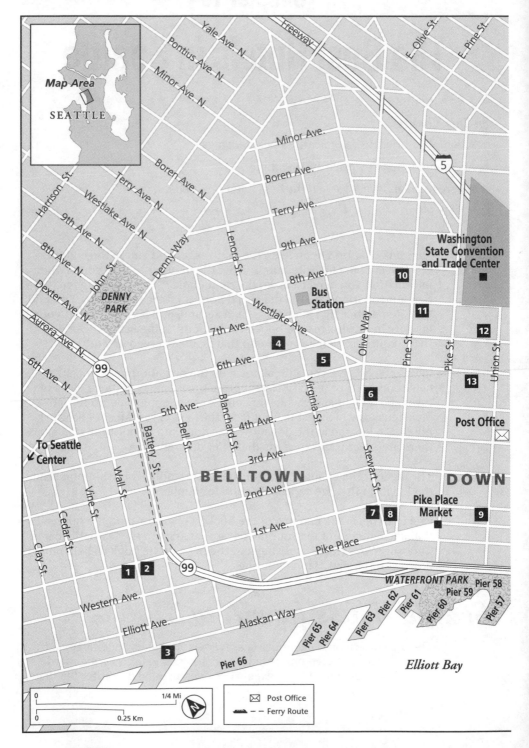

Map Area

SEATTLE

Yale Ave. N.

Pontius Ave. N.

Minor Ave. N.

Freeway

E. Olive St.

E. Pine St.

Minor Ave.

Boren Ave. N.

Boren Ave.

Terry Ave. N.

Terry Ave.

Harrison St.

Westlake Ave. N.

9th Ave. N.

Denny Way

9th Ave.

5

8th Ave. N.

John St.

Lenora St.

8th Ave.

Washington State Convention and Trade Center

Dexter Ave. N.

DENNY PARK

Bus Station

Westlake Ave.

Olive Way

10

Aurora Ave. N.

7th Ave.

11

6th Ave. N.

99

6th Ave.

4

5

Pine St.

Pike St.

12

Union St.

Virginia St.

6

13

5th Ave.

Blanchard St.

4th Ave.

Post Office

To Seattle Center

Bell St.

3rd Ave.

Stewart St.

Battery St.

BELLTOWN

2nd Ave.

DOWN

Wall St.

Vine St.

1st Ave.

Pike Place Market

Cedar St.

7 8

9

Clay St.

99

Pike Place

1 2

WATERFRONT PARK   Pier 58

Western Ave.

Pier 59

Elliott Ave.

Alaskan Way

Pier 63 Pier 62

Pier 61

Pier 60

Pier 57

3

Pier 65 Pier 64

Elliott Bay

Pier 66

0   1/4 Mi
0   0.25 Km

N

⊠ Post Office
⛴ – – Ferry Route

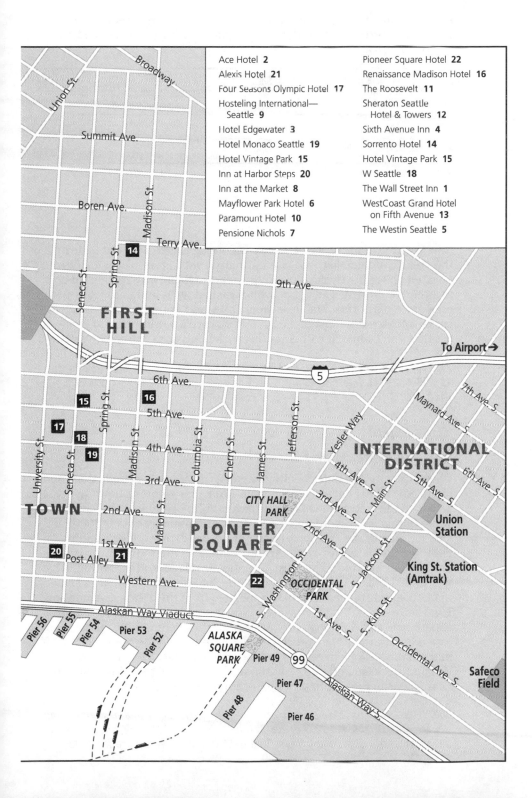

Ace Hotel **2**

Alexis Hotel **21**

Four Seasons Olympic Hotel **17**

Hosteling International—
Seattle **9**

Hotel Edgewater **3**

Hotel Monaco Seattle **19**

Hotel Vintage Park **15**

Inn at Harbor Steps **20**

Inn at the Market **8**

Mayflower Park Hotel **6**

Paramount Hotel **10**

Pensione Nichols **7**

Pioneer Square Hotel **22**

Renaissance Madison Hotel **16**

The Roosevelt **11**

Sheraton Seattle
Hotel & Towers **12**

Sixth Avenue Inn **4**

Sorrento Hotel **14**

Hotel Vintage Park **15**

W Seattle **18**

The Wall Street Inn **1**

WestCoast Grand Hotel
on Fifth Avenue **13**

The Westin Seattle **5**

and rack rates are generally at the top of a hotel's price schedule. You should be able to find considerable discounts during the winter and off-season months.

$	=	$50–$80
$$	=	$80–$125
$$$	=	$125–$175
$$$$	=	$175–$250

Ace Hotel

$ Belltown

New York and San Francisco have tons of places like this, but in Seattle, the trendy, minimalist Ace is a curiosity that caters to the truly hip. Located above the Cyclops bar in the heart of Belltown's restaurant-and-nightclub culture, it's all spare, white-washed walls and floors, low beds on simple platforms, stainless-steel sinks and counters in rooms with cinder-block walls. Most of the 34 rooms share a bathroom, and chances are that you'll share it with a visiting rock band or performance artist.

2423 First Ave. at Wall Street; entry is unassuming, but look for big Cyclops sign. ☎ *206-448-4721. Internet:* www.theacehotel.com. *Rack rates: $75–$95. AE, DISC, MC, V.*

Alexis Hotel

$$$$ Pike Place Market

One of the city's premier boutique hotels, the Alexis is artfully done and hip, from the art gallery on the main floor that rotates shows by local artists to the suites named for the likes of John Lennon, Miles Davis, and Jerry Garcia, each containing drawings and memorabilia of its distinguished namesake. The hotel occupies a handsome older building on First Avenue near the Seattle Art Museum, and the rooms are spacious and well-appointed. The best are the fireplace suites, which have whirlpool baths, wet bars, king-size beds, and black bathrooms trimmed in marble and stocked with bath amenities from the in-house Aveda spa. Light a fire and call for a massage in your room for the ultimate sybaritic experience, and then head to the lobby for the evening wine tastings, followed by dinner at the equally artful Painted Table restaurant. Pets are more than welcome here; they're treated like royalty, with special amenities and packages offered. A perfume shop at street level is one of the best places in the city to pick up a scent for your beloved.

1007 First Ave. on Madison Street, halfway between Pioneer Square and the Market. ☎ *800-426-7033 or 206-624-4844. Fax: 206-621-9009. Internet:* www.alexishotel.com. *Rack rates: $230–$250 (fireplace suites are $440). AE, DC, DISC, MC, V.*

Chambered Nautilus Bed & Breakfast Inn

$$ University District

This six-room B&B in a Georgian Colonial home from 1915 is located in a quiet residential neighborhood a few blocks from the noise and bustle of the University of Washington. Great for visiting parents but perhaps too sedate for a student, the rooms have queen-size beds and private baths and are decorated in antiques and floral motifs. Hardy souls who don't mind a hefty hike may enjoy the third-floor Crow's Nest Chamber, with a fireplace and nautical window that offers mountain views.

5005 22nd Ave. NE. Take I-5 to NE 50th Street, head west, turn left on 20th Ave. NE, right on NE 54th St., and right on 22nd Ave. NE. ☎ *800-545-8459 or 206-522-2536. Fax: 206-528-0898. Internet:* www.chamberednautilus.com. *Rack rates: $99–$124; full breakfast included. AE, MC, V.*

Four Seasons Olympic Hotel

$$$$ Shopping District

An Italian Renaissance beauty in the heart of downtown, the Four Seasons is Seattle's most elegant lodging. The plush lobby is decorated with chandeliers and enormous vases brimming with flowers, and the ballrooms are what brides-to-be dream of. The rooms aren't especially large given the steep tariff you pay for them, but they contain all of the amenities, from ironing boards to terrycloth bathrobes, that you expect from a Four Seasons. The beds are large enough to easily accommodate the NBA players who bunk here. The Garden Court restaurant/lounge is a wonderful place to bring your mother for afternoon tea, and chef Gavin Stephenson turns out classic continental fare in the Georgian Room. Younger children swoon over the Teddy Bear Suite, which is decorated every holiday season with adorable bears and a Christmas tableau, with free cookies for visitors.

411 University St., between 4th and 5th avenues. University Street is one-way heading north. ☎ *800-223-8772 or 206-621-1700. Fax: 206-682-9633. Internet:* www.fourseasons.com. *Rack rates: $325–$355. AE, DC, DISC, MC, V.*

Hosteling International–Seattle

$ Pike Place Market

Popular with the international backpacking set, this hostel lies in an excellent location in the lower reaches of the Pike Place Market, a short walk from Pioneer Square and the waterfront. Clean and comfortable, the 1915 building is broken down into dorm rooms that sleep six to ten and share a bath; semi-private dorm rooms that sleep four, with a shared bath; and private rooms for families or couples. A lounge, library, and self-service kitchen and laundry provide public space for guests to stretch out in, linens are available, and unlike most hostels, it has no curfew.

Seattle Accommodations—North & Northeast

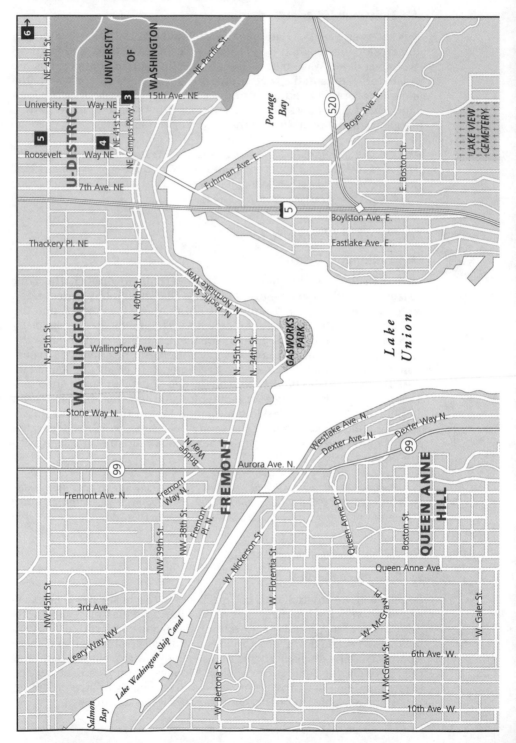

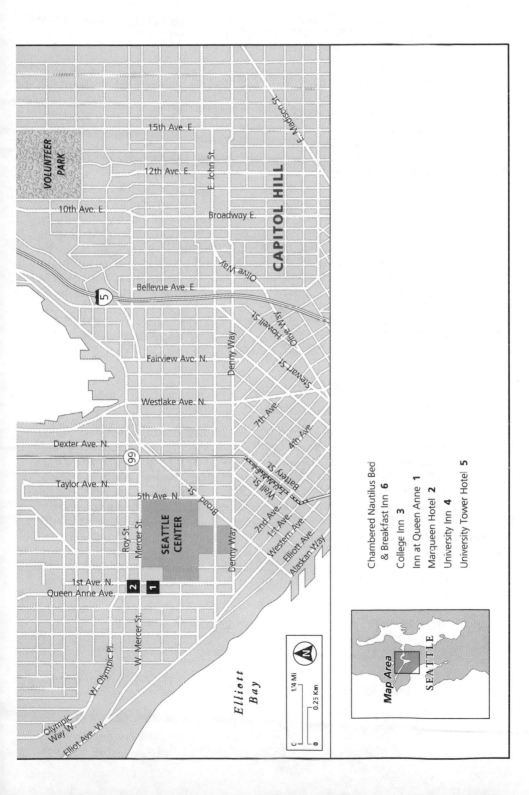

Chambered Nautilus Bed
& Breakfast Inn **6**
College Inn **3**
Inn at Queen Anne **1**
Marqueen Hotel **2**
University Inn **4**
University Tower Hotel **5**

84 Union St. (between Western Avenue and Post Alley on the bottom of the Pike Place Market). ☎ *888-622-5443 or 206-622-5443. Internet:* www.hiseattle.org. *Rack rates: $20–$23 for dorm rooms. AE, MC, V.*

Hotel Edgewater

$$$ Waterfront

How can it be that in a city that is famous for its aquatic environment, the Edgewater is the only full-service lodging on the water? That's one of the reasons this hotel is packed throughout the year. It can't hurt that it's in a marvelous setting on pilings over Elliott Bay with nonstop views of Bainbridge Island, the Olympic Mountains, and ferries crisscrossing Puget Sound. The lodge-style rooms are decorated in plain, peeled pine furniture; fireplaces were added to all the rooms in 2000 to up the charm quotient a notch. Be sure to ask for a water view, and plan to spend some time on your smallish balcony overlooking the bay. Don't miss Myrtle Edwards Park to the north for strolling and biking, and the marvelous Seattle Aquarium to the south. And yes, the Beatles slept here back in 1964, and you can buy a poster of the Fab Four in the hotel's gift shop.

2411 Alaskan Way, north end of the waterfront at the foot of Wall Street. ☎ *800-624-0670 or 206-728-7000. Fax: 206-441-4119. Internet:* www.noblehousehotels.com. *Rack rates: $149 – $239. AE, DC, DISC, MC, V.*

Hotel Monaco Seattle

$$$$ Shopping District

A San Francisco–style export from the Kimpton Group, which has opened Monacos in Denver, Chicago, and San Francisco, the Monaco is anything but a chain hotel. Decorated extravagantly and beautifully, it has a gorgeous lobby of murals and sculptures. The boudoir-like guestrooms, exuding comfortable elegance, are done in striped walls and draped fabrics and bold colors. Rooms are equipped with fax machines and stereos with CD players, and the suites have VCRs and whirlpool tubs in the spacious bathrooms. Billed as a "boutique" hotel, it has a big-hotel feel, with a fitness center, 24-hour room service, evening wine tastings, and a crackerjack concierge and service staff. Next door, the Sazerac restaurant is a Cajun place with terrific food and a crackling urban atmosphere (see Chapter 14).

1101 Fourth Ave., corner of Spring Street. ☎ *800-945-2240 or 206-621-1770. Fax: 206-624-0060. Internet:* www.monaco-seattle.com. *Rack rates: $225–$235. AE, DC, DISC, MC, V.*

Hotel Vintage Park

$$$$ Shopping District

A sister property to the Hotel Monaco, the Vintage Park is a slightly older and more understated version of the boutique hotel, with the Kimpton

Group's same commitment to providing business travelers with an alternative to big, impersonal convention hotels. The lobby is a cozy, living-room-style space, with a fireplace, books, and evening wine tastings. Access to an off-premises health club is offered, as well as valet parking and 24-hour room service. Guestrooms are all named after local wineries, with a purple-and-green grapevine motif on the bedspreads, and walls done in maroon and hunter green. For business travelers, the hotel is wired to the max, with fax machines and high-speed Internet access. Deluxe rooms are a good way to go, with half-canopy beds and granite-trimmed baths. The adjoining Tulio Restaurant is one of the better Italian eateries in town. Businesspersons appreciate the quick access to I-5, but shoppers find that it's a long walk to the best department stores and downtown malls.

1100 Fifth Ave., corner of Seneca Street. ☎ *800-624-4433 or 206-624-8000. Internet:* www.hotelvintagepark.com. *Rack rates: $200–$230. AE, DC, DISC, MC, V.*

Inn at Harbor Steps

$$$ Pike Place Market

Four Sisters Inns, which operates distinctive B&Bs on the West Coast, took a chance on this unique property in the bottom floors of a high-rise apartment/condo building at the Pike Place Market. The spacious rooms, all with sitting areas and fireplaces, have no views, but they open onto a peaceful courtyard garden. Guests can use the building's excellent fitness center, lap pool, and basketball court, and continental breakfast is served. A wood-trimmed library is a great place to read the morning newspaper from the comfort of deep leather chairs.

1221 First Ave. at Seneca Street, just south of Harbor Steps public stairway. ☎ *888-728-8910 or 206-748-0973. Fax: 206-748-0533. Internet:* www.foursisters.com. *Rack rates: $160–$225. AE, DC, MC, V.*

Inn at the Market

$$$$ Pike Place Market

Located in the heart of the Market, this French-inspired inn has long been the boutique getaway of choice for those who want a small, intimate hotel experience in Seattle. It's still pretty tough to beat, with its views of Elliott Bay, expansive rooms trimmed in silk and chenille with bay windows overlooking the waterfront, oversize bathrooms, rooftop patio above the Market, and room service coming from the exquisite Campagne restaurant (see Chapter 14). For a fee, you can use the Seattle Club, one of the better health clubs in town, a few blocks away at the north end of the Market.

86 Pine St. in the Market between Pike Place and First Avenue. ☎ *800-446-4484 or 206-443-3600. Fax: 206-443-0631. Internet:* www.innatthemarket.com. *Rack rates: $190–$265. AE, DC, DISC, MC, V.*

Marqueen Hotel

$$$ Queen Anne

A uniformed doorman with an Eastern-European accent greets you in this converted apartment building in a great location on lower Queen Anne, a short walk from Seattle Center. The hardwood-floor rooms are quirky and old, with small sitting areas and full kitchenettes, which makes this a great bargain for families who don't mind cooking in for some meals. With its refurbished lobby that is all dark mahogany and new carpets, you get the feeling that you've stepped into an elegant, old-city residence. You won't get room service or a restaurant, but a dozen places lie within two blocks; some offer signing privileges for hotel guests.

600 Queen Anne Ave. N. at the corner of Mercer Street. ☎ *888-445-3076 or 206-282-7407. Fax: 206-283-1499. Internet:* www.marqueen.com. *Rack rates: $139–$179. AE, DC, DISC, MC, V.*

Mayflower Park Hotel

$$$ Shopping District

This grand old property in a 1927 building harks back to the days when wealthy businessmen enjoyed grand lodgings in the heart of a big city. The location is superb: in the heart of the downtown shopping district, with an attached walkway to Westlake Center shopping and the monorail to Seattle Center. The lobby is elegant and expansive, and the floor-to-ceiling windows in Oliver's — the bar that makes the best martinis in town — provide a great look at the passing scene on Fourth Avenue. Where the Mayflower Park always comes up a bit short is in its smallish rooms, blandly decorated — the kind of stodgy, faded businessman's lodging that makes you understand why they started building Embassy Suites and Marriotts. Ask for a corner room or suite if you don't want to feel cramped, and be sure to eat at Andaluca, the fine Mediterranean restaurant in the basement (see Chapter 14).

405 Olive Way at Fourth Avenue. ☎ *800-426-5100 or 206-623-8700. Fax: 206-382-6997. Internet:* www.mayflowerpark.com. *Rack rates: $150–$195. AE, DC, DISC, MC, V.*

Paramount Hotel

$$$$ Shopping District

The Paramount has a reputation as an upscale rock-and-roll hotel that houses the big acts that play at the nearby Paramount Theater. The lobby doesn't dispel that image, with its polished marble fireplace and plump sofas. But I find the rooms to be surprisingly mundane, with beige decor and old prints. An Executive King on an upper floor makes up for the lesser rooms with a jetted bathtub and view of downtown, and Pacific Place's shopping and restaurants are right across the street.

724 Pine St. across from Pacific Place. ☎ *800-426-0670 or 206-292-9500. Fax: 206-292-8610. Internet::* www.westcoasthotels.com/paramount/. *Rack rates: $220–$240. AE, DISC, MC, V.*

Renaissance Madison Hotel

$$$ Shopping District

A big convention hotel affiliated with Marriott, the Madison suffers from a less-than-ideal location at the far end of the shopping district, a steep hill climb from the waterfront and Pike Place Market. Fitness buffs and families with kids love the rooftop health club and its indoor swimming pool, whirlpool, and fitness room. For a few extra dollars, the Club Floor offers extra amenities, such as a continental breakfast and afternoon cocktails in a private lounge.

515 Madison St. between 5th and 6th avenues. ☎ *800-278-4159 or 206-583-0300. Fax: 206-624-8125. Internet:* www.renaissancehotels.com. *Rack rates: $140–$240. AE, DC, DISC, MC, V.*

The Roosevelt

$$$ Shopping District

Built in 1929, the centrally-located Roosevelt has benefited from a renovation by its operator, the WestCoast hotel chain. The old dowager still has some pretty tiny rooms at the lower price levels, but the lobby is cheerful and paneled in dark woods, and the new fitness center is top-notch. Upgrade to a hot tub room with a big whirlpool tub if you want a bathroom that doesn't feel tiny and cramped.

1531 Seventh Ave. and Pine Street, across from Pacific Place. ☎ *800-426-0670 or 206-621-1200. Fax: 206-233-0335. Internet:* www.westcoasthotels.com. *Rack rates: $135–$190. AE, DC, DISC, MC, V.*

Sheraton Seattle Hotel and Towers

$$$$ Shopping District

Seattle's biggest, most bustling convention hotel has a little of something for everyone. The lobby resembles Grand Central Station at rush hour, with groups of conventioneers and diners coming and going. Fullers is a tasteful, hushed restaurant that serves exquisite gourmet fare, and the Pike Street Cafe has a calorie-laden (but oh-so-soothing) dessert bar. Standard rooms are modestly appointed and blandly decorated, but big enough to not feel cramped, and concierge-level floors at the top have their own reception and lounge. The health club on the 35th floor is among the best in town, with an indoor pool, whirlpool, and fitness center. Snag a north-facing room for the best views of Lake Union and the Space Needle; a west-facing room looks out on an enormous, view-blocking skyscraper.

1400 Sixth Ave. at Union Street. ☎ ***800-325-3535*** *or 206-621-9000. Fax: 206-621-8441. Internet:* www.sheraton.com. *Rack rates: $240–$280. AE, DC, DISC, MC, V.*

Sorrento Hotel

$$$$ First Hill

This Italianate mansion, with a lovely courtyard and fountain at the entrance, would be one of the finest lodgings in town — if it *were* in town. Instead, the Sorrento is perched on a hillside on busy Madison Street, a steep walk to downtown and more proximate to First Hill's (nicknamed Pill Hill) hospitals. The hotel itself is utterly stylish, with beautifully decorated rooms and public areas, and a complimentary limousine service into the downtown core eases the pain somewhat. A suite upgrade costs as little as $20 more a night and provides an extra sitting area, and views from the west-facing rooms take in all of downtown Seattle. I hear that the penthouse is awfully elegant, too, for those nights when only a $1,000 room will do.

900 Madison St. at Terry Avenue, north of downtown core. ☎ ***800-426-1265*** *or 206-622-6400. Fax: 206-343-6155. Internet:* www.hotelsorrento.com. *Rack rates: $230–$250. AE, DC, DISC, MC, V.*

University Tower Hotel

$$ University District

Art Deco styling is the main attraction of this high-rise hotel, formerly called the Edmond Meany Hotel until new ownership took over and changed it to a Best Western property. The rooms are large, thanks to their corner locations, with smallish baths. Get a room on an upper floor to escape the traffic noise from busy 45th Street and enjoy the best views of the Cascade and Olympic mountains. Proximity to the UW campus and I-5 are big draws, along with the Deco styling and furnishings. Services include a restaurant in the basement and espresso bar and bakery off the lobby, in-room coffeemakers and ironing boards, and a continental breakfast. Parking is free, too, making this a very good bargain.

4507 Brooklyn Ave. NE at NE 45th Street. ☎ ***800-899-0251*** *or 206-634-2000. Fax: 206-547-6029. Internet:* www.meany.com. *Rack rates: $99–$179. AE, DC, DISC, MC, V.*

The Wall Street Inn

$$ Belltown

It may sound businesslike and corporate, but this cheerful inn is a great find in Belltown, with large rooms overlooking Elliott Bay and four-poster beds. A comfy living room with leather furniture and a fireplace doubles as a breakfast room for big, homemade breakfasts, and fresh flowers brighten the sun-filled space nicely. If you'd like to cook in, a patio deck has a barbecue grill, but don't bother: Downstairs is El Gaucho, one of Seattle's best steakhouses.

2507 First Ave. at Wall Street. ☎ *800-624-1117 or 206-448-0125. Fax: 206-448-2406. Internet:* www.wallstreetinn.com. *Rack rates: $85–$145. AE, DC, DISC, MC, V.*

WestCoast Grand Hotel on Fifth Avenue

$$–$$$ Shopping District

Choose a west-facing room on an upper floor for the best views from this business and convention hotel, conveniently located in the thick of the downtown shopping and commercial district. Rooms are larger than most and comfortably furnished, but offer nondistinctive, chain-hotel decor. Coffeemakers and hair dryers are included in the amenities, as well as Nintendo.

1415 Fifth Ave. between Pike and Union streets. ☎ *800-325-4000 or 206-971-8000. Fax: 206-971-8100. Internet:* www.cavanaughs.com. *Rack rates: $109–$159. AE, DC, DISC, MC, V.*

W Hotel

$$$$ Shopping District

Yes, Virginia, there is some style in Seattle. Dressed in dark chocolates and ecrus, with chrome and glass vanity and leather accents, the W Hotel gives stubbornly unfashionable Seattle a rare taste of New York/L.A. style. Not surprising, because it is affiliated with the other new W hotels in New York and L.A., Atlanta, and Sydney. Seattle's version gives you more of the same: a reception desk that's backed by a wall of modernist oils, a lobby that resembles a living room filled with plush, velvety furniture and silver knick-knacks, and rooms wired with great electronics, including a VCR, CD/cassette player, Internet access, and cordless phones. Need some substance to go with the style? The feathery beds are simply the best in town.

1112 Fourth Ave. at Seneca Street, across from Hotel Monaco and Four Seasons Olympic. ☎ *206-264-6000 or 877-W-HOTELS. Fax: 206-264-6100. Internet:* www.w-hotels.com. *Rack rates: $390–$450. AE, DC, DISC, MC, V.*

The Westin Seattle

$$$$ Shopping District

With nearly 900 rooms occupying two cylindrical towers, the Westin, now owned by mega-conglomerate Starwood Resorts, is one of Seattle's top business and convention hotels. Bill Clinton stayed here during the APEC conference and is probably the only head of state to order McDonald's delivered to his room from across the street. Equipped with everything you need in a convention hotel, from an indoor pool and spa to business-equipped rooms with fax machines and Internet access, the Westin bustles with a big-city vibrancy, but it's also curiously cold and impersonal. The hotel's Kid's Club program offers special amenities and services (such as cribs, high chairs, and souvenir items) for the younger set.

1900 Fifth Ave. at convergence of Stewart Street and Westlake Avenue. ☎ *800-WESTIN-1 or 206-728-1000. Fax: 206-728-2259. Internet:* www.westin.com. *Rack rates: $225–$330. AE, DC, DISC, MC, V.*

Index of Accommodations by Price

$
Ace Hotel
Hosteling International—Seattle

$$
Chambered Nautilus Bed
  & Breakfast Inn
University Tower Hotel
The Wall Street Inn

$$$
Hotel Edgewater
Inn at Harbor Steps
Marqueen Hotel
Mayflower Park Hotel
Renaissance Madison Hotel

The Roosevelt
WestCoast Grand Hotel
  on Fifth Avenue

$$$$
Alexis Hotel
Four Seasons Olympic Hotel
Hotel Monaco Seattle
Hotel Vintage Park
Inn at the Market
Paramount Hotel
Sheraton Seattle Hotel
  and Towers
Sorrento Hotel
W Hotel
The Westin Seattle

Index of Accommodations by Neighborhood

Belltown
Ace Hotel
The Wall Street Inn

First Hill/Capitol Hill
Sorrento Hotel

Pike Place Market
Alexis Hotel
Hosteling International—Seattle
Inn at Harbor Steps
Inn at the Market

Queen Anne
MarQueen Hotel

Shopping District
Four Seasons Olympic Hotel
Hotel Monaco Seattle

Hotel Vintage Park
Mayflower Park Hotel
Paramount Hotel
Renaissance Madison Hotel
The Roosevelt
Sheraton Seattle Hotel
  and Towers
W Hotel
WestCoast Grand Hotel
  on Fifth Avenue
The Westin Seattle

University District
Chambered Nautilus Bed
  & Breakfast Inn
University Tower Hotel

Waterfront
Hotel Edgewater

No Room at the Inn?

In high season, Seattle's accommodations choices can be limited. If my favorites (listed earlier in this chapter) are booked solid, the following selections are perfectly fine options.

College Inn

$ **University District**

4000 University Way NE. ☎ ***206-633-4441.*** *Fax: 206-547-1335. Internet:* www.speakeasy.org/collegeinn/. *Rack rates: $65–$80. MC, V.*

Inn at Queen Anne

$$ **Queen Anne**

505 First Ave. N. ☎ ***800-952-5043*** *or 206-282-7357. Fax: 206-217-9719. Rack rates: $99–$109. AE, DC, DISC, MC, V.*

Pensione Nichols

$$ **Downtown**

1923 First Ave. ☎ ***800-440-7125*** *or 206-441-7125. Fax: 206-448-8906. Rack rates: $100. AE, MC, V.*

Pioneer Square Hotel

$$–$$$ **Pioneer Square**

77 Yesler Way. ☎ ***800-800-5514*** *or 206-340-1234. Fax: 206-467-0707. Rack rates: $99–$199. AE, MC, V.*

Sixth Avenue Inn

$–$$ **Downtown**

2000 Sixth Ave. ☎ ***800-648-6440*** *or 206-441-8300. Fax: 206-441-9903. Rack rates: $79–$131. AE, DC, DISC, MC, V.*

University Inn

$–$$ **University District**

4140 Roosevelt Way NE. ☎ ***800-733-3855*** *or 206-632-5055. Fax: 206-547-4937. Rack rates: $92–$119. AE, DC, DISC, MC, V.*

Chapter 11

Orienting Yourself in Seattle and Getting Around

. . . .

In This Chapter

▶ Arriving by air, car, or train

▶ Driving in Seattle

▶ Experiencing the Seattle bus adventure

▶ Taking monorails, streetcars, and ferries

▶ Hitting the town on two wheels — or two feet

. . . .

*H*ere's a little-known civic skeleton-in-the-closet that you can use to goad your new Seattle friends: Seattleites are profoundly envious of Portland's light-rail transportation system. It's a source of local shame that Seattle never got its act together to build a decent public-transportation system, as Portland did, and now you can see the results in the form of daily traffic jams and downtown parking woes. Sure, Seattle has buses, a trolley car, ferries, and even an old monorail that has but two stops, but the bottom line is that Seattle drives to where it's going. (A light-rail system was finally voted in by the local populace in 1999, but it won't be built and ready to use for years.) For travelers whose main objective is to stick to the attractions clustered around the city's downtown core, the lack of public transit matters little. But for those who want to see much more of Seattle and its surrounding environs, it's a good idea to know a bit about your transportation options before you arrive.

Getting from the Airport to Your Hotel

Located 15 miles from downtown Seattle and about the same distance from downtown Tacoma (hence the name, **Sea-Tac International Airport**), Seattle's airport, originally built in the mid-1940s, is surprisingly small for such a large metropolitan area, which is both good and

bad news for travelers. The good news is: It's relatively easy to find
your way around the airport, get your bags quickly, and head over to
ground transportation. The bad news is: The airport is congested and
perennially under construction — last year it moved 27.7 million
people through a facility that was designed to handle about half that
number — with projected expansions into the first decade of the 21st
century that include a much-debated third runway that will add even
more air traffic and subsequent congestion.

You arrive at one of five concourses (a sixth is being renovated and
won't reopen until 2003). From most of these concourses, it's a quick,
easy five-minute walk to the main terminal and lower-level baggage
claims, but from the north and south terminals, you need to take a
subway train to the baggage claim. The train only goes in one direction,
and it's virtually impossible to get lost on it. At the baggage claim, the
15 baggage carousels are clearly marked for each airline, and baggage
retrieval is generally fast. If you need cash, there are ATM machines in
the main concourse between the ticket counters and the gates as well
as on the baggage claim level, and, of course, several espresso vendors
who would love to pour you your first cup of hot Seattle coffee. An
information desk at the baggage-claim level is supposed to assist travelers with ground transportation information, but don't count on
people actually being there to help out, particularly late at night.

You then have a few options for getting into town. Head to either end
of the baggage claim level to find waiting taxis that can drive you the 20
minutes into downtown Seattle (for about $30). You also find represen-
tatives there for Shuttle Express, a shared-van service that can take
you to any address — *except major hotels* — in the metropolitan area
for about $21 for the first passenger and $7 for accompanying passengers. If you'd like a town car, Lincoln Continental transfers are offered
for $50 to downtown points. The cheapest option is to wait (up to a
half-hour) for Gray Line buses that meet in front of the baggage claim
and stop at all of the major downtown hotels — cost: $8.50 per person.
City buses also stop at the airport and head downtown for $1.50, but
it's a long, circuitous trip, and I don't recommend taking them.

If, ten minutes after you leave the airport, you feel as if you're going
around in circles because another airport is visible from the highway,
don't fret or yell at the driver. You're simply passing Boeing Field, a
manufacturing and testing facility for Seattle's favorite aerospace con-
glomerate as well as a small airstrip for charters and private jets.

Rental-car companies are also located on the baggage claim level. They
can sign you up and put you into a courtesy van (keep reading for
more information) for a quick ride to their parking areas.

Courtesy vans for services that use the airport have all been shunted
into the adjoining parking garage. If you're looking for a hotel van,
rental car van, or shuttle to an airport parking lot, you need to continue from the baggage claim up an escalator to a covered bridge that

The million-dollar question: Should you rent a car?

The answer is no and yes, but mostly no. If you're staying in the downtown area and are intent on exploring Seattle's best attractions, you can get by quite well with a judicious use of shoe leather, public transportation, and the odd cab ride. You rarely find that you even need a car. And don't forget that the cost of parking (and the time spent searching for parking) can be prohibitive. If after a few days of scouring Seattle's core you want to venture farther afield — excursions or day trips to the city's far-flung neighborhoods or islands, say to Mount Rainier National Park or Olympic National Park — you can easily rent a car downtown, take your trip, and then return the car to the agency and let them deal with parking. All of the big rental-car agencies have downtown locations, and you can save a considerable amount on taxes if you rent from them rather than picking up your car at the airport.

connects the terminal to the parking garage; go downstairs one level once you get there and wait at one of several courtesy-van stopping points, where phones are available to call your vendor for a pick-up.

Arriving by Car

Driving into Seattle? Lucky you! You get to see right away how hideous traffic can be on Seattle's major transportation arteries. Since the city is surrounded by water to the east and west, you either arrive from the north or south on **Interstate 5,** which can experience major congestion at any time of the day or night, or from the east on **Interstate 90,** which crosses Lake Washington by bridge and grinds to a standstill during rush hours. From I-5, enter downtown from the Seneca Street or Mercer Street exits (both left-lane exits if you're coming from the south). Continuing north on I-5 past Mercer Street puts you onto a bridge over the Ship Canal, with the first exit being NE 45th and 50th streets for the University District, Green Lake, and the near-north neighborhoods. Heading west past Mercer Island and Lake Washington, I-90 dead-ends shortly after you pass the I-5 interchange, putting you into downtown Seattle on 4th Avenue S.

Arriving by Train

Showing up in Seattle on Amtrak's **Coast Starlight** train, which originates in San Diego and runs through Portland, is a fine way to arrive in the Emerald City. The rather dingy and little-used train station is located in the Pioneer Square section of downtown Seattle. A cab ride from the station to a downtown hotel takes just five to ten minutes and costs a few bucks or, if you're traveling light, you can walk to many downtown hotels. But don't do so late at night: That part of Pioneer Square can get rowdy and ominous after the sun goes down.

Getting Around Once You're Here

Transportation, particularly the attendant hassles of keeping and parking a car, can make or break your trip to the Emerald City. Fortunately, most of Seattle is very easily strolled, and buses in the Ride Free Zone can whisk you from one end of downtown to the other. Heed the following advice carefully, and you can spend far more time sightseeing and far less time dealing with transportation hassles as you explore the metro area.

Getting around by car

You can get along just fine in Seattle without a car, particularly if you're only interested in seeing the main attractions in the core of the city. But lots of visitors to Seattle wouldn't think of missing out on the myriad spectacular sights in close range of the city. Whether you're using a car for the full duration of your vacation or simply to take a day trip outside the city, here are some tips on driving the highways and byways of Seattle.

Although they look fat, desirable, and accessible on the map, the main highways of Seattle are frequently the worst places to drive. **Interstate 5,** the major north-south artery, is choked with traffic throughout the day, particularly where it passes under the Convention Center downtown in a bewildering tangle of exits and ramps. **I-90** and **SR520,** the two highway bridges that feed workers and residents into the city from the eastern suburbs, have some of the worst traffic snarls in the country. These tangles exist not only at rush hours but on sports nights when Sonics fans are coming to Seattle Center to watch a basketball game or when Mariners fans are headed to Safeco Field to catch a ballgame. The bottom line: Try to avoid I-5 at all costs during your visit to save yourself lots of time and aggravation (keep reading for an alternative route), or schedule your drives during off-peak hours.

If you're heading east, it's usually better to use I-90 across Mercer Island, but absolutely don't do it during either rush-hour period of the day. On the east side, **I-405,** the bypass route that stretches from just north of the airport to the northern suburb of Lynnwood, can be hellishly plugged throughout the day and is worth avoiding if you can help it.

Street smarts: Where to pick up information

For more information and local maps, head to the **Washington State Convention and Trade Center** at 8th Avenue and Pike Street downtown, where the Seattle-King County Convention and Visitors Bureau (☎ **206-461-5840**) can provide you with brochures and information. If you just need a map, any self-respecting gas station or convenience store should have several of the local area.

Make Route 99 your best friend in Seattle. Also known as Aurora Avenue, this north-south road is the best way to get from downtown to the near-north neighborhoods, or south to the airport. It's much less traveled than I-5 and easier to access. It's also a great way to get to the neighborhood of West Seattle and the ferries to Vashon Island and Southworth.

Most downtown streets are one-way and relatively well-marked. Seattle drivers are, for the most part, very courteous, and they generally give way if you signal your desire to change lanes.

Right on red is the law in Washington, and is restricted only at the few intersections posted with "No Right on Red" signs.

Parking downtown can be a real hassle, not to mention costly if your hotel charges a daily parking fee, but it's doable if you're willing to park a few blocks away from the busiest parts of the city and walk the rest of the way. Here are some tips on where and when to park, how to find free parking, and how to keep your parking cost from becoming prohibitive:

- ✔ On-street parking runs $2 per hour in Seattle and is enforced every day except Sunday and holidays until 6 p.m. The meters accept quarters and dimes only, and most go up to just two hours.

- ✔ Unless you get up at 5 a.m. before the city starts to fill up with workers, you won't find street parking in the downtown core anyway. You may have better luck finding parking in the northern part of downtown, on the streets north of Bell Street as you head toward Denny Way. You can also use the lots at Seattle Center near the Space Needle, which charge about $6 per day, and then take the monorail or a bus into downtown for sightseeing.

- ✔ Downtown parking lots charge between $10 and $15 a day, with early-bird rates offered before 9 a.m. at $6 to $8. Most lots are unattended and require you to stuff your payments into little slots in a central payment box, so make sure you have lots of dollar bills handy. The lots are zealously monitored, and they charge a stiff fine (traceable to you through your rental-car contract) for nonpayment of parking fees.

✔ In the main Shopping District, merchants give you an Easy Streets token for every $20 purchase you make in their stores, which knocks a dollar off the price of parking at most nearby lots.

✔ Neighborhoods like Ballard, Queen Anne, and Capitol Hill, have plenty of free street parking off the main commercial streets. Just drive a block or two away from Market Street, Queen Anne Avenue N., or Broadway, respectively, to find neighborhood parking. Keep an eye out for restricted parking signs in some neighborhoods that only allow street parking by permit (for the use of residents).

✔ If you park your car on one of Seattle's many hills, always point your front tires to the curb, or you may be liable for a fine.

✔ The Pike Place Market's parking garage, located on Western Avenue just opposite the Market, offers free parking for the first hour of shopping. After an hour, you pay $5 for the second hour, and $2.50 an hour after that. An hour gives you plenty of time to run into the Market and grab enough fruit, cheese, and baked goods to make a picnic without having to pay for parking.

Getting around by bus

Chalk it up to Seattle's hilly topography and network of twisting, "arterial" streets (the main routes around town), but the city's **Metro bus system** (☎ **800-542-7876** or 206-553-3000) can get a trifle confusing if you're trying to reach distant points in the city. To reach the Ballard Locks (see Chapter 15), for instance, you need to choose one of eight different routes between First and Fourth avenues downtown, wait for a bus heading north, bump your way around and through parts of Queen Anne, cross the Ballard Bridge, get off on Market Street with a transfer (you get it from the bus driver when you pay), and wait for another bus heading west — a process that can take over an hour for a 15-minute trip. It's not a bad way to see the city, if you have the time and the inclination to sort out bus schedules and wait for transfers, but if you're in a hurry, it's hard to justify. Buses generally run until about midnight, and fares cost $1 to $1.75, depending on the distance you travel and when you travel (riding during commuter hours means higher fares). A big sign on the cash box tells you the fare. You need exact change (dollar bills are accepted), or you can purchase a book of tickets that are valid on all Metro routes and the Waterfront Streetcar (see the section "Getting around by Waterfront Streetcar and monorail") by calling ☎ **206-624-PASS.** Don't forget to ask for a transfer if you need to board a connecting bus.

Riding the bus for free

The best thing about the bus system is that most of downtown Seattle has been established as a Ride Free Zone between 6 a.m. and 7 p.m. This is where you can really use the bus to your advantage, as you hop from Belltown (the Ride Free Zone begins at Battery Street) to the Pike Place Market or Pioneer Square (the Zone ends at South Jackson Street, just a few blocks from Safeco Field), or up the steep hills from the waterfront to Sixth Avenue and the Shopping District without paying a dime. In the Ride Free Zone, you can board the bus from either of the two doors; the driver announces when you're nearing the edge of the Zone. If you continue past the Zone, you exit from the front door and pay on your way out.

Not sure if you're in the Ride Free Zone or if you're past the hours of free rides? You can tell if people are boarding the bus from the front and the rear at the same time, or if the driver holds his hand over the cash box when you board, signaling that you don't have to pay.

The great thing about the Ride Free Zone is that you can board nearly any bus heading in your direction, and you don't have to deal with schedules or routes. Just stay on the bus until it approaches your destination, or if it veers off in another direction, get off at the next exit and grab the next bus going your way. Since it's free, you won't need transfers or tickets.

The electric Kool-Aid bus system

Seattle's one big concession to easing downtown traffic was to build a 1.3-mile-long tunnel underneath the downtown area that is used solely by electric buses. There are five stations between the Convention Center (entrance at 8th Avenue and Pine Street) and the International District, with a central stop near Pioneer Square at 3rd Avenue and James Street. Since it's in the Ride Free Zone, trips through the tunnel are all free (during the Ride Free hours of 6 a.m. to 7 p.m.). It's a quick way to get from the Shopping District to Pioneer Square, and the underground stations are all decorated with interesting public art.

Getting around by taxi

Seattle is not a city where you can hail taxis on the street, but it has a number of competing cab companies that can come and get you at a hotel or attraction. And you can always find cabs lined up and ready to be boarded at major downtown hotels like the Sheraton, the Four Seasons Olympic, and the Westin. Taking cabs is a good way to fill in transportation needs, but if you find that you're taking cabs more than two or three times a day, it can quickly get cost-prohibitive (versus renting a car). The fare is $1.80 for the flag drop and $1.80 for every mile. Try **Yellow Cab** (☎ **206-622-6500**), **Farwest Taxi** (☎ **206-622-1717**), or **Graytop Cab** (☎ **206-782-TAXI**).

Taxis have been chided in Seattle in recent years for their less-than-stellar customer service, and it can take forever to dispatch a car to an out-of-downtown location. If you take a cab to a far-flung corner of the city (like the Arboretum or the Museum of Flight), make sure that they know when to pick you up again for the return trip. You might even plead with the driver to wait for you for an hour (try to get him to do it off the meter). Don't expect to just call and get a quick pick-up from any spot in the city; it might take an hour or more for them to pry a driver away from the downtown area.

If you want to make sure that you always have a ride, and you don't mind paying a premium for the service, call a limousine company to have a town car and driver at your disposal. **Express Car,** a division of Shuttle Express (☎ **425-981-7077**), provides Lincoln Continental town cars for one-way trips or hourly charters ($55 per hour).

Getting around by Waterfront Streetcar and monorail

Downtown Seattle has two quaint transportation alternatives that aren't much for moving the masses but that work great for tourists who want to see the city. **Metro** (☎ **800-542-7876** or 206-553-3000) operates an old-fashioned streetcar along the Alaskan Way waterfront from Pier 70 (near the Edgewater Hotel) to Pioneer Square. The fare is $1 ($1.25 during peak hours), exact change, and during the summer months it runs about every 20 minutes until 10:45p.m.

If you have a car to park, you have a much better chance of finding a spot for it under the Alaskan Way viaduct near Pioneer Square or all the way north on Alaskan Way near Myrtle Edwards Park. Then you can take the Waterfront Streetcar to waterfront attractions like the Aquarium and the Omnidome Film Experience and to elevators or steps leading up to the Pike Place Market.

Similarly, the **Seattle Monorail** (☎ **206-441-6038**) can shoot you directly from its station at Seattle Center near the Space Needle and Experience Music Project to the heart of the downtown shopping district at Westlake Center in just 90 seconds. Alas, these are its only two stops (lots of local people want it to be extended), and the ride is more of a tourist attraction than serious public transportation. It's a great way to get around between those two central points, however, and costs but $1.25 each way, with attendants on hand to make change. It runs until 11 p.m. most nights.

Getting around by ferry

Although it's long past the heyday of the Mosquito Fleet days, when all manner of ships dotted Puget Sound, delivering people and goods to far-flung communities on the water, the **Washington State Ferry system** (☎ 206-464-6400 or 800-84-FERRY) is a quintessential Northwest experience that you shouldn't miss. Ferryboats can't get you around Seattle proper, but they make for great getaway trips to Bainbridge and Vashon islands or the Kitsap Peninsula towns of Bremerton and Southworth (see Chapter 17). You can go by car or on foot to Bainbridge Island, with fares set at $3.70 for passengers and $6.50 for car and driver ($8.25 during peak tourist months in the summer). Ferries leave from Pier 52 on the downtown waterfront and from the Fauntleroy Terminal in West Seattle.

Getting around by bike

Keeping in mind that Seattle is a big, active city, getting around by bicycle can be an alternative if you're an experienced rider. Many Metro buses (see "Getting around by bus," earlier in this chapter) are equipped with bike racks that can take on the steeper hills for you, and the city has several dedicated bike paths. On the downtown waterfront, for example, **Blazing Saddles Bike Rentals** (☎ 206-341-9994; 1230 Western Ave.) has computerized equipment that puts you on the best ride for your shape and size. You could easily negotiate Alaskan Way and the lovely waterfront path at Myrtle Edwards Park by bike, but I wouldn't recommend riding through the busy shopping district unless you're very experienced. North of the Ship Canal, the Burke-Gilman Trail, along with a few side streets, connects all of the neighborhoods from Ballard to the University District with a dedicated bike-and-jogging trail that easily allows you to explore Ballard and its Locks, Fremont, Gasworks Park, Wallingford, and U-District by bike.

To get to the near-north neighborhoods and the Burke-Gilman Trail from downtown by bike, take Westlake Avenue, a wide, safe thoroughfare that runs down the west side of Lake Union, turn right onto the Fremont Bridge (you can use the sidewalk to safely cross it), and then look for the bike path going in either direction on the north side of the ship canal. Going right leads to Wallingford and the U-District; left heads to Ballard.

Getting around on foot

Downtown Seattle is surprisingly compact and, except for a few nasty, San Francisco–style hills, easy to walk. The Pike Place Market and Belltown, for instance, are just a few blocks apart from one another on flat First Avenue, and the center of the Shopping District, at 5th and Pine, is just four long blocks from the Market. An ambitious walker could scour the entire downtown area in one long day (with several stops for rejuvenating lattes). You face some nasty hills from the water-front heading east toward the Shopping District — if you head in that direction, you might consider taking a bus instead. Otherwise, when faced with a steep hill to climb from one avenue to the next, simply head a block or two north or south and you find that the inclines recede. In some places, like Queen Anne Hill, you won't have any option but to suck it up and climb the steep hill, but your effort is rewarded at the top with some marvelous vistas of the city, the mountains, and the water below.

You can see many of Seattle's neighborhoods on foot. Simply take the bus or park your car on one edge of Fremont, Capitol Hill, or Wallingford, and then spend a few hours strolling among the old houses and retail corridors. The Burke-Gilman Trail (see the preceding section) is also a great way to get from one near-north neighborhood to another without encountering any traffic.

 Jaywalking is taken seriously in Seattle. It might seem comical or out-right crazy to you to be standing at a clear intersection with no cars in sight, particularly if you're from New York, but Seattleites won't cross that street until the light changes. And if one of Seattle's Finest catches you jaywalking, you have some 'splainin' to do and a hefty fine to pay.

Chapter 12

Money Matters

● ●

In This Chapter

▶ Accessing your cash on the road

▶ Salvaging your vacation if your wallet is stolen

▶ Taxing tourists, the Seattle way

● ●

*Y*ou've plotted your budget in advance, figuring what it will cost you (and your family) on average to stay, dine, and enjoy the sights in Seattle during your vacation. Now you need to know exactly where in the city you can access cash, where to get more if your wallet is stolen, and just how deep a bite the local taxman plans to take out of your finances.

Where to Get Cash in Seattle

You won't have any problem accessing cash in Seattle. The city is loaded with ATM machines, and there seems to be a bank on every corner of most neighborhoods. With the exception of Washington Mutual (keep reading for more information), most banks charge a service fee ($1 to $1.50) for noncustomers to use their ATMs. So it's smart to try to minimize the number of cash withdrawals you make. The major banks in town are **Bank of America** (☎ 206-461-0800), with dozens of locations; **Washington Mutual** (☎ 800-756-8000), which at the time of this writing was not charging noncustomers a service fee to use its ATMs; **KeyBank** (☎ 800-KEY-2YOU); **Wells Fargo Bank** (☎ 800-869-3557); and **U.S. Bank** (☎ 800-US-BANKS).

Prominent tourist areas that also have ATM machines are **Safeco Field,** the **Pike Place Market** (one is located right behind the Ticket/Ticket booth near Rachel, the Pig; another is inside near the chili parlor), **Pacific Place,** and **Seattle Center.** Many convenience stores also have ATMs, but they charge the highest service fees ($1.50 to $2). Debit cards with a Visa logo are widely accepted at shops and restaurants.

A smart way to use your debit card to access cash without having to pay a service charge is to buy something at a grocery store like **Safeway** (☎ 425-455-6444) or **QFC** (☎ 425-455-3761), pay for it with your debit card, and get cash back.

What to Do If Your Wallet Is Stolen

Almost every credit card company has an emergency 800-number that you can call if your wallet or purse is stolen. Your credit card company may be able to wire you a cash advance off your credit card immediately; in many places, it can get you an emergency credit card within a day or two. The issuing bank's 800-number is usually on the back of the credit card, but that won't help you much if the card was stolen. Copy the number on the back of your card onto another piece of paper before you leave, and keep the copy in a safe place just in case. **Citicorp Visa's** U.S. emergency number is ☎ **800-645-6556. American Express** cardholders and traveler's checks holders should call ☎ **800-221-7282** for all money emergencies. **MasterCard** holders should call ☎ **800-307-7309.**

If you opt to carry traveler's checks, be sure to keep a record of their serial numbers so you can handle just such an emergency, and you should always keep the list of numbers in a safe and separate place so that you're ensured a refund if the checks are lost or stolen. Also, dual checks are available for traveling couples, and either person can sign for them.

If you need quick cash, you can always have someone wire you money in Seattle. Western Union has several offices in Seattle; among them are locations at 539 Queen Anne Avenue N. (☎ **206-285-1400**) and 201 Broadway E. (☎ **206-324-8740**).

Odds are that if your wallet is gone, you've seen the last of it, and the police aren't likely to recover it for you. However, after you realize that it's gone and you cancel your credit cards, you should call to inform the police. You may need the police report number for credit card or insurance purposes later.

Taxing Matters

Washington's sales tax is a hefty 8.8 percent, which partially makes up for the zero state income tax that residents (don't) pay. Visitors get hit with additional taxes. On hotel rooms within the Seattle city limits, it's a total tax of 15.6 percent (after a "convention and trade tax" of 7 percent is tacked on to the existing sales tax). Car rentals get hit the hardest, with an 18.3 percent rental surcharge (which includes taxes levied to pay for the lovely new baseball stadium — remember *that* when you're stuck in ballgame traffic), and yet another 10 percent if you pick up the car at the airport. Holy Toledo, that's 28.3 percent! You can save some of that cost by renting from a downtown agency.

Chapter 13

The Lowdown on the Seattle Dining Scene

● ●

In This Chapter

▶ Dress code? What dress code?

▶ Dining out among the locals

▶ Discovering the hottest trends and happenings in Seattle's restaurants

▶ Keeping food costs down

▶ Knowing where and when to make reservations

● ●

C all it Seattle's Golden Age of good eating. The Internet and high-tech money that fueled the city's economic growth in recent years also brought a whole lot of seared salmon, foie gras, fat steaks, and crème brûlée to town. Today, the city's explosion of new restaurants, particularly in the Belltown area of downtown, continues unabated, and a potential shakeout brought on by the cooling of technology stocks and failure of many e-businesses never happened, at least as of this writing. The competition among restaurateurs is nothing but good news for diners, who can enjoy delicious Pacific Northwest cuisine at any number of venues in a variety of price categories. If, by some chance, you tire of salmon and chowder, Seattle offers plenty of places to sample excellent Italian, pan-Asian, Mexican, and French dishes.

Discovering the Latest Trends, the Hot Seats, and the Star Chefs

Steak has arrived in town with a vengeance, thanks in large part to the success that **El Gaucho** has enjoyed by unashamedly serving up huge portions of tender cow. In the last two years, Seattle has found room for several upscale steakhouse chains, such as **Fleming's, Morton's,** and **Ruth's Chris Steak House.** I include descriptions of my favorites in Chapter 14.

After tucking away your two pounds of prime beef, you'll be thinking about a luscious dessert, of course, and the best restaurants in town go out of their way to provide unique dessert menus with the name of the pastry chef prominently featured. Wrap yourself around a warm pumpkin brioche, a molten chocolate cake, or a perfect *tarte tatin* (upside-down apple tart), and you'll never go back to colored gelatin again. Local star chef Tom Douglas has gone so far as to open a retail bakery alongside the new **Dahlia Lounge** to meet the demand for his insanely delicious coconut-cream pie, which is tall and creamy and covered in shavings of white chocolate.

The hottest restaurant neighborhood of late has been **Belltown,** where you can hardly walk down the street without bumping into a chef who has just opened his own fine-dining establishment. But the sheer saturation of restaurants in the neighborhood, as well as the dearth of available rental space, is good news for other up-and-coming sections of town, such as **Ballard** and **Capitol Hill.** The city's general mania for good food extends also to new delis and take-out kitchens that are popping up in communities and cooking whole meals for families to take home and reheat.

Seattle's top chefs have begun to move on to second-generation projects, and the results are spectacular. Standout cooks like Kerry Sears, Tamara Murphy, and Christine Keff have moved into new ventures with, respectively, **Cascadia, Brasa,** and **Fandango.** With them comes a new level of confidence and experience, as they apply their skills to new variations of Northwest, Mediterranean, and Latin foods. They're on the move literally as well: Tom Douglas picked up and moved his first restaurant (out of the three he now runs), the **Dahlia Lounge,** a few blocks down Fourth Avenue into a bigger, better space, as did **Wild Ginger,** the city's favorite Asian restaurant, which left its nook under the Pike Place Market for more expansive digs on Third Avenue.

Eating Like a Local

Yes, Seattle has its fair share of hot-shot chefs and big-city dining experiences, but the culinary landscape would be much diminished if the regional bounty were not as rich and varied as it is. Here are the staples of land and sea that drive the local diet.

Seafood is king

Seafood is king in Seattle, and I don't just mean king salmon. I'm talking chinook salmon, silver salmon, farm-raised salmon, hook-and-line-caught salmon, and salmon that comes with a pedigree from a specific fishery in Alaska. People around here know the difference between a

Yukon River salmon and a Copper River salmon (they hail from different parts of Alaska, and have slightly different textures and flavors), or a Judd Cove oyster from Orcas Island versus a Quilcene oyster from the Olympic Peninsula. Go to any supermarket in town or visit the fishmongers who hawk (and throw) fresh fish at the Pike Place Market, and you begin to discover the myriad varieties of coldwater fish that Northwesterners love. Besides salmon, there's black cod, a buttery, rich fish that is a wonder in either fresh or smoked form; halibut steaks from Alaska or the chewier, lobsterlike halibut cheeks that resemble large scallops; monkfish that has been known as "the poor man's lobster"; and trout and steelhead from local rivers.

Puget Sound is also a huge producer of shellfish, much of which winds up on local tables. Oysters, clams, mussels, and crab are all available throughout the year (less so during the summer months, when harvests are leaner), and the harvesting of rare, wild razor clams is allowed by the state — people race to their fish markets to get some of the sweet, chewy meat. See Chapter 14 for some of my favorite restaurants for seafood.

To many people, the word "seafood" equals "expensive." That's not necessarily so in Seattle. You can get a fine plate of fish and chips made from lingcod or halibut for under $6 at many places around the city (see Chapter 14 for more on quick and cheap eats), and the local clam chowder — a thick, creamy white soup laden with clams and potatoes — is a steal at under $3 a bowl. Look for more tips on saving money while still eating well, later in this chapter.

Seattle's coffee fix

Seattleites love their coffee and develop strong loyalties to the local coffee shops and brands, whether it's Seattle's Best Coffee, Tully's Coffee, or Starbucks (otherwise known as McCoffee, thanks to their global expansion). In Seattle, expect to find a coffee bar or three on most major intersections of the city and drive-through espresso shacks serving up quick fixes of the local elixir. I list some of my favorites in Chapter 14.

Fresh from the farm to your table

Finally, I can't overemphasize the value of the **Pike Place Market** to the local culinary scene. It's so much more than just a tourist experience; it's the best place to find Washington fruits, fish, and vegetables in season. The success of the market has spawned satellite markets in neighborhoods around the city where farmers come to sell their produce. You can find them on weekends, during the summer and fall months, in the University District, Fremont, and South Seattle.

Dressing to Dine, Seattle Style

Seattle is utterly casual and informal in its attitudes towards dressing up to eat. I know of only one restaurant, **Canlis,** that even *suggests* that men wear a jacket to dinner. Ties are about as prevalent as spats. Even in upscale places like **El Gaucho** that attract a suit-and-tie crowd of attorneys and downtown professionals, it's not unusual to find a casual blue-jeaned and sweater crowd chowing down at the next table from the suits.

Indeed, you are more likely to feel out of place in most Seattle restaurants if you're overdressed, not underdressed. Dress casually and comfortably, and you should fit in fine nearly everywhere. When in doubt, call the restaurant ahead of time if you're not sure what to wear.

Making Reservations

Seattle's best restaurants do fill up, especially on weekends, but you won't be shut out if your schedule is flexible. You definitely need a reservation if you're trying to arrange seating for more than four diners at a time. Lunch rarely calls for a reservation, and if you don't mind eating dinner before 7 p.m., you have a better chance of getting into a hot spot. Be sure to call ahead in any event, because sometimes a whole restaurant may be taken over by a private party. If you have one or two eateries on your list that you absolutely don't want to miss, call ahead at least a week in advance to be sure to secure a table.

For a unique dining opportunity, check to see if your restaurant offers a Chef's Table in the kitchen, where you can watch the staff prepare your dinner. You'll feel as if you have the whole place to yourself. Restaurants like **Buca di Beppo** and the **Georgian Room** have very popular Chef's Tables that sell out well in advance, and more restaurants are following suit.

Cost-Cutting Tips for Dining Out

It would be a pity to miss out on trying some Northwest food favorites like salmon, crab, and oysters because you're trying to keep food costs down. Spend your vacation eating at fast-food joints or national chains and you miss a big part of what makes the Northwest unique. You can minimize your food costs by remembering some of the following suggestions, and then use your savings to splurge for a fine meal:

✔ Coffee bars and espresso stands are cheap spots to go for breakfast, with muffins, rolls, and bagels available alongside the brew. Many of them also carry ready-made sandwiches and salads for lunch.

✔ Don't forget to take advantage of the continental breakfast if your hotel offers one.

✔ Kids are often perfectly happy with a big bowl of inexpensive cereal in the morning, available with milk from any corner grocery store in the city.

✔ You can make one of your daily meals an inexpensive one by ordering takeout food, pizza, or sandwiches, or by grazing the inexpensive food stands at **Seattle Center,** the **Pike Place Market,** or **Westlake Center.**

✔ Seattle's supermarkets, such as **Safeway, QFC,** and **Thriftway,** have all expanded their ready-made-foods departments, with extensive offerings of inexpensive sandwiches, sushi, fresh soups and chili, and Chinese food. Buying a whole roasted chicken, fresh bread, tossed or prepared salads, and a pie for dessert is a delicious and cheap way to feed the family at a picnic in the park.

✔ Dungeness crabs are always cooked directly at sea when they're caught. You can save a bundle on restaurant prices by buying your crabs in season (September through May) from fish markets or supermarkets and making them the featured attraction of a picnic or in-room meal. Ask the store to clean your crab by removing its hard cap and washing out the insides; they should do it at no additional charge. Then crack the shells with your hands or a fork, and pick the meat out. It's delicious cold, especially with a zesty cocktail sauce.

Chapter 14

Seattle's Best Restaurants

· ·

In This Chapter

▶ The top restaurants in the city

▶ Lists of restaurants by location, price, and the type of food served

▶ Snacks and quick bites

▶ Oysters and eggs: The Northwest breakfast

▶ A coffee bar on every corner

▶ Market-grazing and food for picnicking

· ·

I wish that you had a month in Seattle to try out all of the restaurants that I recommend, but even a month won't be enough time to sample all the wonderful places the city has to offer. The dining scene here is varied, prosperous, and very exciting, where great chefs compete in a world-class culinary arena. Food is an important part of the local culture, and many of the places on this list represent the state of the art in Northwest cuisine.

Here I give you a good selection of different cuisines and price ranges. None of the restaurants on the list were thrown in just because they were cheap or offered an unusual type of food, nor do you find the names of any big chain restaurants, because almost without exception they don't measure up to the quality and service that you get from an independent eatery. If budget is a big consideration, see Chapter 13 for some tips on cutting food costs in order to maximize your food budget.

Each listing includes typical prices for standard entrees, along with a quick-reference guide to prices that follows these guidelines for a three-course meal of appetizer, entree, dessert, a beverage, and a tip (from 15 to 20 percent of the total check), per person:

$	Under $20 (cheap eats in a place with little or no decor)
$$	$20–$30 (moderate prices for an ethnic dinner or fancy lunch at a nice restaurant)
$$$	$30–$40 (nicer decor and service and finer dining opportunities)

$$$$	$40–$50 (top-of-the-line at most of the finer places)
$$$$$	over $50 (most exclusive places in town, with multiple courses and great decor)

Seattle Restaurants from A to Z

Andaluca
$$$$ Downtown/Shopping District MEDITERRANEAN

Dark and atmospheric, with carved booths and hand-painted finishes on the walls, this is one of Seattle's finest restaurants for a pan-Mediterranean fare of Spanish paellas, Italian risottos and bruschettas, and a marvelous *meze* of artfully prepared vegetables. You could easily make a meal of several of the small plates from the "shareables" menu of appetizers. But then you'd miss out on the Spanish beef tenderloin entree with its exquisite Marsala glaze and side of grilled pears.

407 Olive Way at the Mayflower Park Hotel. ☎ 206-382-6999. Reservations suggested. Main courses: $18.50–$27.95. Open: Daily 5–10 p.m. (to 11 p.m. Fri and Sat); lunch served Mon–Sat, 11:30 a.m.–2:30 p.m. AE, DC, DISC, MC, V.

Brasa
$$$$$ Belltown CONTINENTAL

Enjoy one of Seattle's finest top-end meals from one of its most celebrated chefs: Tamara Murphy, formerly the executive chef at Campagne. With co-owner Bryan Hill overseeing an eclectic wine list of hundreds of bottles from the Mediterranean region, and pastry chef Valerie Mudry doing wonders with ice creams, *brûlées*, and chocolate creations, Brasa adds up to a memorable dining experience. Put yourself in Murphy's capable hands for dishes such as a roasted monkfish with gnocchi, or suckling pig served with chorizo and clams. Many of the dishes on the menu are cooked in the wood-fired oven (*brasa,* after all, is Portuguese for "live coals"). One of Belltown's favorites, Brasa was named "Best Restaurant in Seattle" in *Food & Wine* magazine's 2000 Restaurant Poll.

2107 Third Ave., at Lenora St. ☎ 206-728-4220. Reservations highly recommended. Main courses: $22–$30. Open: Daily 5–10:30 p.m. (Fri–Sat to midnight). AE, DC, DISC, MC, V.

The Brooklyn Seafood, Steak & Oyster House
$$ Downtown SEAFOOD

This bustling businessmen's restaurant is a great place to try Northwest seafood, particularly the oysters that are served chilled on the half-shell from more than a dozen different producers, allowing you to taste the difference between a Quilcene and a Kumamoto. You also can't go wrong with the grilled fish or crab dishes. If the restaurant looks historic and venerable, that's because it's housed in one of the city's oldest buildings. The Oyster Bar is a great place for a happy-hour snack and microbrew.

1212 Second Ave., at University Street, near Benaroya Hall. ☎ 206-224-7000. Reservations generally not necessary. Main courses: $16–$34. Open: Mon–Fri, 5–10 p.m. (to 10:30 p.m. Fri), 4:30–10:30 p.m. Sat, 4–10 p.m. Sun; open for lunch Mon–Fri, 11 a.m.–3 p.m. AE, DC, DISC, MC, V.

Buca di Beppo
$$ Lake Union   ITALIAN

I don't usually recommend chain restaurants, but I make an exception for Buca di Beppo, offshoots of which are springing up all over the country. Why? Because it is riotous fun, and the spaghetti-and-meatballs cuisine is done awfully well. Beppo's is a crowd-pleaser that kids adore, with kitschy decor and walls plastered with photos. The food comes in huge portions on platters, and if you order more than three things for six people, you end up taking food home. Try the four-cheese pizza and linguine *frutti di mare;* the meatballs are as big as softballs. For the ultimate experience, reserve the Pope's Room in advance (for parties of 8 or more), or the Kitchen Table, where you can watch the chefs cook.

701 Ninth Ave. N. at Roy Street. ☎ 206-244-2288. Limited reservations accepted, but call ahead to put your name on the seating list. Go early for the best chance for a short wait. Main courses: $15–$25, but they're made for 2 to 4 people each. Open: Mon–Thurs, 5–10 p.m., Fri 5–11 p.m., Sat 4–11 p.m., Sun noon–10 p.m. AE, DC, DISC, MC, V.

Cafe Juanita
$$$$ Kirkland   NORTHERN ITALIAN

We hesitate to send you across Lake Washington for food (the traffic can be brutal), but there's no denying that Chef Holly Smith is creating some of the most exquisite Italian food in town. You won't find a tomato on the menu most days as she sticks to Northern Italian favorites like hand-cut tagliatelle pasta with local chanterelles, great risottos, or creamy fonduta cheese with bruschetta and white truffle oil. The ambience is warm and cozy, and the wine list is loaded with top bottles from the Piedmont region of Italy. Allow plenty of time for crossing the lake on the SR520 bridge and plan to spend several hours eating your way through Smith's menu.

9702 NE 120th Place, Kirkland. Call for directions. ☎ 425-823-1505. Reservations essential. Main courses: $15–$28. Open Tues–Sun, 5–10 p.m. (Sun to 9 p.m.).AE, DC, MC, V.

Downtown Seattle Dining

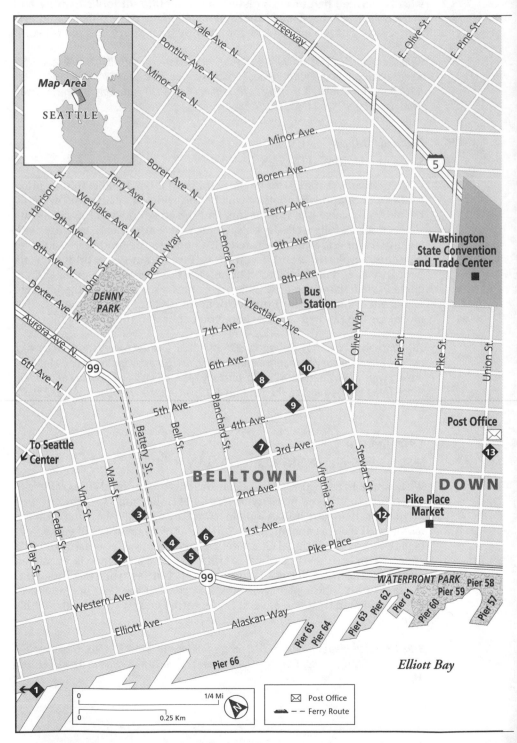

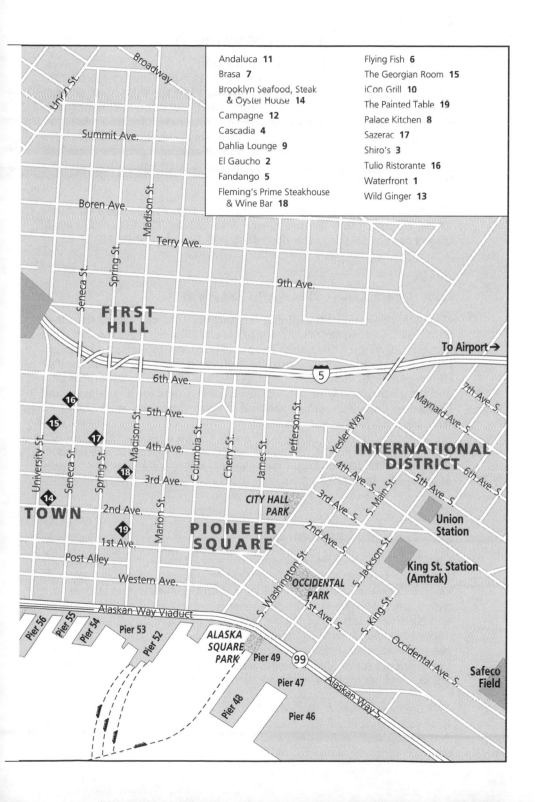

Andaluca **11**

Brasa **7**

Brooklyn Seafood, Steak & Oyster House **14**

Campagne **12**

Cascadia **4**

Dahlia Lounge **9**

El Gaucho **2**

Fandango **5**

Fleming's Prime Steakhouse & Wine Bar **18**

Flying Fish **6**

The Georgian Room **15**

iCon Grill **10**

The Painted Table **19**

Palace Kitchen **8**

Sazerac **17**

Shiro's **3**

Tulio Ristorante **16**

Waterfront **1**

Wild Ginger **13**

Campagne

$$$$ Pike Place Market COUNTRY FRENCH

For 16 years, Campagne has been one of Seattle's favorite French bistros, stubbornly sticking to its populist roots in making country French fare available to the whole family. As such, its fit in the Pike Place Market couldn't be better. Try the *tarte flamiche* with leeks and bacon, or three-course family dinners that might be *poulet roti* (roast chicken) one night, steak frites another. The adjoining Café Campagne does a bistro menu and packs them in for Sunday brunches of croque madames (ham and Gruyère on thick slices of fresh bread with a fried egg on top) and big bowls of coffee.

86 Pine St., at the Inn at the Market, between First Avenue and Pike Place.
☎ *206-728-2800. Reservations suggested. Main courses: $24–$30; prix fixe family dinners begin at $25 per person. Open: Daily 5:30–10 p.m. AE, DISC, MC, V.*

Canlis

$$$$ Queen Anne STEAK AND SEAFOOD

One of Seattle's oldest fine-dining restaurants, this was always the place where you took Grandma out for a special dinner. Second-generation owners Chris and Alice Canlis have worked hard to bring it up to contemporary standards, and with the help of chef Greg Atkinson, they've succeeded. With views high atop Lake Union, it's still a memorable site, and the service and wine list are impeccable. Come for filet mignon and Dungeness crabcakes, grilled salmon, or lamb chops,and finish things off with a fluffy soufflé.

2576 Aurora Ave. N., just before the Ship Canal Bridge, and reachable only on north-bound lanes. ☎ *206-283-3313. Reservations required; jackets advised for men. Main courses: $24–$41. Open: Mon–Sat, 5:30 p.m.–midnight. AE, DC, DISC, MC, V.*

Carmelita

$$$ Fremont VEGETARIAN

Chef Dan Braun's vegetarian menu isn't just bean sprouts and lettuce leaves: He fashions a thoughtful, interesting menu out of organic foods and produce that is more about flavor than vegetarian dogma. Start out with a bowl of elephant-garlic potato soup served with truffled croutons, and consider a homemade pizza topped with roasted eggplant or a red pepper tapenade. Entrees include pastas, gnocchis, and tofu dishes in generous portions. Set in two rooms elegantly decorated with paintings, Carmelita's is one of the few vegetarian places I've been to where I never felt like looking for meat alongside the potatoes.

7314 Greenwood Ave. N., just past the west side of the zoo. ☎ *206-706-7703. Reservations suggested. Main courses: $13.95–$15.95. Open: Tues–Sun, 5–10 p.m. (to 10:45 p.m. on Fri and Sat). MC, V.*

Cascadia

$$$$$ Belltown   NORTHWEST

This private venture by Aussie chef Kerry Sears and his hostess wife, Heidi Grathwol, gets it all right. The idea was to apply Kerry's fine-dining skills to preparing ingredients that only come from the Pacific Northwest, and the result is a sensational series of tasting menus offered daily that might include baked mussels with leek sauce and stuffed mushrooms, an herb-baked partridge with blackberry reduction, or a perfect sage crepe in a wine demi-glaze. Whimsical touches like a "chocolate catch of the day" for dessert, or a sensational mushroom soup served from a can (which Sears also designed) keep it fun, and the room is a cool, flowing space of hardwoods and cut glass. Cascadia has been one of the top tables in town since it opened in 1999, and it hasn't slipped an inch since. The prix fixe menus are the way to go, but feel free to mix and match from the many categories of food. Portions are small, and five courses just begin to satisfy big eaters. Early birds get great deals on a three-course meal.

2328 First Ave., between Bell and Battery streets. ☎ 206-448-8884. Reservations advised. Main courses: $28–$30; 6- and 7-course tasting menus run $65–$90. Open: Mon–Sat, 5–10 p.m. (to 10:30 p.m. Fri and Sat). AE, DC, DISC, MC, V.

Cassis

$$$ Capitol Hill   COUNTRY FRENCH

French farmhouse cooking comes to a quiet corner of Capitol Hill in this charming little bistro that serves up big, satisfying portions of classic French food. A different country favorite is featured each weekday, such as a rich cassoulet on Sundays and choucroute garni on Wednesdays, and an early-evening three-course prix fixe is a bargain at $24. The room is small and loud, and tables are close together as patrons tuck into steak frites, braised wild boar, or a fragrant fish soup.

2359 Tenth Ave. East about a half-mile north of the Broadway retail district. ☎ 206-329-0580. Reservations suggested. Main courses: $17–$22; 3-course prix fixe 5–7 p.m: $24. Open: Daily 5–10 p.m. (Fri and Sat to 11 p.m.). AE, MC, V.

Chinook's at Salmon Bay

$$ Magnolia   NORTHWEST SEAFOOD

A working fishing-boat anchorage is the perfect setting for this bright, bustling restaurant that specializes in oyster stews, clam chowders, and big servings of fresh salmon and halibut that come on plates piled with roasted potatoes and vegetables. The fish and chips are among the best in town, and salads and sandwiches are available for lighter eaters.

1900 W. Nickerson St. at Fisherman's Terminal (exit Elliott Avenue W. just before the Ballard Bridge). ☎ 206-283-HOOK. Reservations not necessary. Main courses: $8–$15. Open: Daily from 4 p.m.; lunch served Mon–Fri, 11 a.m.–4 p.m. and Sat 11:30 a.m.–4 p.m.; breakfast served Sat and Sun, 7:30 a.m.–11:30 a.m. AE, MC, V.

Seattle Dining—North & Northeast

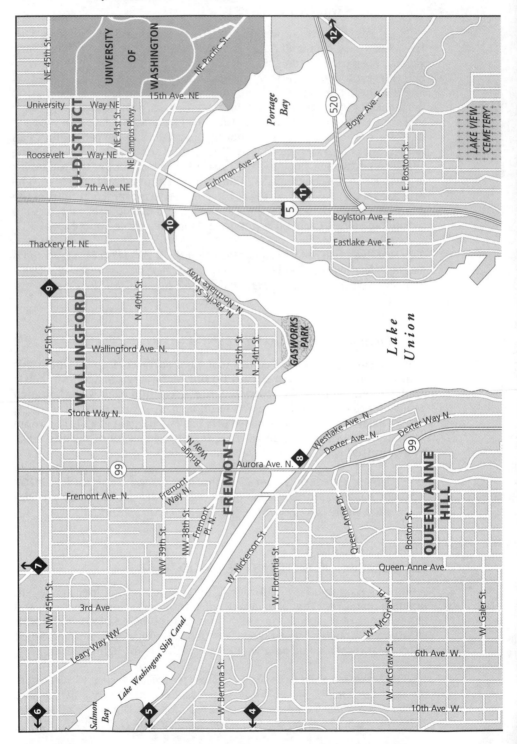

VOLUNTEER PARK

15th Ave. E.

12th Ave. E.

E. John St

10th Ave. E.

Broadway E.

CAPITOL HILL

E. Madison St

Olive Way

Bellevue Ave. E.

Howell St.

Olive Way

Fairview Ave. N.

Denny Way

Stewart St.

Westlake Ave. N.

7th Ave.

4th Ave.

Dexter Ave. N.

99

Wall St.

Battery St.

Taylor Ave. N.

5th Ave. N.

Broad St.

2nd Ave.

1st Ave.

Western Ave.

Elliott Ave.

Alaskan Way

SEATTLE CENTER

Denny Way

Roy St.

Mercer St.

1st Ave. N.
Queen Anne Ave

W. Mercer St.

Elliott Bay

W. Olympic Pl.

Olympic Way W.

Elliot Ave. W.

1/4 Mi

0.25 Km

0

0

Map Area

SEATTLE

Buca di Beppo **3**
Cafe Juanita **12**
Canlis **8**
Carmelita **7**
Cassis **11**
Chinook's at Salmon Bay **5**
Dick's Drive-Ins **2, 9**

Ivar's Salmon House **10**
Kaspar's **1**
Nishino **13**
Palisade **4**
Ray's Boathouse and Café **6**
Rover's **14**

Dahlia Lounge

$$$ **Belltown** NORTHWEST FUSION

Local star Tom Douglas moved this, his first solo restaurant in Seattle (out of three that he now operates), to a bigger, better space in Belltown in 2000, and it benefits greatly from the upgrade. The menu still has the most sensational crabcakes in town, as well as Asian-influenced dishes of meat and fish. The Sea Bar offers varieties of fresh seafood with interesting sauces, and the coconut-cream pie is a local legend, with shavings of white chocolate and coconut cascading off the plate. If you can't live without it, it's now available at a bakery that Douglas opened alongside the restaurant.

2001 Fourth Ave. at Virginia Street. ☎ 206-682-4142. Reservations advised. Main courses: $16–$31. Open: Mon–Sat, 5:30–10 p.m. (to 11 p.m. on Fri and Sat); Sun 5–9 p.m.; lunch served Mon–Fri, 11:30 a.m.–2:30 p.m. AE, DC, DISC, MC, V.

Dick's Drive-Ins

$ **Queen Anne, Ballard, and Wallingford** BURGERS

Seattle's local hamburger joint competes with the national fast-food chains to offer cut-rate burgers, fries, and terrific milkshakes made, naturally, with real milk. Try a Dick's Deluxe burger (a Big Mac by any other name) and a thick chocolate shake to fuel up for a day of sightseeing or revive after a night of dancing.

500 Queen Anne Ave. N., at Republican Street. ☎ 206-285-5155; 9208 Holman Rd. in north Ballard (15th Ave. NW becomes Holman above 90th Street). ☎ 206-783-5233; 111 NE 45th St., in Wallingford between 1st and 2nd avenues NE. ☎ 206-632-5125. Burgers and shakes under $3 each. Open: Daily 10:30 a.m.–2 a.m. No credit cards.

El Gaucho

$$$$ **Belltown** STEAK

Seattle's favorite place to tuck into a slab of beef is this big, cavernous dining room in Belltown with elegant waiters dressed in livery who attend to your every need. The meat is sensational, with classic cuts of sirloin and porterhouse and lamb and veal chops, and the tableside service of desserts, like bananas Foster or flaming Spanish coffees, are nearly worth the considerable price. Plan to eat big and spend big. The bar area is one of Belltown's liveliest for the after-work business crowd, and downstairs, the Pampas Room nightclub has live music and dancing most nights.

2505 First Ave. at Wall Street. ☎ 206-728-1337. Reservations suggested. Main courses: $13.50–$39. Open: Daily 5 p.m.–2 a.m. (Sun to 11 p.m.). AE, DC, MC, V.

Fandango
$$$ Belltown LATIN

Christine Keff, who made her name locally with nearby Flying Fish, opened this bright, fun restaurant to bring a little needed culinary diversity to the local dining scene. The result is a menu of Latin dishes rarely seen in these parts, like a Brazilian crab soup, oxtail stew served with plantains and yucca, and a rich vegetarian *posole* stew from Mexico. True to form, the locals are eating it up, making Fandango one of the newer hits on the Belltown restaurant scene.

2313 First Ave. between Bell and Battery streets. ☎ 206-441-1188. Reservations advised. Main courses: $14.85–$18.95. Open: Daily 5 p.m.–midnight. AE, DC, MC, V.

Fleming's Prime Steakhouse & Wine Bar
$$$$ Shopping District STEAK

A great location puts this urban steakhouse at the top of the heap of recent additions to the local steak scene. The handsome room in the Expediter building has comfortable booths, high ceilings, and large windows looking out over Madison Street. The filet mignon and strip steaks are perfectly broiled, and appetizers of Dungeness crab or sauteed scallops are a delicious way to prepare for the meat. A wine list with over 100 wines by the glass allows you to explore Northwest wines quite well.

1001 Third Ave. at Madison Street. ☎ 206-587-5300. Reservations suggested. Main courses: $17.50–$26.95. Open: Daily 5–10 p.m. (to 11 p.m. Fri and Sat). AE, DC, MC, V.

Flying Fish
$$ Belltown SEAFOOD

Northwest seafood meets Asian preparations in this chic, crowded restaurant that draws a hip young Belltown crowd. Christine Keff brought her flair and considerable cooking talents to this, her first solo restaurant. People come for the ambience and dishes like a perfectly seared ahi tuna or a Northwest steelhead spiced with Asian accents. An "Oyster Happy Hour" brings out the best shellfish in the region and accompanies them with crisp, white wines, and the desserts are worth waiting for. In the summer, the whole scene spills out onto sidewalk tables.

2234 First Ave. at Bell Street. ☎ 206-728-8595. Reservations suggested. Main courses: $9–$17. Open: Daily 5 p.m.–1 a.m. AE, DC, MC, V.

The Georgian Room
$$$$$ Downtown/Shopping District CONTINENTAL

Under the tutelage of chef Gavin Stephenson, this fine-dining room at the Four Seasons Olympic delivers expert preparations of standards like grilled salmon, rack of lamb, and beef tenderloin. The room is everything you'd want from an urban oasis, all vaulted ceilings and high windows dressed in long drapes. If you want to impress your clients, book (well in advance) the chef's table in the kitchen, which gives a small group a bird's-eye view of the cooks at work.

411 University St. at the Four Seasons Olympic Hotel. ☎ 206-621-7889. Reservations advised. Main courses: $26–$38. Open: Mon–Sat, 5:30–10 p.m. (to 10:30 p.m. Fri and Sat); Sun brunch 7 a.m.–1 p.m. AE, DC, MC, V.

iCon Grill

$$$ Downtown/Shopping District   REGIONAL AMERICAN

The decor declares that the place is pure fun, with dozens of blown-glass balls hanging in nets and small lamps dotting nearly every available surface. Don't miss the hysterical treatments accorded the bathrooms, with dramatic music and video screens running clips of gushing waterfalls. And the food? It's an equally entertaining mix of comfort foods (even macaroni and cheese and meatloaf) and standards like broiled salmon or a merlot-braised lamb shank.

1933 Fifth Ave. at Virginia Street. ☎ 206-441-6330. Reservations suggested. Main courses: $10–$27. Open: Daily 5:30–9 p.m. (to 10 p.m. Tues–Thurs, and to 11 p.m. Fri and Sat); lunch served Mon–Fri, 11:30 a.m.–2 p.m. AE, MC, V.

Ivar's Salmon House

$$ Lake Union   SEAFOOD

You see Ivar's fish and chips shops around the city thanks to a local restaurateur who staked his claim here to inexpensive seafood. This flagship restaurant, located on a quiet stretch of Lake Union waterfront near Gasworks Park, is decorated to look like an American Indian longhouse, with totem poles, a long canoe, and an open-pit area where salmon is cooked on alderwood. Yes, the fish and chips are first-rate, and Ivar's has always made one of the best clam chowders in town — but it's the flavorful salmon that is the real hit here.

401 NE Northlake Way between Fremont and the University District on the north shore of Lake Union. ☎ 206-632-0767. Reservations suggested. Main courses: $12–$30. Open: Mon–Sat, 11 a.m.–10 p.m. (to 11 p.m. Fri and Sat); Sun 10 a.m.–2 p.m. for brunch, and 3:30–10 p.m. for dinner. AE, MC, V.

Kaspar's

$$$ Queen Anne   CONTINENTAL

A secret favorite of many locals, this homey place is situated on a quiet Queen Anne street. It's presided over by chef Kaspar Donier, who serves an eclectic continental menu that is long on seafood and fresh, local products. Try his chef's table in the kitchen for a very personal dining experience, or the wine bar for excellent, low-priced bites and glasses of wine.

19 W. Harrison St. ☎ 206-298-0123. Reservations suggested. Main courses: $15 $23. Open: Tues–Sat, 5–9 p.m. (to 10 p.m. Fri and Sat) AE, MC, V.

Nishino
$$$ Madison Park SUSHI

A favorite of high-rollers and Microsofties (original vice-president of sales Scott Oki is a co-owner), this is one of the top spots in town for sushi and Japanese food, thanks to the talents of Japanese chef Tatsu Nishino. Try the Arboretum Roll, named after the nearby park, for an unusual pairing of avocado, rice, and the freshest fish, and a $60 prix fixe *omakase* meal makes a believer out of anyone who harbors doubts as to the splendors of Japanese cuisine. Expensive but exquisite.

3130 E. Madison St. near Lake Washington. ☎ 206-322-5800. Reservations necessary. Main courses: $4–$17; sushi, $2.50–$7 a pair. Open: Daily 5:30–10:30 p.m. (Sun to 9 p.m.). AE, MC, V.

The Painted Table
$$$$ Pike Place Market NORTHWEST FUSION

Hand-painted chargers on the table and colorful, high-backed booths announce an unusual and delightful dining experience in this room near the Seattle Art Museum. Chef Tim Kelley doesn't disappoint, serving a unique blend of Northwest favorites like Ellensburg lamb alongside small, exquisite plates of Asian fare. Everything is beautifully displayed and presented on lacquered plates. For a memorable meal, put yourself into Kelley's hands by ordering the chef's tasting menu, or accompany him on special meals that begin with shopping at the nearby Pike Place Market to pick out ingredients.

92 Madison St. (at First Avenue), at the Alexis Hotel. ☎ 206-624-3646. Reservations suggested. Main courses: $16–$28. Open: Daily 5:30–10 p.m.; lunch served Mon–Fri, 11:30 a.m.–2 p.m. AE, DC, DISC, MC, V.

Palace Kitchen
$$$ Downtown/Shopping District REGIONAL AMERICAN

Local star Tom Douglas's base of operations is also his hippest restaurant, which stays open late into the evening to serve an eager club-going crowd his signature Burger Royale, grilled salmon, or a plate of artisan cheeses. The big, horseshoe-shaped bar is a premier see-and-be-seen place in town, and the kitchen is open and bustling into the wee hours.

2030 Fifth Ave. ☎ 206-448-2001. Reservations advised. Main courses: $10–$23. Open: Daily 5 p.m.–2 a.m. AE, DISC, MC, V.

Palisade
$$$ Magnolia   SEAFOOD

It's a bit hard to find, but well worth the drive to Elliott Bay Marina to find this gorgeous, sprawling restaurant. Outside are views of the Olympic Mountains and ferries skimming Puget Sound; inside are slate floors and an enormous saltwater fishpond with anemones and swimming trout. Seafood is the order of the day, and frequently the kitchen offers selections from all points of the world, such as prawnlike Moreton Bay Bugs (a saltwater shellfish from Australia). You always find Northwest salmon and oysters on the menu. Sunday brunches are a good buy, with a fruit (and chocolate) buffet to go with your breakfast entree.

2601 W. Marina Place at Elliott Bay Marina; exit Elliott Avenue for the Magnolia Bridge and follow the signs to the marina. ☎ *206-285-1000. Reservations advised. Main courses: $15–$33. Open: Mon–Sat, 5:30–9:30 p.m. (to 10 p.m. on Fri and Sat); Sun brunch 10 a.m.–2 p.m. and dinner 4–9 p.m.; lunch Mon–Fri, 11:30 a.m.–2 p.m.; Sat 12–2 p.m. AE, DC, DISC, MC, V.*

Ray's Boathouse and Cafe
$$$ Ballard   SEAFOOD

A splendid view of Puget Sound and the Olympic Mountains draws flocks of people to this popular seafood restaurant near the Ballard Locks. Downstairs is a fine-dining restaurant specializing in salmon, clams, and other seafood in exquisite preparations. Upstairs it's a bit more casual, and cheaper, and the outdoor deck is a huge hit during the summer months. Waiting times can be long and service spotty, so I don't recommend it for families with restless kids.

6049 Seaview NW, past the Ballard Locks. ☎ *206-789-3770. Reservations advised; drop-in chances are better for the upstairs bistro. Main courses: $16–$45 (boathouse); $9–$17 (cafe). Open: Daily 11:30 a.m.–10 p.m. AE, DC, DISC, MC, V.*

Rover's
$$$$$ Madison Park   CLASSIC FRENCH

This may well be the best restaurant in town, at least according to the readers and food editors of *Seattle Magazine.* I certainly wouldn't argue the point. Chef Thierry Rautureau, a transplanted Frenchman, is getting national recognition for his exciting, classically-based French cooking. The setting is a handsome frame house in an affluent neighborhood, and the excellent service and Rautureau's ready smile make you feel like part of the family. Some of his meals, such as an 11-course Halloween feast with chef and diners *en costume,* are legendary and sell out close to a year in advance. On any ordinary night, though, you select a prix fixe menu and watch as an array of wonders arrives at your table, such as spot prawns with foie gras and a celeriac puree, a perfect squab breast with caramelized turnips and Armagnac sauce, or scallops with foie gras in a chestnut puree — heavenly. Pair an eight-course chef's menu with Northwest and French wines for each course, and you'll reach dining Nirvana.

2808 E. Madison St. ☎ *206-325-7442. Reservations required. Main courses: 5-course tasting menu, $69.50; 8-course menu, $97.50. Open: Tues–Sat, 5:30–9:30 p.m. AE, DC, MC, V.*

Salty's on Alki Beach
$$$ West Seattle   SEAFOOD

The food isn't the reason that people make the trek to this eatery in the bedroom community of West Seattle; it's the view. Seattle's downtown skyline is in full panoramic splendor from Salty's dining room and outdoor deck, and that makes the basic menu of salmon, fish and chips, and steamed clams go down easily — very popular in the summer months when the deck is open. Try to hold out for a late table after dusk (which can be 9 p.m. or later in the middle of summer) for the best view of the city skyline.

1936 Harbor Ave. SW. Take the West Seattle Bridge exit on I-5 or Rte. 99 south, and then the first exit in West Seattle to reach Alki Beach. ☎ *206-937-1085. Reservations advised. Main courses: $17.50–$36. Open: Daily 5–10 p.m. (Sat from 4–10 p.m. and Sun from 4–9 p.m.); lunch served Mon–Fri, 11 a.m.–2:30 p.m., Sat noon–3 p.m.; Sun brunch 9 a.m.–2 p.m. In summer Salty's keeps later hours; call for times. AE, DISC, MC, V.*

Sazerac
$$$ Downtown/Shopping District   CAJUN

A San Francisco–style restaurant attached to the Hotel Monaco, Sazerac is a big, exuberant place with an open kitchen that produces huge portions of Cajun-style comfort foods. The jambalaya and fried catfish are terrific, and steak comes out in thick slabs smothered in a spicy sauce. The small bar area is a lively meeting place during happy hours, and the restaurant is named after a New Orleans cocktail of whiskey and Pernod. Try one: It will put you in the festive, Sazerac mood.

1101 Fourth Ave. at Spring Street, adjacent to the Hotel Monaco. ☎ *206-624-7755. Reservations advised. Main courses: $10–$25. Open: Mon–Thurs, 5–10 p.m. (Fri and Sat 5–11 p.m.); lunch served Mon–Sat, 11:30 a.m.–2:30 p.m.; breakfast served Mon–Fri, 6:30–10 a.m., Sat and Sun 7–10:30 a.m.; Sun brunch 9 a.m.–2:30 p.m. AE, DISC, MC, V.*

Shiro's
$$ Belltown   SUSHI

Japanese chef Shiro Kashiba is the undisputed master of preparing fresh sushi in Seattle. He earned his stripes at the Nikko restaurant at the

---

Serendipity in a savory bowl of soup

In this chapter, I barely scratch the surface of the sheer number of eating opportunities in Seattle. When it comes down to it, however, sometimes the most fun of a trip comes in seeking out and finding your own favorite place. Serendipity in Seattle comes in many forms: in a savory bowl of soup at a plant-filled coffeehouse, in a basket of fish and chips at the Pike Place Market, or in a sexy little tapas bar along a side street. Check out the following neighborhoods, all of which offer plenty of opportunities to discover your own great place or simply to enjoy a quick bite as you look around.

On **Capitol Hill,** the food is mostly concentrated on the retail strip of Broadway between Pike Street and Roy Street. You find pizza, great burgers, and ethnic food that includes good Thai, Mexican, and Mongolian barbecue.

The **Fremont** neighborhood has plenty of good places to grab a bite as you stroll around the kitschy antique shops and public art. Look for the Still Life in Fremont coffeehouse for vegetarian fare, great soups, and homemade pastries and cookies. There are two good Thai places, pizza, and a restaurant solely devoted to desserts that sells some great ones. Of course, the bars and brewpubs that cater to college students and neighborhood regulars all have good eats, too. At the top of the hill, a few blocks south of the zoo, the Marketime grocery store has great prepared sandwiches and salads.

The **Wallingford** shopping district on NE 45th Street houses a great variety of medium-priced restaurants. You find a stretch of ethnic restaurants in a five-block area, including a Pakistani place, curry houses, a Japanese noodle and sushi place, and a Spanish tapas restaurant. Look in the Wallingford Center shopping center in a former public grade school for several good choices. The grocery store on the corner of Wallingford Avenue has prepared foods (you could take them to the park a block south), and the bakery on NE 45th has portion-size packages of cheese and patés to go with the bread and croissants.

In the **Queen Anne** neighborhood, look to both the lower and upper parts of Queen Anne Avenue N. for lots of inexpensive food shops. You have your choice of submarine sandwiches, wraps, Italian food, a Chinese buffet, and a place that brags about its New York–style bagels. The coffee shops here have terrific desserts, too.

Westin before striking out on his own with this small, crowded Belltown restaurant that packs them in every night for exquisite sushi preparations. Get there early to avoid the masses, and if Shiro says "try the mackerel," don't think twice. The man has an eye for fresh fish, and his diners are the better for it.

2401 Second Ave. at Battery Street. ☎ 206-443-9844. Reservations suggested. Main courses: $16–$20.50. Open: Mon–Sat, 5:30–10 p.m., Sun 4:30–9 p.m. AE, MC, V.

Tulio Ristorante

$$$ **Downtown/Shopping District NORTHERN ITALIAN**

Chef Walter Pisano named the place after his Italian father, and Tulio's indeed has the atmosphere of a warm, family gathering. Sometimes Tulio himself is on hand to greet guests. The fare is elegantly prepared Northern Italian, with some standout dishes that linger in memory, such as a smoked salmon ravioli or sweet-potato gnocchi. Service is topnotch; larger parties should try to reserve a private banquet table located on the mezzanine above the somewhat crowded main dining room.

1100 Fifth Ave. at Seneca Street at the Hotel Vintage Park. ☎ *206-624-5500. Reservations advised. Main courses: $12–$24. Open: Daily 5–10 p.m. (to 11 p.m. Fri and Sat); lunch served Mon–Fri, 11 a.m.–2 p.m., Sat and Sun, noon–3 p.m. AE, DC, DISC, MC, V.*

Waterfront

$$$$ **Belltown NORTHWEST FUSION**

The Seattle waterfront has had plenty of room for an upscale restaurant to go along with the tourist traps, and it got one in mid-2000 with the opening of this spacious and airy eatery at the north end of the commercial zone. The food is basic seafood fusion, with fish served in Asian preparations (such as a Thai seafood stew), but the menu offers something for everyone, including thick steaks patterned after the fare at sister restaurant El Gaucho. While the prices suggest something very special, you won't find it in the food — the real hit here is the view, with a deck surrounding the restaurant that offers wonderful, breezy walks suspended over Elliott Bay. The long, curving bar is becoming a favorite meeting place.

2801 Alaskan Way at Pier 70 at the north end of the downtown waterfront. ☎ *206-956-9171. Main courses: $26.50–$39. Open: Daily 5–10 p.m. (to 10:30 p.m. Fri and Sat). AE, DC, MC, V.*

Wild Ginger

$$$ **Downtown ASIAN**

Seattle's favorite Asian fusion restaurant didn't miss a beat when it moved to spacious new quarters near Benaroya Hall in 2000. People still flock to get their hands on delicious Thai satays, Seven Flavors Soup, and exquisite preparations of duck. It remains a tough reservation to get as well, and the service staff isn't any friendlier, but after you get in and get seated, you're bound to be satisfied with the flavors and artful presentations.

1401 Third Ave. at Union Street. ☎ *206-623-4450. Reservations advised. Main courses: $8.50–$21. Open: Mon–Sat, 11:30 a.m.–1 a.m.; Sun 4:30 p.m.–1 a.m. AE, DC, DISC, MC.*

Index of Restaurants by Price

$
Dick's Drive-Ins

$$
The Brooklyn Seafood, Steak & Oyster House
Buca di Beppo
Chinook's at Salmon Bay
Flying Fish
Ivar's Salmon House
Shiro's

$$$
Carmelita
Cassis
Dahlia Lounge
Fandango
iCon Grill
Kaspar's
Nishino
Palace Kitchen
Palisade

Ray's Boathouse and Café
Salty's on Alki Beach
Sazerac
Tulio Ristorante
Wild Ginger

$$$$
Andaluca
Cafe Juanita
Campagne
Canlis
El Gaucho
Fleming's Prime Steakhouse & Wine Bar
The Painted Table
Waterfront

$$$$$
Brasa
Cascadia
The Georgian Room
Rover's

Index of Restaurants by Neighborhood

Belltown
Brasa
Cascadia
Dahlia Lounge
El Gaucho
Fandango
Flying Fish
Shiro's
Waterfront

The Brooklyn Seafood, Steak & Oyster House
Fleming's Prime Steakhouse & Wine Bar
The Georgian Room
iCon Grill
Palace Kitchen
Sazerac
Tulio Ristorante
Wild Ginger

Capitol Hill/Madison Park
Cassis
Nishino
Rover's

Downtown/Shopping District
Andaluca

Kirkland/Eastside
Cafe Juanita

North of Downtown
Buca di Beppo
Carmelita

Chinook's at Salmon Bay
Dick's Drive-Ins
Ivar's Salmon House
Palisade
Ray's Boathouse and Café

Pike Place Market
Campagne
The Painted Table

Queen Anne
Canlis
Dick's Drive-In
Kaspar's

West Seattle
Salty's on Alki Beach

Index of Restaurants by Cuisine

Asian
Wild Ginger

Burgers
Dick's Drive-Ins

Cajun
Sazerac

Continental
Brasa
The Georgian Room
Kaspar's

French
Campagne
Cassis
Rover's

Italian
Buca di Beppo
Café Juanita
Tulio Ristorante

Latin
Fandango

Mediterranean
Andaluca

Northwest
Cascadia
Dahlia Lounge

The Painted Table
Waterfront

Regional American
iCon Grill
Palace Kitchen

Seafood
The Brooklyn Seafood, Steak &
   Oyster House
Canlis
Chinook's at Salmon Bay
Flying Fish
Ivar's Salmon House
Palisade
Ray's Boathouse and Cafe
Salty's on Alki Beach

Steak
Canlis
El Gaucho
Fleming's Prime Steakhouse &
   Wine Bar

Sushi
Nishino
Shiro's

Vegetarian
Carmelita

On the Lighter Side: Top Picks for Snacks and Meals on the Go

If you'd rather spend your time (and money) in Seattle on the go rather than sitting down to elaborate meals, you're in no way out of luck, nor do you have to resort to eating all your meals under the Golden Arches. Here I give you some worthy alternatives for finding quick bites and food on the run, including foods that are specific to this region and one of the great grazing opportunities in the world. And don't forget coffee, the favorite snack food around here; I give you some good tips on finding plenty of that famous Seattle brew.

Breakfast on the half-shell

The standard bacon, egg, and pancake breakfast gets a Northwest lift when you substitute the favorite local mollusk, the Puget Sound oyster, for the meat. Oysters and eggs, also called the "Hangtown Fry" on menus, makes for a delicious, briny breakfast with toast and hash browns. Look for it on the menu at the **Bay Cafe** (Fisherman's Terminal in Magnolia; ☎ **206-282-3435**), a bustling diner with windows over-looking the Alaskan fishing fleet. In the Pike Place Market, check out **Lowell's** (1519 Pike Place; ☎ **206-622-2036**), an aging institution with great views of Elliott Bay. You order breakfast from the cafeteria-style line, and servers then deliver the meal to you after it's cooked.

For more standard breakfast fare at good prices, I like the **Salmon Bay Cafe** in Ballard (5109 Shilshole Ave. NW, just west of the Ballard Bridge; ☎ **206-782-5539**) for a wonderful stuffed French toast and working-man's portions, and **Donna's Diner** (1760 First Ave. S. near Safeco Field; ☎ **206-467-7359**) for ridiculously cheap meat and egg breakfasts. If you're the kind of person who likes to have breakfast in the middle of the night, **13 Coins** (125 Boren Ave. N., just north of Denny Way; ☎ **206-682-2513**) is a local institution that slings the hash 24 hours a day. For a breakfast treat that isn't cheap, **Café Campagne** (86 Pine St., at the Market; ☎ **206-728-2233**) makes fabulous baked egg dishes, quiches, or simple baguettes and jams served with big bowls of caffe latte.

Living the high life in caffeine city

Speaking of coffee, a cuppa Joe and a baked good serve as a perfectly satisfying breakfast for many people, and you won't find a shortage of either in Seattle. Indeed, you may be overwhelmed by the sheer number of coffee possibilities in Caffeine City: Espresso carts on street corners; drive-through espresso shacks on major streets; quaint neighborhood coffee shops; and chain places, sometimes two or three on major retail corners, designed to look like little living rooms with fireplaces and easy

Know your coffee lingo

A snotty Starbucks employee once said to a visitor from New York, "If you speak to me in my language, you'll get what you want." When ordering coffee in Seattle, try to follow these rules:

✔ State the size of drink you want (i.e. short, tall, or Grande).

✔ State the number of espresso shots you want in it (single or double).

✔ If you're ordering anything but full, caffeinated coffee, mention it now.

✔ State the type of drink you're ordering (latte, Americano, or mocha).

✔ Call the kind of milk you want: whole, 2 percent, or "skinny" (skim).

✔ Add any extras you might want, such as a hazelnut or vanilla flavoring.

So it goes like this: *"I'll have a short, single, half-decaf latte, 2 percent, with hazelnut."*

More tips: A regular cup of coffee is an Americano; order it with "room for cream" if you're going to add milk. Always get the whipped cream on a mocha (live a little; you're already getting plenty of extra calories and fat from the chocolate). And if somebody ever says, "If you speak to me in my language, you'll get what you want," turn around, walk out, and go to the next coffee place.

chairs from which to sip your latte and nibble your muffin. The original **Starbucks** (1912 Pike Place Market; ☎ 206-448-8762) is still doing business in the Market (with the original coquettish mermaid logo that has since been removed from the corporate identity), but many locals prefer to settle down at one of the numerous locations of **Tully's Coffee, Seattle's Best Coffee,** and **Caffe Ladro,** all of which make fine coffee and tea drinks and serve pies, bagels, and fresh muffins. If you're in the neighborhood, stop by **Cafe Bambino** (405 NW 65th St. in Ballard; ☎ 206-706-4934), which is owned by artist Andhi Spath and contains his original paintings, and **Uptown Espresso** (525 Queen Anne Ave. N. in lower Queen Anne; ☎ 206-281-8669), which makes terrific pies, scones, and muffins. In the Fremont retail district, **Still Life in Fremont** (709 N. 35th St.; ☎ 206-547-9850) is a throwback coffeehouse with art on the walls, fresh baked goods, and excellent soups and vegetarian sandwiches.

Exploring the food stalls at Pike Place

It's no exaggeration to say that you could spend a week eating from the food vendors at the Pike Place Market and not taste the same thing twice. The Market is the epicenter of the local food scene, where farmers and grocers sell fresh fruits and produce, and dozens of stalls offer prepared foods and delicatessens. Most of the food stalls are open from the early morning hours to about 5 p.m., with restaurants continuing on from that hour. Explore the inner and outer reaches of the Market, and you encounter fresh cinnamon rolls and Greek specialties, Turkish delight, and Filipino stir-fries, French bread, cookies, pastries, big Philadelphia-style cheese steak sandwiches, Chinese and Italian food, and lots of coffee. You're sure to find a place that hits the spot for what you're craving, but do yourself a favor and don't miss **Piroshky, Piroshky** (1908 Pike Place; ☎ 206-441-6068), which is run by Russian expats and makes consistently tasty rolls filled with salmon, vegetables, or meat — wonderful desserts, too — the apple tarts are to die for. For seafood, **Jack's Fish Spot** (1514 Pike Place; ☎ 206-467-0514) is not only a fish vendor, but it has a stainless-steel counter where you can buy excellent fish and chips or Dungeness crab cocktails served with crunchy celery and a homemade cocktail sauce. **World Class Chili** (1411 First Ave. inside the south arcade building; ☎ 206-623-3678) is the best in town, and **Biringer Farms** (1530 Post Alley; ☎ 206-467-0383) sells generous slices of pies that include local favorites like fresh blackberry or huckleberry when the fruits are in season.

Quick eats on the street

When food on the fly or cheap eats are the order of the day, find your way to one of these bargain places.

Bakeries

If loaves of fresh bread and artfully crafted pastries make you happy (in my case, ecstatic), then seek out one of these bakeries, all of which have small areas in which to sit and devour your purchase. In Wallingford it's the **Boulangerie** (2700 N. 45th St.; ☎ 206-634-2211), a French place with baguettes, croissants, and lovely brioche baked around a circle of brie. Pioneer Square workers line up to get their bread and muffin fix at the **Grand Central Bakery** (214 First Ave. S.; ☎ 206-622-3644), which makes several varieties of artisan breads. At the Market, it's the **Three Girls Bakery** (1514 Pike Place; ☎ 206-622-1045), which not only has a dozen varieties of bread but also fine Danish, cookies, and fresh macaroons. For exclusively Danish products from an old Ballard family, the **Larsen Brothers Danish Bakery** (8000 24th NW; ☎ 206-782-8285) fills the bill with buttery Danish pastries and breads. After walking around Green Lake, you can put back some of the calories you lost with a visit to the **Honey Bear Bakery** (2106 N. 55th St., a few blocks east of the lake; ☎ 206-545-7296), which always has a broad selection of cakes, pies, and cookies to sample.

Burgers

Besides the fast-food outlets of **Dick's Drive-Ins** (see "Seattle Restaurants from A to Z" earlier in this chapter for listings), Seattle has a few burger places that stand out above the rest. Locals flock to the two locations of

Red Mill Burgers (1613 W. Dravus, between Queen Anne and Magnolia, ☎ 206-284-6363; and 312 N. 67th St. in Greenwood, ☎ 206-783-6362) for thick burgers and good, thin-cut fries. Order ahead and they'll have it waiting for you. On Capitol Hill, the **Deluxe Bar & Grill** (625 Broadway E.;☎ 206-324-9697) is a sit-down restaurant that makes fine, oversize burgers.

Burritos and wraps

The craze of wrapping foods in a large tortilla that might be red from sun-dried tomatoes or green from spinach and pesto has hit Seattle's fast-food scene hard in recent years. **Taco del Mar** (numerous locations) is a good source for cheap, enormous, sloppy burritos made with whole or refried beans and either meats or fried fish. **World Wrapps** (numerous locations) is another chain that does a good job mixing Asian- or Mexican-style preparations in a big tortilla. For terrific, authentic Mexican burritos and tacos, get yourself to **Malena's Taco Shop** on upper Queen Anne (620 W. McGraw St.;☎ 206-284-0304).

Fish and chips

Seattle's trademark fish and chips is made from fresh lingcod that comes out of Puget Sound, or flaky, white Alaskan halibut, and any shop worth its salt also offers fried oysters and excellent chowder. You can make a fine, cheap Northwest meal at any of the following locations. Opposite the Ballard Locks, the tall, carved totem poles signal the location of the **Totem House Seafood & Chowder** restaurant (3058 NW 54th St.;☎ 206-784-2300). Take your catch back across the street to the park near the Locks, or sit at the restaurant's outdoor picnic tables. In most parts of town you find a blue-and-white **Ivar's** restaurant (several locations), which are fast-food shops that sell fried fish and one of the best chowders in town. Fisherman's Terminal between Queen Anne and Magnolia wouldn't be the same without **Little Chinook's** (Fisherman's Terminal;☎ 206-283-HOOK), a take-out place with picnic tables overlooking the long piers where fishing boats tie up for the winter months.

Pizza

Pagliacci Pizza gets consistently high marks for quality pizza; their "Brooklyn Bridge" pie is loaded with pepperoni, sausage, mushrooms, and vegetables. They deliver throughout the city (☎ 206-726-1717) and have sit-down restaurants in lower Queen Anne (550 Queen Anne Ave. N.; ☎ 206-285-1232), Capitol Hill (426 Broadway E.; ☎ 206-324-0730) and the University District (4529 University Way NE; ☎ 206-632-0421). On upper Queen Anne, the **Elliott Bay Pizza Co.** (2115 Queen Anne Ave. N.; ☎ 206-285-0500) sells by the slice or the pie and makes hearty grinder-style sandwiches. **Zeek's Pizza** has a nice sit-down restaurant near the zoo in the upper Fremont/Greenwood neighborhood (6000 Phinney Ave. N.; ☎ 206-789-0089).

Packing up for a picnic

Eat inside on a beautiful summer day? No way! says the ardent Seattleite who knows only too well how fleeting fine weather can be and takes every opportunity to be outside. The perfect way to enjoy one of the city's many parks is armed with a basket of food, of course. The Pike Place Market has everything you need. For Italian fare, go to **DeLaurenti's Specialty Food Market** (1435 First Ave.; ☎ 206-622-0141) for a great selection of breads, meats, and cheeses. In the upstairs room, you also find a selection of Italian wines at good prices. Farther down Pike Place, **Cucina Fresca** (1904 Pike Place; ☎ 206-448-4758) has gorgeous prepared Italian foods, from mozzarella and tomato salads to grilled chicken, roasted vegetables drowning in olive oil, and specialty pizzas. Round out your meal with fresh fruits or desserts from the Market's vendors and then head to the north end of the waterfront and Myrtle Edwards Park to enjoy it.

Part IV
Exploring Seattle

The 5th Wave
By Rich Tennant

"We've seen where they filmed parts of 'Sleepless in Seattle', the TV show 'Twin Peaks', and several documentaries on Sasquatch. I'm not sure why, but I feel like just going back to the hotel room and watching TV."

In this part . . .

You've arrived in Seattle, you've settled in to your hotel, and you're ready to see the sights. Here I describe the city's top attractions — giving advice on what to see and what to avoid — and offer an insider's look at other cool things to see and do. I offer advice on the best places to take kids and teens, and where to go to enjoy Seattle's glorious natural spaces. In addition, I outline several specific city itineraries as well as day trips to the surrounding mountains, parks, and islands. For shoppers, I give a breakdown of Seattle's great shopping neighborhoods and where to find items that are uniquely Pacific Northwest. Finally, the nightcrawler in you can appreciate the chapter on Seattle nightlife, from performing arts to theater to bars and clubs with attitude.

Chapter 15

Seattle's Top Sights and Cool Things to Do

Don't feel bad if all you want to do during your first days in Seattle is walk the streets, sit at a sidewalk cafe sipping lattes and eating pie, or stroll a waterfront path at sunset. Those things are all intrinsic parts of the Seattle experience. But after you soak up the atmosphere of the city — and there is loads of it — you may want to try out some of the unique attractions that the city has to offer. Just be sure to build in plenty of time for relaxing, too, because this town has as pleasant a cafe society as you're likely to encounter anywhere.

The Top Attractions from A to Z

Ballard Locks
Ballard

Officially known as the Hiram M. Chittenden Locks, this little park and engineering feat by the U.S. Army Corps of Engineers turns out to be one of the most pleasant diversions in the city on a nice day. The Locks were built to allow boats to navigate the different water levels of Lake Union and Puget Sound, and it's fun to watch everything from canoes and dinghies to yachts and commercial barges tie into a lock, have a door close behind them with a clang, and then ascend or descend on a pillow of water. Added to this are the fish ladders on the south side of the waterway (reached by walking over the dam that holds back Lake Union) with viewing windows that allow you to see full-grown salmon fighting their way upstream to return to their spawning grounds. Most salmon runs take place from June to September, but it varies each year. The combination of technology and nature is a hit with every age we've ever taken there, and the Locks are always on the itinerary when friends and relatives come to town.

3015 NW 54th St. (in Ballard; continue west on Market Street; it passes the Locks about 1 mile past the main commercial district). ☎ *206-783-7059. Open: All daylight hours; boat traffic is heaviest on weekends. Admission: free.*

Benaroya Hall
Downtown

The $118-million home of the Seattle Symphony, built in Beaux Arts–style in the heart of downtown and funded in large part by private donors that included several Microsoft millionaires, opened in 1998 and has been the center of the city's cultural scene ever since. The acoustics have been compared to Carnegie Hall's for sheer, crystal-clear brilliance, and in 2000, a state-of-the-art concert organ was added, broadening the symphony's range even more. Book your tickets early; this is a perennial sell-out. If you'd like to tour the hall, meet in the Grand Lobby on the Third Avenue and University Street side, Monday through Friday at noon or 1 p.m.

200 University St. at Second Avenue, near the Seattle Art Museum. ☎ *206-215-4747. Internet:* www.seattlesymphony.org *for a calendar and online purchase option. Admission: $10–$77 for concerts; tours are free. No children under 5 allowed into concerts.*

Boeing Plant
Everett

Here's a neat doubleheader to impress your kids. At Boeing's largest assembly plant, they can see how airplanes are built and also stand inside the single largest building under one roof in the world. Cool! Boeing remains the single largest employer in Washington, and this guided tour on raised catwalks in the massive space (for extra credit, tell them that you could fit all of Disneyland into the building) is an impressive inside look at great sections of airplanes coming together.

Boeing Tour Center on SR 526 in Everett, 30 miles north of Seattle. Take I-5 north, and then head west on 526; give yourself at least an hour from downtown Seattle. ☎ *800-464-1476 or 206-544-1264. Open: One-hour tours are first-come, first-served and run Mon–Fri from 9 a.m.–11 a.m. and 1 p.m–3 p.m. Admission: $5 adults, $3 seniors and children under 16. Children must be at least 4 feet, 2 inches tall.*

Downtown Seattle Attractions

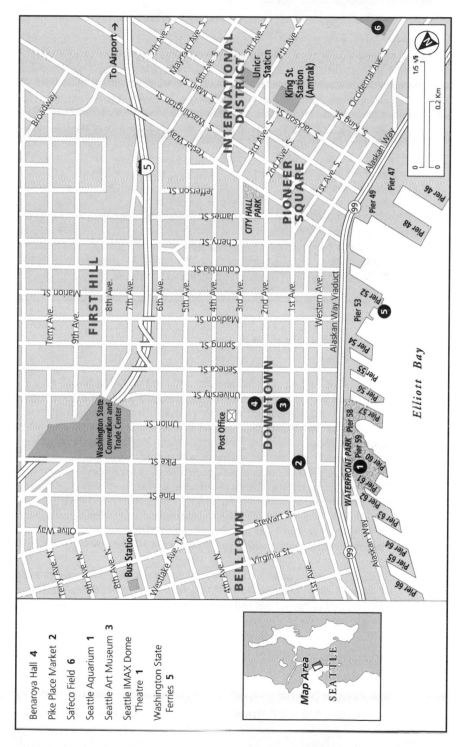

Benaroya Hall **4**

Pike Place Market **2**

Safeco Field **6**

Seattle Aquarium **1**

Seattle Art Museum **3**

Seattle IMAX Dome
Theatre **1**

Washington State
Ferries **5**

Celebrating at the Seattle Center

Seattle Center's grounds and buildings (see the listing for Seattle Center later in this chapter) get turned into an enormous, groovin' street party three times a year for major festivals that attract hundreds of thousands of visitors over the course of three- and four-day weekends. **Bite of Seattle,** the city's homage to local food and drink, takes place every July, with more than 90 food vendors who represent the city's restaurants, live music, and beer gardens from which to wash it all down. Labor Day weekend is the time for **Bumbershoot,** an enormous arts festival of music, dance, fine arts, and literature performed simultaneously in a dozen different Seattle Center venues, with one admission price buying access to everything. The earthier **Northwest Folklife Festival,** held over Memorial Day weekend, is devoted to folk music and performances. Food is served at each event, and the people-watching and entertainment values are unsurpassed. Go early to beat the crowds, and try to pick up advance tickets whenever possible to avoid the enormous lines to get in. **Bite of Seattle:** ☎ 206-232-2982; Internet: www.biteofseattle.com; admission is free; $2–$5 for samples of food items. **Bumbershoot:** ☎ 206-281-8111; Internet: www.bumbershoot.org; admission varies. **Northwest Folklife Festival:** ☎ 206-684-7300; Internet: www.nwfolklife.org; admission varies.

Experience Music Project
Seattle Center

It started out as a small museum to house Paul Allen's collection of Jimi Hendrix memorabilia and mushroomed into a $100-million shrine to rock-and-roll music. People either love or hate the curving, multihued building by architect Frank Gehry that sits like a basket of dumped laundry under the Space Needle. The admission fee is steep, but once inside, grown-ups appreciate the galleries with artifacts like Janis Joplin's feather boa and Elvis's motorcycle jacket, while kids love playing instruments in the Sound Lab, riding a motion-simulator into the heart of a James Brown concert, or performing "Wild Thing" karaoke-style before a simulated crowd. Skip the MEGs (CD-ROM devices that provide running commentary on the exhibits) for smaller children; they're bulky and ponderous. The Turntable restaurant and Liquid Lounge bar are fine hangouts, too.

2901 Third Ave., at Seattle Center (adjacent to the Space Needle and Monorail). ☎ *206-770-2700. Open: Sun–Thurs, 10 a.m.–6 p.m. (galleries open to 11 p.m. on Fri and Sat); call for restaurant and lounge hours. Admission: $19.95 adults, $15.95 seniors and teens 13–17, $14.95 children 7–12, children 6 and under free.*

Lake Union
Downtown

For a quintessential Seattle experience, spend some time on or around Lake Union, the teardrop-shaped body of water just north of downtown.

Sailboats and pleasure craft ply the waters, rowers do their thing in canoes and kayaks, and seaplanes take off and land in a roar of engines. Big, family-friendly restaurants with outdoor patios offering great views line the eastern shore. For the best experience, head to the Northwest Outdoor Center and rent big, steady kayaks (doubles and triples are great for taking kids along) with foot-controlled rudders and spray skirts that keep the drips off your clothes, and paddle among the communities of dollhouse-like houseboats on either shore, with the city's buildings providing a backdrop.

North of Mercer Street in downtown Seattle. **Northwest Outdoor Center:** *2100 Westlake Ave. N., on the west side of the lake in the commercial strip of buildings.* ☎ *206-281-9694. Internet:* www.nwoc.com. *Fees: Single kayak, $10 per hour; double, $15 per hour. Canoes and kayaks also available from the* **Center for Wooden Boats,** *1010 Valley St., at the north end of the lake just west of the Burger King* **(**☎ *206-382-BOAT), and the* **University of Washington Waterfront Activities Center,** *just behind Husky Stadium on Lake Washington (*☎ *206-543-9433).*

Mount Rainier
South-central Washington

Seattle's favorite sight, the one that evokes a collective sigh from its citizenry, is of 14,410-foot Mount Rainier looming above the city on a clear day from its vantage point, 100 miles south of the city. The postcard view from the city is at Kerry Park (3rd Avenue W. and Highland Drive, in the Queen Anne neighborhood), where a small strip of grass perched on a hilltop looks south over the city's buildings and Elliott Bay, with the big mountain in the background. Otherwise, keep your camera at the ready for Rainier sightings when you head south on Aurora Avenue toward downtown, crossing Lake Washington in either direction on the I-90 and SR520 bridges, or from numerous viewpoints on the University of Washington campus. For a closer look, head south to the mountain itself, which has numerous hiking trails to explore and fields of wildflowers that pop up in July and August. The best approach is from the visitor center located at Paradise, at the 5,400-foot level of the mountain in Mount Rainier National Park.

Mount Rainier National Park, 110 miles from downtown Seattle on SR706. ☎ *360-569-2211. Admission: $10 per vehicle, $5 per person, cyclist, or motorcyle. Call ahead in the winter months to be sure the roads are open.*

Museum of Flight
South Seattle

Seattle loves its airplanes, and this imposing steel-and-glass museum is a fine way for kids and aviation buffs to immerse themselves in aircraft. It should be: It's on the grounds of one of Boeing's main plants, and part of the museum is the little Red Barn that was the company's original factory back in 1910. Inside is a spectrum of aircraft (many of them built by

Seattle Attractions—North & Northeast

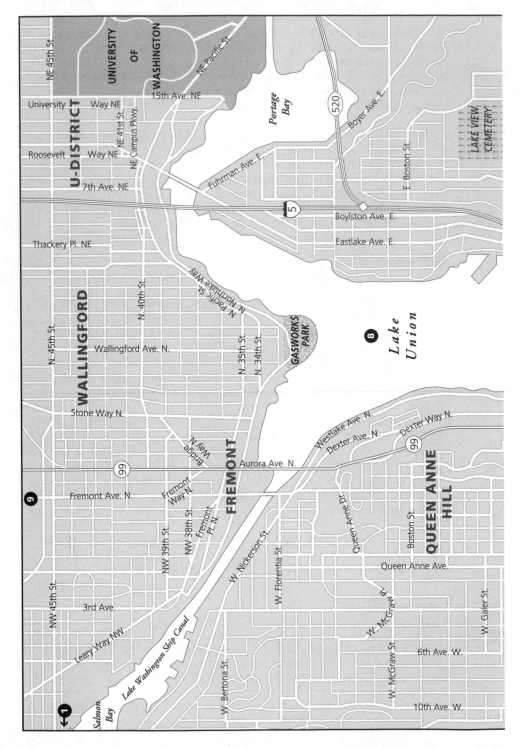

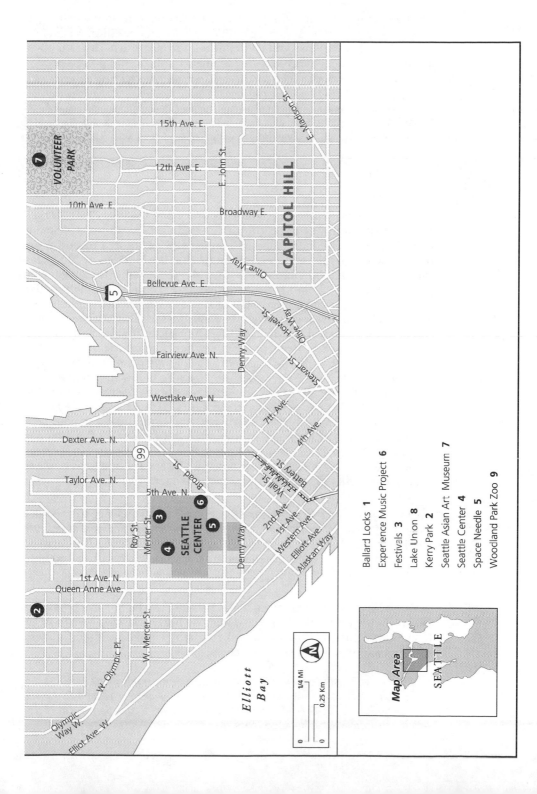

Ballard Locks **1**

Exper ence Music Project **6**

Festivals **3**

Lake Un on **8**

Kerry Park **2**

Seattle Asian Art Museum **7**

Seattle Center **4**

Space Needle **5**

Woodland Park Zoo **9**

Boeing), including a DC3 and a Blackbird suspended from the ceiling, a biplane, and an Apollo space capsule that you can peer into. A small area of toy planes allows younger children to get some of their climbing and interactive energy satisfied. A snackbar is on the premises; allow a half-day for getting there and exploring the galleries.

9404 E. Marginal Way S. on the west side of Boeing Field. Take I-5 South to exit 158. ☎ *206-764-5720. Admission: $8 adults, $7 seniors, $4 ages 6–15, children 5 and under free; first Thurs also free. Hours: Daily 10 a.m.–5 p.m.; until 9 p.m. on Thurs.*

Pike Place Market
Downtown

City officials have worked overtime to ensure that the Pike Place Market, begun in 1907 and one of Seattle's most enduring institutions, remains true to its roots. A big push was made a few years ago to add more tourist-friendly T-shirt and souvenir shops, but the Market fought to keep the emphasis on food and flowers. The Market remains the single best place in the city to find fresh produce and seasonal specialties like Rainier cherries, Washington asparagus, fresh king salmon, and Northwest hazelnuts. The food grazing is unsurpassed: Don't leave without trying a Dungeness crab cocktail, a fresh-baked piroshky or cinnamon roll, and, of course, coffee from any number of vendors, including the original Starbucks (with the original randy mermaid sign that you won't see at worldwide McStarbucks outlets). Explore below the main floor to find wonderful specialty shops, including one of the best stores devoted to magic and old magic posters in the country, a fragrant store dedicated to spices, and an exotic bird store where the parrots squawk in your face. A 90-minute Market Heritage Tour is offered daily during the summer, beginning at the Market Heritage Foundation Visitor Center on Western Avenue. At night the vendors clear out, and the Market becomes home to several excellent restaurants, bars, and a theater.

Do not, repeat *not,* drive into Pike Place itself, lest you want to get stuck in a jam of delivery trucks and hordes of pedestrians. You will never find parking there; the vendors all took it at the crack of dawn. Park instead in the lot on Western Avenue adjacent to the Market, where the first hour is free.

Seattle's favorite meeting place is Rachel the Pig, the life-size brass piggybank in the crook of Pike Place under the big clock. Kids love to sit on Rachel and pose for pictures, and frequently musicians and clowns making balloon animals entertain the crowds.

Pike Place, which starts at First Avenue and Pike Street, with shops spread out in several buildings on First Avenue and Western Avenue between Union Street and Virginia Street. ☎ *206-682-7453. Hours: Mon–Sat, 9 a.m.–6 p.m.; Sun 11 a.m.–5 p.m. Admission: free. Market Heritage Tours are $7.*

Safeco Field
Downtown

The Seattle Mariners ballpark was the most expensive ever built, at $517 million, when it opened in July 1999. A large portion of the cost was for the retractable roof that closes after every home game while the P.A. system plays "Flight of the Valkyries." It's a truly wonderful place to watch a ballgame; the seats in the upper deck on the first base line have the best views of the Space Needle and downtown skyline. Feel free to wander about and check out the playground for kids behind centerfield and food venues that offer such goodies as Northwest chowder, salmon, sushi, and microbrews. Artwork and decorative touches are everywhere, including placards of famous ballplayers from around the world that decorate the upper deck concourse. Tours are offered daily, and when the team is out of town these tours include dugouts and locker rooms.

First Avenue S. at S. Atlantic St., just south of Pioneer Square. ☎ *206-622-HITS for ticket information and schedules. Internet:* www.seattlemariners.com. *Admission: $6–$36; box offices are located on the south side of the stadium, and a Mariners team store with complete merchandise is located on the First Avenue S. side. Admission for tours is $7 adults, $3 children (tour information:* ☎ *206-346-4000).*

Seattle Aquarium
Downtown

God knows that Puget Sound is too cold to swim in or snorkel, but you can get an eel's-eye perspective on the teeming life in the Sound at this waterfront aquarium. The Puget Sound tank features bizarre wolf eels, lingcod and rockfish, and a giant Pacific octopus named Neah. A shark tank has plenty of action to excite the kids, and they can pet a starfish (not exactly a cuddly experience) in a hands-on tank. The Aquarium also houses the IMAXDome Theater, with films that unfold in a giant panorama overhead.

Pier 59 on the Waterfront, a few blocks south of the Edgewater Hotel. Take the elevator or steps from the Pike Place Market to Alaskan Way and then walk or catch the waterfront streetcar heading north. ☎ *206-386-4320. Open: Daily 10 a.m.–7 p.m. Admission: $8.25 adults, $7.25 seniors, $5.50 children 6–18, $3.50 children 3–5. Extra charges and package rates for the Omnidome Film Experience.*

Seattle Art Museum and Seattle Asian Art Musuem
Downtown and Capitol Hill, respectively

Sculptor Jonathon Borofsky's enormous *Hammering Man* points the way to the Seattle Art Museum's (SAM) new location downtown near the Market. Major traveling exhibitions stop here, and the standing galleries, with Native American art and Northwest contemporary art, provide a good orientation to the region's history of art. One knock on the museum is that it offers everything under the sun, from African art to European masters, but little of any one thing. The positive aspect of this, however, is that visitors are bound to find something here to interest them. In Volunteer Park on Capitol Hill, the Seattle Asian Art Museum is as tranquil a setting as you can find in the city, in SAM's former Art Deco digs, with a fine collection of pan-Asian art and an emphasis on Japanese and Chinese exhibits.

Be sure to get a personal CD-ROM headset and one for each child at SAM. There are programs geared to all age levels, and it's a great way to keep kids occupied and involved with the museum tour, which they can do at their own pace while you linger over your personal favorite items.

Seattle Art Museum: 100 University St., on First Avenue. ☎ 206-654-3100. Open: Tues–Sun, 10 a.m.–5 p.m. (to 9 p.m. Thurs); closed Mon. Admission: $7 adults, $5 seniors, children 12 and under free. Free first Thurs of the month.

Seattle Asian Art Museum: Volunteer Park, 14th Ave. E. and E. Prospect Street. Find street parking anywhere on the perimeter of the park and enjoy the walk to the museum. ☎ 206-654-3100. Open: Tues–Sun, 10 a.m.–5 p.m. (to 9 p.m. Thurs); closed Mon. Admission: $3 adults, children 12 and under free. Free first Thurs of the month.

Seattle Center
Seattle Center

At some point in your trip you're bound to wind up at Seattle Center: This multiblock complex, located just north of downtown in the Queen Anne neighborhood, is not only home to many of the city's arts venues, such as the Pacific Northwest Ballet, Seattle Children's Theatre, and Seattle Opera, but it houses the crowd-pleasing Space Needle, Experience Music Project, and Pacific Science Center. Seattle Center is also a great place to blow off steam with the younger set. The computerized fountain is a huge hit on warm days for kids who don't mind getting wet, and an amusement park offers rides and a videogame parlor. The Centerhouse stages dances and exhibitions such as Winterfest, which provides games and activities for children and is the venue for several inexpensive fast-food-type vendors. Be sure to call ahead for information on festivals and events: During the three major festivals of the year, the place gets incredibly crammed.

305 Harrison St. is the official location, but the entire area is within the boundary of First Avenue N. and Fifth Avenue, and Denny and Mercer streets. Parking lots are more abundant on the Fifth Avenue side; Monorail from Westlake Center goes directly to Seattle Center's Centerhouse. ☎ 206-684-7200 for program information. Admission: free. Hours vary with programs.

Space Needle
Seattle Center

Still the most beloved symbol of Seattle, the Space Needle continues to be a must-see landmark. Built for the 1962 World's Fair, it has been

Seattle Center

Roy St.

2nd Ave. N.

3rd Ave. N.

4th Ave. N.

1

Mercer St.

1st Ave. N.

Warren Ave. N.

2 **3** **4** **5** **6**

7

Republican St.

11

8

5th Ave. N.

10 **9**

Harrison St.

12

14

15

16

PARKING

24 **13**

17

18

23

Thomas St.

19

20

21

John St.

22

Seattle
Center

SEATTLE

Broad St.

Monorail

Denny Way

0		1/8 mi
0		1/8 km

N

Amusement Park Areas **16**
Bagley Wright Theatre **2**
Center House & Children's Museum **15**
Exhibition Hall **4**
Experience Music Project **23**
Flag Pavilion **18**
Flag Plaza **14**
International Fountain **9**
Intiman Playhouse **3**
The Key Arena **12**
Memorial Stadium **8**
Mercer Arena **6**

Mercer Street Parking Garage **1**
Monorail Terminal **17**
Mural Amphitheatre **20**
Northwest Crafts Center **10**
Northwest Rooms **11**
Opera House **5**
Pacific Arts Center **19**
Pacific Science Center **22**
Seattle Center Pavilions **13**
Seattle Children's Theater **24**
Space Needle **21**
Veterans Hall **7**

spruced up of late, with a new visitor center and gift shop on the lower levels. At 520 feet, the observation deck has nice signage pointing out what you can see in all directions (on a sunny day), and just enough space through the railings to give you a chilling, *Vertigo* look down. If you're too scared to go outside, you can linger in the Observation Deck's gift shop for a souvenir. The lounge and revolving restaurant can be fun, but they're generally packed and expensive, and the food definitely doesn't match the views. Fireworks here on New Year's Eve are the best in town. For views and pictures of the Needle, head to Kerry Park on West Highland Avenue in Queen Anne, or take your photographs from a ferry boat. Expect long lines for the Observation Deck elevator, but a nearby video-game parlor can occupy the kids while a parent waits in line.

219 Fourth Ave. N. at Seattle Center. Take the monorail to Seattle Center from Westlake Center, or park on lots off Fifth Avenue. ☎ *206-443-2100. Open: Daily 9 a.m.–11 p.m. Admission: $9 adults, $8 seniors, $4 ages 5–12.*

Washington State Ferries
Downtown

Washington State maintains one of the most extensive ferry systems in the world, and much of it is centered around Seattle. For a scenic, inexpensive way to see Puget Sound, you can't beat standing on the top deck of a ferry crossing from downtown Seattle to Bainbridge Island or Bremerton. Go at sunset for the best views, and on the way back you can admire the city skyline as the downtown buildings light up. Keep an eye out for dolphins and sea lions. The outdoor areas on the bow can get pretty chilly, but the upper-deck outdoor area is heated, and there is less wind chill in the stern.

Car decks on the boats are first-come, first-served, so if you're going to drive onto the ferry, particularly at the beginning or end of a holiday weekend, plan to get to the terminal early and bring some reading material, because the parking lots get packed and you might have to wait up to two hours to get onto a boat. If you can avoid driving onto the ferry during rush hours, do so at all costs, or you'll encounter considerable commuter traffic.

Pier 52 on the Waterfront, just north of Pioneer Square. Pedestrian walkway directly to terminal from First Avenue and Columbia Street. ☎ *206-464-6400. Numerous daily departures and returns. Fees: Foot passengers pay $3.70, westbound only (free to return to Seattle); $6.50 for car and driver ($8.25 during peak tourist months in the summer) each way to Bainbridge Island.*

Woodland Park Zoo
Fremont

A number of exhibits have been added in recent years, including a Komodo dragon exhibit and a jaw-dropping look at black bears and gorillas, the latter of which have produced offspring here. Habitats are big and as natural as possible, from an African savannah to a tropical rain forest. Don't miss the Nocturnal House, a dark, quiet place where creatures of the night zip by the viewing windows, and the collection of snakes and spiders. The zoo also has a petting zoo for the little ones, as well as pony rides. In the summer, the zoo offers a concert series that is quite popular and sells out quickly.

5500 Phinney Ave. N. in Fremont; main parking area on Fremont Avenue N. & N. 50th Street Drive north on Aurora Avenue, exit at Green Lake Way, turn left onto N. 46th Street and right on Fremont Ave. N. to reach the main gate and parking area. ☎ *206-684-4800. Open: Daily 9:30 a.m.–6:30 p.m. Admission: $8.50 adults, $7.75 seniors, $6 children 6–17, $3.75, ages 3–5.*

More Cool Things to Do and See

Ever the magnanimous one, I say a rousing "To each his own" to my multifaceted readers who, after meeting atop the Space Needle and snapping pictures, scatter to all parts of the city to pursue their diverse interests. Parents with children can expect a full slate of museums and attractions geared specifically to the younger set, with visits to parks and pools to burn off energy. Teens who make it out of the Experience Music Project with time and money to spare find unusual tours into unexpected corners of the city and great places to hang out with their own kind. The blissfully romantic (you can spot them by their serial hand-holding and sappy grins) can stroll through charming neighborhoods and find world-class places for bonding, and outdoor lovers adore the city's parks and biking trails.

Seattle just for kids

Spend a few days in Seattle with your kids and you may see why all of those Californians moved up here for quality-of-life issues. Utilize the whole city to keep the children happy and entertained, from the downtown museums and attractions to neighborhood parks that are equipped with wading pools and playground apparatus, or the indoor public pools dotted around the city.

Enchanted Village and Wild Waves
Federal Way

The biggest and best amusement park in the state is located some 20 miles south of the city. The Enchanted Village side has rides, including merry-go-rounds and a big roller coaster, and the water park has lots of fast slides and tubes, and spraying stations to keep all ages happy and cool on hot summer days. Keep in mind that despite the high prices, the park gets utterly jammed by locals who are thrilled by the sunny weather.

36201 Enchanted Pkwy. S., Federal Way. Take I-5 South to Exit 142-B (direction Puyallup). ☎ *253-661-8000. Admission: $21.95 adults and children over 4 feet tall; $19.95 all other children; $14.95 seniors. Open mid-May to Sept; call for hours.*

Fun Forest Amusement Park
Seattle Center

Seattle Center's amusement park is smaller than Enchanted Village's, but it's also a heck of a lot closer and cheaper. It has a log-flume ride and a smallish roller coaster, as well as a fun house of horrors and a couple of those upside-down rides that only teenagers can stomach. You get lots of cotton candy, popcorn, and carnival games of chance, too, and next door is a huge video-game parlor.

Adjacent to the Monorail and Experience Music Project. ☎ *206-728-1585. Open noon–7 p.m. in summer (to 11 p.m. Fri and Sat; to 8 p.m. Sun); hours vary during the winter. Admission charged per ride; purchase ride tickets at kiosks.*

Pacific Science Center
Seattle Center

Seattle's science museum is a big, sprawling building with several wings and a courtyard that features a pond with replica dinosaurs bathing. Everything is hands-on and interactive, as kids learn things about physics and natural sciences without even knowing it. A cool dinosaur exhibit has life-size animatronic models that move and roar, and a technology center allows you to play virtual basketball against a 7-foot-tall pro. It's geared more for grade-school ages and below, but your teenagers can enjoy the IMAX theater on the premises (see the section "Seattle just for teens," later in this chapter).

200 Second Ave. N. ☎ *206-443-2001. Open daily 10 a.m.–6 p.m. Admission: $7.50 adults, $5.50 ages 3–13 and seniors.*

Playgrounds

The city has lots of neighborhood playgrounds that are equipped with swings, slides, merry-go-rounds, and, in many cases, wading pools that are filled up in the summer and provide hours of entertainment for toddlers. If sightseeing and city-scouring gets to be a bit too much for your youngsters, and everyone needs a break, head to a park to let them play while you sit on a bench and gather yourself. Ask your hotel's front desk or concierge to recommend a playground close by, or give one of the ones in the following listing information a try.

Green Lake Park, *Green Lake Dr. N., at the north end of the lake, just west of the community center. Unnamed playground in Wallingford at Woodlawn Avenue N. and N. 43rd Street, two blocks south of the Wallingford commercial district.* ☎ *206-386-4320 for Seattle Parks and Recreation. Open: Daylight hours. Admission: free.*

Ride the Ducks
Seattle Center

This land/sea tour on a refurbished military amphibious craft is a riot for kids, since everyone is handed a duck-bill-shaped "quacking" noisemaker to honk early and often throughout the narrated tour. For more details, see "And on Your Left: Seeing Seattle by Guided Tours," later in this chapter.

Tickets at Seattle Center kiosk adjacent to the Space Needle. ☎ *206-441-3825. Multiple tours throughout the day. Admission: $20 adults, $10 kids.*

Seattle Children's Museum
Seattle Center

In the basement of the Seattle Center Centerhouse, this museum is a hands-on buffet of attractions for younger children, from toddlers to grade-school age. There is a great bubble station and kinetic sculptures to play with, and an enormous carved volcanic mountain with stations for sliding, touching, and learning about trees and nature.

The Centerhouse. ☎ *206-441-1768. Open Tues–Sun., 10 a.m.–5 p.m. Admission: $5.50 per person.*

Seattle Children's Theatre
Seattle Center

One of the best theaters in the country that is dedicated solely to producing works for children, this spiffy new theater programs old classics and world premieres alike, with a repertory that goes beyond kiddie entertainment to explore issues of self and society that speak to children. It's well-attended by local grade schools and the public, so inquire into ticket availability early in your trip planning.

The Charlotte Martin Theatre, 2nd Ave. N. at Thomas Street. ☎ *206-441-3322. Open Sept–June, with public shows and matinees on weekends only. Admission varies with each production.*

Swimming pools

It is the hardy child indeed who would brave a swim in frosty Puget Sound, which never gets above 55 degrees, even on the hottest summer days. Instead, take your kids to an indoor swimming pool for a family swim. Pools are located near community centers around the city and are equipped with locker rooms with keyed lockers and showers, and, in some cases, saunas or whirlpool baths.

Ballard pool, 1471 NW 67th St., just north of Ballard High School; ☎ *206-684-4094. Queen Anne pool, 1920 1st Ave. W., atop the hill and across from McClure Middle School;* ☎ *206-386-4282. Call ahead for hours for family and public swims. Admission: $2.50 adults, $1.75 children.*

The Waterfront
Downtown

Not so much a neighborhood as a commercial strip, this piece of Alaskan Way in downtown Seattle is a fun attraction for families with kids. The old-fashioned streetcar plies a railroad track from one end to the other, competing with horse-drawn carriages for your transportation buck. In between are lots of souvenir shops, hot dog stands, restaurants, and terminals for pleasure cruises and ferries. In summer, one of the piers turns into an outdoor concert venue with national acts, and a big, new cruise-ship terminal docks megaliners every week during the summer. It's a glitzy part of Seattle that kids enjoy, and the views of Puget Sound and the Olympic Mountains are terrific.

Downtown Seattle on Alaskan Way from Myrtle Edwards Park to Pioneer Square.

Ye Olde Curiosity Shop
Downtown

This souvenir store on the Seattle waterfront ups the gawking ante considerably with the authentic shrunken heads and real mummies on display in glass cases alongside the T-shirts and tacky tourist items. The gross-out factor is high; kids love it.

Pier 54, Alaskan Way on the Seattle Waterfront (just north of the ferry terminal). ☎ *206-682-5844. Open daily 9:30 a.m.–6 p.m. (weekends 9 a.m.–6 p.m.). Admission: free.*

Seattle just for teens

Sure, I know what teens want. They want to be around kids their own age doing cool things. And when I figure out what things are cool all of the time to every teen, I'll issue a special bulletin and let you know, too. In the meantime, here are a few activities around Seattle that your older kids might enjoy. Keep in mind, too, that they might appreciate being handed a fistful of dollars and being left to their own devices for a few hours at the Pike Place Market or Experience Music Project. In that vein, a night off from the family to catch a movie in one of Seattle's many theaters could go a long way toward maintaining family harmony.

Fremont

Seattle's funkiest neighborhood is a great place to explore. Teens appreciate the kitschy stores that sell vintage clothing, pop culture paraphernalia and knick-knacks, and public art that ranges from an enormous bronze sculpture of Lenin that was hauled over from a Russian fire sale to the hammered-tin Fremont rocket that is propped up on the side of a commercial building. On weekends, an open market sells crafts and handmade goods, and at night, the parking lot clears out and classic movies are screened on the side of a building, with people arriving with their own folding chairs and coolers to enjoy the show. A pleasant footpath on the north side of the ship canal makes for pleasant walks.

Begins just after the Fremont Bridge on Fremont Ave. N. and N. 35th St.

GameWorks
Downtown

The video-game parlor by Steven Spielberg's Dreamworks company debuted here, and it's far and away the best electronic entertainment in the city. The multilevel space has all the top, state-of-the-art video games, including simulated jet-ski and skiing games and an incredible electronic version of shoot-'em-up that has you strapped into a seat that rises and falls some 30 feet — great french fries and pizza, too. Buy your kid a pass card, and turn him or her loose while you shop at the nearby stores. After 10 p.m., it's only open to people ages 18 and above.

1511 Seventh Ave. at Pike Street ☎ 206-521-0952. Open Mon–Thurs, 11 a.m.– midnight; Fri to 1 a.m.; Sat 10 a.m.–1 a.m.; Sun 11 a.m.–midnight. Admission: free. Games cost $1–$3 each. Ask about special weekday and weekend promotions.

Gasworks Park
Fremont/Wallingford

This very urban park between the Fremont and Wallingford neighbor-hoods is more about happenings than playing on kiddie swings and slides. Named for the rusty, Gothic-looking old boilers and machinery that constituted the city's power source way back when, it's a hilly expanse overlooking downtown and Lake Union. On most days it's a great place to fly kites and hang out, and it's frequently the venue for outdoor concerts and festivals throughout the summer, including a huge Fourth of July bash that culminates in a fireworks show over the lake.

N. Northlake Way and Meridian Avenue N. Take the Fremont Bridge from down-town and turn right, then right on Stone Way, and stay on it as it turns into N. Northlake Way.

IMAX Dome Theatre
Seattle Center

The impressive, six-story IMAX movie screen at Pacific Science Center has debuted stellar new films, including the breathtaking *Everest,* which was made by Seattle climbers and photographers. Don't miss the 3-D pre-sentations when they're offered; the images pop off the screen and hover before your eyes with the best 3-D effects I've ever seen. It's a great way to soak up some cultural and natural history in a crowd-pleasing format that impresses even the most jaded teens.

Pacific Science Center at Seattle Center. Ticket kiosk for IMAX films is located behind the museum on the 2nd Avenue N. and John Street side. ☎ 206-443-2001. Admission: $6.75–$7.50 adults, $5.75–$6.50 ages 3–13 and seniors. Showtimes throughout the day.

University of Washington
University District

The stately, classical buildings of UW (universally pronounced U-Dub) and the stellar views of Mount Rainier in the distance make this tree-lined campus a great place to stroll, particularly if your teenager wants a taste of the college atmosphere. Red Square, in the center of campus, is a paved redbrick area surrounded by libraries and classroom buildings where students rollerblade, skateboard, and play Frisbee. It's well worth a visit if college is starting to enter the family conversation, and adjacent University Avenue NE features a great strip of cheap food places and student-oriented shops.

Main entrance at 15th Ave. NE and NE 45th Street; take I-5 north to first exit after bridge (NE 45th and 50th sts.) and turn right. ☎ 206-543-2100. Best to visit during daylight hours. No admission; campus parking lots fill up early, so find parking on nearby streets.

Seattle for romantics

With its ever-present water views, drawbridges, green, tree-filled parks, and ubiquitous coffee shops, Seattle is a great place for exploring with your sweetheart. Combine some of these attractions with a romantic dinner for two in a cozy Belltown boite to keep the old heartstrings twanging.

The bridges of King County

Seattle's downtown is connected to the north-side neighborhoods by several bridges, three of which are lovely little drawbridges that go back decades. They all have pedestrian walkways and offer nice views of the canal, with pleasure craft and commercial barges slowly traveling to and from Lake Union and Puget Sound. The lowest, the Fremont Bridge, is the most-opened drawbridge in the country.

Ballard Bridge on Elliott Avenue W. as it becomes 15th Ave. W. Fremont Bridge at Westlake Avenue and Fremont Avenue N. University Bridge on Eastlake Avenue as it becomes Roosevelt Way N.

Emerald Downs
Auburn

Seattle's new, state-of-the-art horse-racing track makes for a grand afternoon out. Even if you don't like to wager, it's fun to watch the thoroughbred horses parade in the paddock before each race, the jockeys in silks boosted onto their backs. The competition is first-rate, and there are plenty of opportunities for wining and dining.

2300 Emerald Downs Dr., about 40 minutes southeast of the city. Take Rte. 167 from I-405 S. to 15th Ave. NW exit. ☎ 888-931-8400 or 253-288-7711. Daily post times during April–Sept season. Admission fee: $3–$5.50.

Golden Gardens Park
Ballard

Seattle's idea of a beach is this rocky point on a tip of land on the edge of the Ballard neighborhood. A paved path leads past the chilly beach and a restroom station to a natural wetlands where you can see starfish that wash up in the tidal flats and waterfowl. Sea lions bark from the rocky areas alongside the adjacent marina, and the views of water, islands, and mountains are stellar. Dog lovers can climb the steep stairs up the adjacent hill to find a large fenced area where dogs come to play leash-free.

Seaview Avenue NW in Ballard, past the Ballard Locks. Plenty of free parking at the park.

Myrtle Edwards Park
Downtown

This strip of the downtown waterfront is north of all of the shops and attractions, and it receives far less traffic than most of the city's parks, which is a pity, because it has great views of Puget Sound, ferryboats crossing to Bainbridge Island, and the towering Olympic Mountain range in the background, with a paved path for walkers and cyclists and strips of green grass dotted with park benches. On the Fourth of July the park hosts a huge festival that culminates in a dramatic fireworks show.

Alaskan Way, north of Pier 70 and the cruise ship terminal. Free parking available.

Seattle Center dances
Seattle Center

Known around town as "the old people's dance," the ballroom dances held weekly at Seattle Center attract an adorable crowd of seniors, couples, and kids on dates. Musical combos that invariably consist of three or four elderly gents produce a smooth sound to which you can foxtrot, Lindy hop, and even jitterbug, and the dance floor at the Seattle Centerhouse is smooth and spacious. It's very sweet entertainment, and free to boot.

Seattle Center Centerhouse, adjacent to the monorail station. ☎ 206-684-7200. Dances most Saturdays 8–10 p.m. and occasional matinees. Admission: free; dance lessons usually offered at 7 p.m. for $5.

Seattle for nature and outdoors lovers

Want to immerse yourself in trees and nature without even leaving the city? It's easy, because Seattle is graced with an abundance of parks that preserve the Northwest's natural setting of tall cedars and pines. The following offer some great options for getting outside and exploring.

Burke-Gilman Trail

This terrific urban bike trail was born when an old, abandoned railroad bed that ran through several northside neighborhoods was paved over. The Burke-Gilman stretches from Fremont past the University district and all the way up to the top of Lake Washington, with extensions on the way that will connect it to Ballard and the Locks. Walkers and joggers enjoy the pedestrian-only path and views of Lake Union and Lake Washington, while cyclists whiz past. Skaters can rent wheels for the path at **Urban Surf** (2100 N. Northlake Way; ☎ **206-545-9463**), opposite Gasworks Park.

Best place to park and begin trail is at Gasworks Park, N. Northlake Way and Meridian Avenue N. between Fremont and Wallingford. Free parking. Continue east on trail toward UW and points north.

Carkeek Park
Ballard

The salmon are returning to Piper's Creek after careful reclamation efforts in this wild, rugged park on a chunk of hillside in north Ballard. Park the car at an unassuming lot off NW 105th Street and leave all urban sights and sounds behind in this tree-filled natural wonderland. The creek meanders past the footpath as you make your way to a small, rocky beach on Puget Sound. In the fall, the whole place is blanketed in large oak leaves colored red and yellow. Look for salmon from the number of viewpoints along the creek.

8th Avenue NW and NW 105th Street in north Ballard. Look for trailheads and parking behind big shopping center. Cars can also continue to parking lot near the beach from Carkeek Park Road, but walking the path from the hilltop down is more fun.

Discovery Park
Magnolia

This mammoth, 513-acre park packs a variety of Northwest experiences into one long day of exploring. A rocky beach reached by a steep path is studded with driftwood and tidal pools that reveal all sorts of Puget Sound critters, from mussels to bright starfish. Walk the length of the beach to discover a working lighthouse. The upper sections of the park have big meadows of wildflowers and swaying grasses, as well as paths that lead through stands of tall, native trees. The park is so big that you might want to spend a half-day on one side of it, and then drive to the other to begin anew. Guided nature tours are offered on weekends.

3801 W. Government Way in the Magnolia neighborhood; several entrances to the park. Call ☎ 206-386-4236 for programs and information.

Green Lake
Fremont

The best place in the city for jogging and roller-skating is the three-plus-mile paved path around this smallish, manmade lake. Seattleites of every shape and size use the path for exercise on all but the gloomiest days. Rent skates from **Gregg's Green Lake Cycle** (7007 Woodlawn Ave. NE; ☎ 206-523-1822). You can rent bikes there, too, but the path is generally too crowded for cyclists, so stick to the roads that circle the lake or head south to the Burke-Gilman Trail (see the listing earlier in this section) for cycling.

W. Green Lake Way N., just east of Woodland Park and the zoo. Ample parking is available at the south end of the lake.

Olympic National Park

This range of rugged mountains on the Olympic Peninsula, west of Seattle, rivals Mount Rainier and the Cascades for sheer scenery and rugged beauty. A network of hiking trails surrounding 7,965-foot Mount Olympus is centered at Hurricane Ridge on the northeast side of the park. Stop there for backcountry hiking, or continue to the western edge of the park for views of the crashing Pacific Ocean and visits to the lush rain forest at Hoh.

Route 101N, about 2 hours' drive from Seattle. Begin by taking the car ferry to Bainbridge Island, cross the island, and continue north on Rte. 101. ☎ 360-452-0330. Open daily. Admission charged.

University of Washington Waterfront Activities Center
Lake Washington/University District

A shop adjacent to the university's Husky Stadium is a prime spot to rent canoes and kayaks for exploring the marshy areas of Lake Washington and the ship canal. Paddle among peaceful, reedy areas where the lake meets the canal and look for otters and waterfowl, and then cross under the Route 520 bridge (don't forget to snicker at the motorists above who are no doubt stuck in traffic) toward little islands near the Washington Park Arboretum. It's an idyllic paddle, and if you want to turn it into serious exercise, you have 30-mile-long Lake Washington before you.

Montlake Boulevard NE behind Husky Stadium in the University District. ☎ 206-543-9433. Open daily. Various fees for renting watercraft.

Washington Park Arboretum
Washington Park

This 200-acre park has walking trails that lead past hundreds of trees, many of which are identified by signs. Inside is a gorgeous Japanese garden, as well as thousands of cultivated plant and flower varietals. The best time to come is in the spring, when the cherry trees and rhododendrons are flowering and the park is fairly bursting with color and life. The grounds can get pretty mushy during wet seasons, so wear appropriate footwear.

2300 Arboretum Dr. E. at Lake Washington Boulevard across the ship canal from the University of Washington. ☎ *206-543-8800.*

And on Your Left, the Space Needle: Seeing Seattle by Guided Tour

Seattle is a very manageable city to explore on your own, which is to say that the core areas are not so big that you get lost, nor are there crime-ridden areas that are best to avoid. Still, you may prefer the comfort and convenience of a guided tour, especially if you're pressed for time or would like a fast orientation to the city so that you can decide which spots you want to focus on. In the case of Seattle, guided tours are also the only way to see certain inaccessible places (such as Bill Gates's house or an uninhabited San Juan island), unless by chance you bring along your own boat, seaplane, or World War II amphibious landing craft (more on that later).

The downside of guided tours? You have to come and go on someone else's schedule, not your own, and if you find a place you'd really like to stay and explore, chances are that you have to reboard the bus just when you found the perfect cafe for an espresso. You also travel in a pack with other tourists, and as such you probably won't enjoy much interaction with the locals or vendors.

Touring Seattle on land

The mode of travel for land tours of Seattle run the gamut, from big buses to trains to walking shoes. Here are some of the best of the bunch:

✔ The major tour operator in town is **Gray Line of Seattle** (☎ 206-626-5208 or 800-426-7532; Internet: www.graylineofseattle.com), which operates sightseeing tours on big, comfortable buses. Gray Line's **Seattle City Tour** ($27 adults, $13.50 children) is a three-hour spin that takes in the downtown shopping district and waterfront, the Space Needle, Pioneer Square, and the Ballard Locks. You get more time to linger during the six-hour **Grand City Tour** ($39 adult, $19.50 children), which spends a bit more time at the above-mentioned places and adds a visit to the Pike Place Market. A more self-guided option is the company's **Seattle Trolley Tours** ($16 adult, $8 children), which are offered in the summer and consist of an all-day pass to an open-air trolley bus that winds its way around the city and offers narration on the attractions and neighborhoods. You get off the trolley at an attraction that you like, and then reboard when it swings back around. Gray Line also ventures out to all points in the Northwest, and they can package up combinations of tours that take in Mount Rainier or head to Victoria, British Columbia (see Chapter 5).

✔ **See Seattle Walking Tours** (☎ 425-226-7641; Internet: www.see-seattle.com) leads you through the major stops in downtown Seattle, including Pioneer Square, the International District, and the Market. Tours are split into two groups and are contingent on six or more people signing up. The cost is $15 per person for one part and $10 per person for the second part of the tour.

✔ The **Pike Place Market** offers daily 90-minute, guided Market Heritage Tours throughout the summer (call for availability other times of the year). The tours offer a lively walk around the Market, with good, behind-the-scenes stories and glimpses of the Market's many buildings and shops. Tours all begin at the Market Heritage Foundation Visitor Center at 1531 Western Ave. (☎ **206-682-7453**, ext. 653 for information); admission is $7.

✔ Want to really get under the skin of Seattle? A popular and highly unusual tour in Pioneer Square explores a section of the city that has long been out of commission. The **Seattle Underground Tour** (☎ **888-608-6337** or 206-682-4646; $8 adults, $7 college students and children 13–17, $4 kids 6–12) literally goes beneath the city to show you turn-of-the-century storefronts and alleys that were once street level and were buried when Seattle raised itself up a story or two to get away from the utter mud bogs that the streets had become. The tour is anything but dull: Tour guides jazz up the script with a rapid-fire patter of jokes and gags that are a riot to some people and an utter annoyance to others. Don't try this one if you have a bad back: You may have to bend over or skitter through a few narrow openings in the old underground passages.

✔ For a pleasant rail tour of the eastside communities of Renton, Bellevue, and Woodinville, the **Spirit of Washington Dinner Train** is a set of renovated antique railroad cars that make tours from the train depot in Renton, WA (a half-hour's drive southeast of Seattle), and chug slowly through the woodsy communities of Seattle's eastside suburbs. Dinner is served along with vintage wines on starched white linens, and you wind up at a winery in Woodinville for browsing and shopping before turning around and heading back. Lunchtime tours are also offered on weekends. More a wining and dining opportunity than a bona-fide tour, it does offer some narration and information along the route. (☎ **800-876-RAIL** or 206-27-RAIL. Tours: Oct–May, Tues–Sat 6:30 p.m., Sat noon, Sun 11 a.m. and 5:30 p.m.; June–Sept, Mon–Sat 6:30 p.m., Sat noon, Sun 11 a.m. and 5:30 p.m. Admission: $59–$69, including dinner and dessert).

Touring Seattle by air

Just as ferryboats are a quintessentially Northwest experience across Puget Sound, taking a tour on a seaplane that takes off and lands on the water is a unique local attraction. Several companies use Lake Union and Lake Washington as their bases of operations, flying the same solid, reliable DeHavilland Beaver floatplanes with pontoons that Alaskan bush pilots use. The planes seat six passengers and are operated by a single pilot. Get the co-pilot's seat and you have an unsurpassed view of the city and the islands of Puget Sound.

Here are a few of the companies that can take you up, up, and away over Seattle:

✔ In Seattle, **Seattle Seaplanes** (☎ **800-637-5553** or 206-329-9683; 1325 Fairview Ave. E.) flies from Lake Union and offers 20-minute flight tours of the city for $42.50. It can also accommodate charters of up to six passengers to fly to the San Juan Islands or Canada's Gulf Islands. The small terminal is at the southeast corner of Lake Union, just north of Chandler's Cove.

✔ **Kenmore Air** (☎ **800-543-9595** or 425-486-1257; 950 Westlake Ave. N., just south of the Northwest Outdoor Center; Internet: www. kenmoreair.com) is a scheduled-service floatplane operator that flies directly to Victoria and the San Juan Islands, with several departures per day. Kenmore acts as a mini airline, boarding passengers on docks adjacent to its modest terminal on the lake, but the service provides the same opportunity for flight-seeing as a charter, with a route that heads directly up Puget Sound and over Whidbey Island and the San Juans. The cost is $150 roundtrip for adults and $135 for children to the San Juans, with the same fare applicable for a one-day round-trip excursion. It has another terminal on the north end of the lake in the community of Kenmore.

✔ In Renton, **Sound Flight** (☎ **800-825-0722;** 243 W. Perimeter Rd. on the southern shore of Lake Washington) is a charter service that offers two-hour flight-seeing tours to the San Juans or Mount Rainier for $269 per person. If you have a group, you can save money by chartering the whole plane for $717, and the pilot can stop wherever you like, such as in a deserted cove on an uninhabited island for a picnic lunch.

Touring Seattle by water

On the water, Seattle is unsurpassed for touring opportunities, whether you make a short crossing to Bainbridge Island or ride for several hours to the San Juan Islands or Victoria, British Columbia. Make sure that you schedule some time in your vacation to get on the water; the views and environment are sensational on Puget Sound as you cruise among islands with the city perched on one shore, Mount Rainier to the south, snowcapped Mount Baker to the north, and the jagged Olympic Mountain range looming to the west. Sailboats, yachts, and huge commercial ships share the waterways with you, and seagulls gracefully ride the airstreams trailing the big ferryboats, hoping for a handout. You might even see dolphins or a rare pod of killer whales swimming by.

Here is a sampling of the many tour operators that cruise the local waters:

- ✔ The least expensive option for getting on the water is to take a **Washington State ferry** (☎ 206-464-6400; see Chapter 17 for more information) from Pier 52 on the Waterfront, just north of Pioneer Square. These are not guided tours, but you still see plenty of great Puget Sound views. Boats leave two or three times an hour bound for Bainbridge Island or the town of Bremerton, and foot passengers pay only $3.70 for a round-trip fare (it costs more for cars).

- ✔ **Argosy Cruises** (☎ 800-426-7505 or 206-623-4252), which is affiliated with Gray Line of Seattle, has a number of packages available on big, double-decker tour boats. A popular one-hour harbor cruise ($12.45 adults, $46.90 children 5–12) departs from Pier 55 in the center of the Seattle waterfront and offers some nice views of the city from Elliott Bay. A **Cruise the Locks** package gives you the rare opportunity to navigate the Ballard Locks from Puget Sound to Lake Union ($33 adults, $22 children), and a combination land-and-water tour not only gets you through the Locks but lets you walk around a bit and see some of the city's neighborhoods by bus ($59 adults, $35 children). For a "Who Wants to Be a Millionaire" kind of crowd, Argosy also offers tours of Lake Washington that depart from Lake Union's Chandler's Cove and make their way past the magnificent mansions that are perched on the eastern shore of the grand lake, including Bill Gates's modest waterfront estate (which includes a fishpond where Bill raises and releases his own salmon).

- ✔ Located on the north end of the waterfront at Pier 70, just south of Myrtle Edwards Park, the **Spirit of Puget Sound** (☎ 206-674-3500), a harbor cruise ship that offers lunch, dinner, and party cruises throughout the day, frequently including live music. Fares usually begin at $32.50 for lunch and $58 for dinner.

✔ Next door, at Pier 69, is the terminal for **Victoria Clipper** (☎ 800-888-2535 or 206-448-5000; Internet: www.victoriaclipper.com), whose high-speed and very comfortable cruising catamarans shoot to Victoria, British Columbia, in under three hours, passing the San Juan Islands on the way. You could conceivably make the round-trip in a day if you wanted to see a lot of water all at once. Fares are $54 to $109 for adults and $27 to $54.50 for children 1 to 11, with discounts and land tour options available. These very popular cruises are frequently sold out during the summer months, so reserve your seats well ahead of time.

✔ For a flavor of Northwest Native American culture, the **Tillicum Village Tour** is an interesting dinner cruise that leaves daily from Pier 55 on the Seattle waterfront bound for Tillicum Village on tiny Blake Island, which is opposite of West Seattle and just north of Vashon Island. The tour includes narration, a Northwest salmon dinner cooked on an open fire and served in a decorated long-house, and Native American dances and entertainment. A little time is built in for you to explore the remote shores of the island, which is a state park (☎ 206-443-1244; $55.25 adults; $22 children 5–12).

Touring Seattle by Duck

"By land or by sea? I just can't decide!" you wail. You obviously need **The Duck,** a novel tour of Seattle and Lake Union that is conducted on board a renovated WWII amphibious landing craft (the same kind you saw in *Saving Private Ryan* landing soldiers on the beaches of Europe). This is a covered, open-air vehicle that plies the streets of downtown Seattle showing you the sights while, equipped with duck-billed noise-makers, you quack at any and all passersby. The driver doubles as nar-rator and chief quacker. Making its way to Fremont and the northern edge of Lake Union, it plops into the water and chugs along by pro-peller as it tours houseboat communities and the shores of Gasworks Park before clambering, dripping wet, back onto the road and returning to its Seattle Center base. The 90-minute tours begin and end near the Space Needle (☎ 800-817-1116 or 206-441-DUCK; $20 adults, $15 kids).

Chapter 16

A Shopper's Guide to Seattle

* *

In This Chapter

▶ Tuning in to the local shopping scene

▶ Browsing the big names in Seattle retailing

▶ Getting a smart shopping guide to the Pike Place Market and other outdoor markets

▶ Hitting the stores, neighborhood by neighborhood

▶ Discovering Seattle's stores from A to Z

* *

Seattle has a long and storied tradition as a shopping mecca, starting with the Alaska gold-rushers who came to town to load up on supplies before heading north. Seattle is still a center for rugged outerwear for active lifestyles, but in recent years the shopping scene has grown to include major retailers and international and specialty shops. In this chapter, I acquaint you with the city's broad spectrum of shopping opportunities.

Making the Shopping Scene

Ever tried shopping in downtown Los Angeles or Phoenix? I don't *think* so. Seattle, on the other hand, has managed to maintain a vibrant downtown shopping core while other Western cities have abandoned theirs. Most of the action is centered here, so it's easy to hit many of the hot spots from a downtown base. I provide some tips in this section on finding exactly what you want and concentrating your shopping in certain zones of the city.

Store hours vary and change seasonally, so it's best to call ahead. Plan on most department stores opening between 9 and 10 a.m. and closing between 5 and 6 p.m., with 11 a.m. to 5 p.m. being the standard on Sunday and later hours offered during the holiday buying season. The downtown shopping malls (**Pacific Place, City Centre,** and **Westlake Center**) stay open until 9 p.m., and some stores, such as bookstores and music shops, go as late as 11 p.m. Don't plan on arriving late at the **Pike Place Market,** however: It gets deserted by 6 p.m. Conversely, don't rush out the door after breakfast to go shopping at boutiques and independent stores, which frequently don't open until 11 a.m.

Seattle has a rather hefty 8.8 percent sales tax, which consists of the 6.5 percent charged in the rest of the state of Washington plus a surcharge tacked on for the sheer pleasure of it. If you tour the Northwest and plan on making any large purchases, you should consider (as Seattleites often do) waiting to buy it in Oregon, which has no sales tax (see my coverage on Portland in Chapter 26 for more information).

The Big Boys (and Girls) of Retailing

Seattle has its share of big-name stores, many of which originated here and continue to be major draws for shoppers:

- ✓ **Eddie Bauer:** 1330 Fifth Ave. at Union Street (☎ 206-622-2766); also in University Village. Eddie was a Seattle boy with a fondness for designing rugged clothes for fishing and hiking. Who knew he'd grow up to be the Godfather of casual chic?

- ✓ **Fred Meyer:** 915 NW 45th St., Ballard (☎ 206-297-4300) and 417 Broadway E., Capitol Hill (☎ 206-328-6920); open until 11 p.m. The Northwest equivalent of a Target or an upscale Woolworth's is this discount department chain that originated in Seattle. It is the locals' favorite choice for toys, housewares, sundries, and casual clothes.

- ✓ **NIKETOWN:** 1500 6th Ave. at Pike Street (☎ 206-447-6453). Lovers of the swoosh can find their favorite gear here, at astonishing prices, in a store that is a shrine to mega athletes. Browsers like the autographed gear and nonstop video entertainment of Nike athletes in action.

- ✓ **Nordstrom:** 500 Pine St. at Fifth Avenue (☎ 206-628-2111). Seattle's upscale and locally owned department store practically saved downtown in 1998 by moving into a vacant space in the center of town. It boasts the best service in the city, and an unrivaled shoe department.

- ✓ **REI:** 222 Yale Ave. N. at Thomas Street, just north of Denny Way (☎ 206-223-1944). The name stands for Recreational Equipment, Inc., which has long been Seattle's co-op of choice for gearing up for the great outdoors. Now located in a cavernous flagship space with its own climbing wall, mountain bike track, and waterfalls.

Prowling the Market (s)

The **Pike Place Market** is a great place to eat, drink coffee, and purchase fresh vegetables, fruit, and fish (see Chapter 14 for my gushing review of the eating opportunities), but it's also a very cool place to shop, with lots of little stores dotted among the Market's buildings and alleys. Be sure to go below the main level to the **"Down Under"** shops to find all kinds of interesting things, right down to **Western Avenue** on the waterfront side of the Market, which has, among other things, an exotic spice store and a shop that sells live parrots and macaws. At the end of the main arcade of produce vendors, you also find crafts merchants who come daily to hawk their handmade flutes and jewelry, silk-screened T-shirts, and tie-dyed dresses.

Among the many stores, the exotic **Market Magic** (Down Under shops; ☎ 206-624-4271) has wonderful, wall-size posters of great magicians and a large selection of gags and books on performing magic tricks; **Sur La Table** (84 Pine St. on Pike Place; ☎ 206-448-2244) is a serious kitchenware shop for the gourmet cook that has a huge selection of utensils and heavy-duty cookware, as well as an impressive array of cookbooks and gift items like dish towels and serving dishes; **Made in**

Tourist-at-the-market syndrome: Don't let this happen to you!

It's funny at first, and then segues quickly into being downright annoying, to see a group of tourists fresh off the bus standing in a clump at the Pike Place Market and staring at the fish on sale as if at any moment it might spring to life and dance the Macarena. They take pictures of the fish, they have their pictures taken with the fish, and then they move on to do the same with meats, cheeses, and produce. People who actually come to buy the stuff (as opposed to being entertained by it) get shut out or stuck behind groups of gawkers, all of which sort of defeats the purpose of a working food market. Do me a favor, folks, and keep it moving — don't clog the aisles, and buy a few things to separate yourself from the mobs.

The success of the Pike Place Market has spawned a number of smaller markets around the city. In Fremont, the **Fremont Sunday Market** (600 N. 34th St., just west of the Fremont Bridge) is a major center for arts and crafts, with dozens of vendors who set up tables and booths for their handmade furniture, jewelry, pottery, and clothing. It's outdoors in the summer but moves into a covered space the rest of the year. In the summer and fall months, farmers and food vendors come to the U-District every weekend for the **University Market** (corner of University Way NE and NE 50th St.), a neighborhood event that is a good way to find produce in season from nearby farms. If antiques are your passion, the **Antiques at Pike Place** market (92 Stewart St. near the Pike Place Market) is a collection of as many as 80 vendors who gather to display and sell their antiques and collectibles.

Washington (Post Alley; ☎ 206-467-0788) is great for souvenirs from the Northwest; **Isadora's Antique Clothing** (1915 First Ave. between Pine and Lenora streets; ☎ 206-441-7711) has exquisite replicas of 1930's and '40s gowns and tuxedoes; and **The Great Wind-Up** (Economy Market Atrium; ☎ 206-621-9370) carries a broad selection of clever wind-up toys, some of them antiques, and other oddities.

Seattle's Great Shopping Neighborhoods

Seattle's shopping zones are scattered about the city, with a great deal of the action taking place downtown. As in other discussions of the downtown area (such as restaurants and lodgings), I break up downtown into smaller sections here.

Belltown

Seattle's trendiest downtown neighborhood is the site of designer boutiques and interesting shops selling home furnishings and accessories. Be warned that the neighborhood is in constant flux these days, with the prices of retail spaces going through the roof, so stores tend to come and go quickly. Some keepers that you should check out include **Great Jones Home** (1921 2nd Ave; ☎ 206-448-9405) for furnishings and accessories (the vanilla candles look like they've been plucked from classic old farmhouses), and **Fast Forward** (1918 First Ave.; ☎ 206-728-8050), which carries designer fashions from the likes of Helmut Lang and Vivienne Westwood. Sturdy outdoor wear is the stock in trade of **Patagonia** (2100 First Ave.; ☎ 206-622-9700), with its own line of weather-resistant shells and parkas (practically evening wear in casual Seattle). **Mint** (91 Wall St.; ☎ 206-956-8270) may remind you of your Dad's cool old office equipment; vintage Swingline staplers and Smith-Corona typewriters lie under glass domes or are mounted on side tables from the 1960s and sold as retro-chic accessories.

The Shopping District

There's no other way to describe this section in the heart of downtown, home to Seattle's biggest and grandest stores, with **Nordstrom** (500 Pine St. at Fifth Avenue; ☎ 206-628-2111) serving as its epicenter. Within just a few blocks you find **The Bon Marche** (3rd Ave. and Pine Street; ☎ 206-506-6000), another major department store; national chain retailers like **Eddie Bauer** (1330 Fifth Ave. at Union Street; ☎ 206-622-2766) and **Old Navy** (601 Pine St.; ☎ 206-264-9341), and three major indoor shopping centers (okay, urban malls). These are **Pacific Place** (600 Pine St. at 6th Avenue), the newest downtown shopping area which houses the most upscale retailers, such as Seattle's first **Tiffany & Co.** (☎ 206-264-1400); **City Centre** (6th Ave. and Union Street), which is home to major chain retailers like **Ann Taylor** (☎ 206-652-0663) and **FAO Schwartz** (☎ 206-442-9500) and has gorgeous displays of handblown glass from artist Dale Chihuly; and **Westlake Center** (400 Pine St.), with a load of specialty shops and a food court, as well as the downtown station for the Seattle Center monorail.

Pioneer Square

Seattle's oldest district (Yesler Way was the original Skid Row, from when the loggers skidded their cut timber down the steep hillside to the waterfront) is now an artsy area of galleries and shops. Among the standouts are **Bud's Jazz Records** (102 S. Jackson St.; ☎ 206-628-0445), with one of the greatest selections of jazz in the country, and the **Elliott Bay Book Company** (101 S. Main St.; ☎ 206-624-6600), which is widely regarded as Seattle's best bookstore. Just south of Pioneer Square, Safeco Field houses the **Seattle Mariners Team Shop** (1250 First Ave. S.; ☎ 206-346-4287), with everything from baseball caps to replica jerseys. For a broader range of sporting goods, **Warshal's Sporting Goods** (1000 First Ave.; ☎ 206-624-7300) has been supplying Seattle kids with baseball mitts, fishing gear, and footballs long before anyone ever heard of Wal-Mart. Clever toys of another sort can be found at **Magic Mouse** (603 First Ave.; ☎ 206-682-8097), which carries lines of hand-crafted toys from Europe and a great selection of plush stuffed animals.

The Waterfront

Starting from just south of the Pike Place Market to Myrtle Edwards Park to the north, the **Seattle Waterfront** on Alaskan Way is loaded with souvenir shops and amusements. You don't find much of substance here, but you do find the bizarre and indeed curious **Ye Olde Curiosity Shop** (1001 Alaskan Way at Pier 54; ☎ 206-682-5844), which hawks genuine oddities like real shrunken heads and a mummy alongside the T-shirts and Space Needle pencil sharpeners.

Queen Anne

The neighborhood that encompasses Seattle Center has a few retail strips worth perusing. At Key Arena, basketball fans can find their favorite hoop gear at the **Sonics Team Shop** (312 First Ave. N.; ☎ 206-269-SHOP), where a great bite out of your paycheck can procure a Seattle SuperSonics jersey with a player's name stitched onto the back. **Tower Records** (500 Mercer St.; ☎ 206-283-4456) continues to be a major supplier of music and video, and has a TicketMaster outlet inside. For an unusual activity that kids love, check out the **Paint 'N Place** ceramics studio (2226 Queen Anne Ave. N.; ☎ 206-281-0229) at the top of the hill, where you can paint your own designs on plates, mugs, or pottery, and they fire it for you in their kilns.

Neighborhoods north of downtown

The neighborhoods just north of the ship canal that connects Lake Union and Lake Washington to Puget Sound have plenty of distinctive character, which is seen in their shopping opportunities. The neighborhood of **Fremont** in particular, which likes to jokingly bill itself as "the center of the universe," is well worth a visit. It's here that you find a great concentration of antique stores that lean more towards the artful kitsch side of retro goods. Within a couple of blocks you find **Deluxe Junk** (3518 Fremont Place N.; ☎ 206-634-2733), with lots of kidney-shaped tables, retro clothes, and knick-knacks that hail from the 1950s and 1960s. Across the street is **Fritzi Ritz** (3425 Fremont Place N.; ☎ 206-633-0929), which concentrates on antique clothes and accessories. **GlamOrama** (3414 Fremont Ave. N.; ☎ 206-632-0287) plays it strictly for laughs with pop culture kitsch like lunch boxes interspersed with retro clothes, and the **Fremont Antique Mall** (3419 Fremont Place N.; ☎ 206-548-9140) has a little of everything in its cavernous basement space. Also well worth a visit for music is **Dusty Strings** (3406 Fremont Ave. N.; ☎ 206-634-1662), which houses the work of fine craftsmen who make beautiful dulcimers and folk instruments, as well as acoustic guitars, mandolins, and banjos. **Shorey's Bookstore** (1109 N. 36th St.; ☎ 206-633-2990) specializes in rare editions and has an enormous inventory of hard-to-find books to peruse.

The **Ballard** neighborhood to the west of Fremont has always been known for its Scandinavian roots, which are reflected in **Olsen's Scandinavian Foods** (2248 NW Market St.; ☎ 206-782-8288), where you can find house-pickled herring, cookies, and lingonberries to take home to your Swedish grandma. Another Olsen, craftsman **Sten Olsen,** runs a violin-repair shop that sells high-quality used violins and cellos (6508 8th Ave. NW; ☎ 206-783-7654). Ballard is also home to the city's greatest collection of novelty items, gags, punching nun puppets, plastic Martians whose eyes pop out when you squeeze them, and tons of other goodies at **Archie McPhee** (2428 NW Market St.; ☎ 206-297-0240), which is great fun to browse and perfect for kids. Record lovers may want to make the pilgrimage to **Bop Street Records & Tapes** (5512 20th Ave. NW; ☎ 206-783-3009), which has hung around a long time with a huge collection of used records to take advantage of the rebirth of vinyl.

The **U-District** at the very eastern end of the ship canal and bordering Lake Washington, is home to **University Village** (NE 45th St. and 25th Ave. NE), a big urban shopping center with a **Barnes & Noble** bookstore (☎ 206-517-4107), an **Eddie Bauer** outlet, and lots of clothing and accessory stores that are geared to college students. Adjacent to the UW campus is the **University Book Store** (4326 University Way NE; ☎ 206-634-3400), which has a fine selection of contemporary books and hosts frequent author visits. It has a good selection of UW souvenir gear, too. A few blocks away, **Half-Price Books** (4709 Roosevelt Way NE; ☎ 206-547-7859) is a big, spacious store where you can buy many of your favorite books used; they have a great selection of used software, too.

Seattle Stores by Merchandise

Here is a breakdown of stores sorted by the kind of merchandise they carry.

Antiques and retro wares

Antiques at Pike Place: 92 Stewart St.; ☎ 206-441-9643.

Deluxe Junk: 3518 Fremont Place N.; ☎ 206-634-2733.

Fremont Antique Mall: 3419 Fremont Place N.; ☎ 206-548-9140.

Fritzi Ritz: 3425 Fremont Place N.; ☎ 206-633-0929.

GlamOrama: 3414 Fremont Ave. N.; ☎ 206-632-0287.

Isadora's Antique Clothing: 1915 First Ave.; ☎ 206-441-7711.

Books and music

Barnes & Noble: University Village; ☎ 206-517-4107.

Bop Street Records & Tapes: 5512 20th Ave. NW; ☎ 206-783-3009.

Bud's Jazz Records: 102 S. Jackson St.; ☎ 206-628-0445.

Dusty Strings: 3406 Fremont Ave. N.; ☎ 206-634-1662.

Elliott Bay Book Company: 101 S. Main St.; ☎ 206-624-6600.

Half-Price Books: 4709 Roosevelt Way NE; ☎ 206-547-7859.

Olsen's Violins: 6508 8th Ave. NW; ☎ 206-783-7654.

Shorey's Bookstore: 1109 N. 36th St.; ☎ 206-633-2990.

Tower Records: 500 Mercer St.; ☎ 206-283-4456.

University Book Store: 4326 University Way NE; ☎ 206-634-3400.

Fashion

Ann Taylor: City Centre; ☎ 206-652-0663.

Betsey Johnson: 1429 5th Ave.; ☎ 206-624-2887.

Bon Marche: 3rd Ave. and Pine St.; ☎ 206-506-6000.

Eddie Bauer: 1330 Fifth Ave. (also in University Village); ☎ 206- 622-2766.

Fast Forward: 1918 First Ave.; ☎ 206-728-8050.

NIKETOWN: 1500 6th Ave. at Pike St.; ☎ 206-447-6453.

Nordstrom: 500 Pine St.; ☎ 206-628-2111.

Old Navy: 601 Pine St.; ☎ 206-264-9341.

Home decor

The Best of All Worlds: 523 Union St.; ☎ 206-623-2525.

Great Jones Home: 1921 2nd Ave.; ☎ 206-448-9405.

Mint: 91 Wall St.; ☎ 206-956-8270.

Sur La Table: 84 Pine St.; ☎ 206-448-2244.

Outdoor clothing and gear

Patagonia: 2100 First Ave.; ☎ 206-622-9700.

REI: 222 Yale Ave. N.; ☎ 206-223-1944.

Warshal's Sporting Goods: 1000 First Ave.; ☎ 206-624-7300.

Salmon and specialty food items

DiLaurenti Specialty Food Market: 1434 First Ave.; ☎ 206-622-0141.

Jack's Fish Spot: 1514 Pike Place; ☎ 206-467-0514.

Olsen's Scandinavian Foods: 2248 NW Market St.; ☎ 206-783-8288.

Pike Place Fish: 86 Pike Place; ☎ 206-682-7181.

Wild Salmon Seafood Market: Fisherman's Terminal; ☎ 206-283-3366.

Souvenirs and collectibles

Archie McPhee: 2428 NW Market St.; ☎ 206-297-0240.

Made in Washington: Post Alley; ☎ 206-467-0788.

Mariners Team Shop: Safeco Field; ☎ 206-346-4287.

Market Magic: Pike Place Market; ☎ 206-624-4271.

Paint 'N Place: 2226 Queen Anne Ave. N.; ☎ 206-281-0229.

Sonics Team Shop: 312 First Ave. N. at Key Arena; ☎ 206-269-SHOP.

Tiffany & Co: Pacific Place; ☎ 206-264-1400.

Ye Olde Curiosity Shop: 1001 Alaskan Way; ☎ 206-682-5844.

Toys

FAO Schwartz: City Centre; ☎ 206-442-9500.

The Great Wind-Up: 93 Pike Place; ☎ 206-621-9370.

Magic Mouse: 603 First Ave.; ☎ 206-682-8097.

Top Ten Toys: 104 N. 85th St.; ☎ 206-782-0098.

Chapter 17

Four Great Seattle Itineraries and Three Dandy Day Trips

. . . .

In This Chapter

▶ Seeing the sights in three days

▶ Enjoying the Emerald City's natural pleasures

▶ Sipping and snacking in Seattle

▶ Hanging out with the cool crowd

▶ Day-tripping outside of Seattle

. . . .

*I*f you really want to experience Seattle, take it easy. Don't run around like a maniac. The Space Needle isn't going anywhere, and if your only option for visiting it today means making a mad dash across the city in rush-hour traffic, see it tomorrow. Start your day with a simple plan: Include a few top attractions and/or parts of the city you want to see; try to plot your schedule so that you're not spending too much of the day driving from one end of the city to another; more important, be flexible. If the kids decide they want to spend twice the allotted time at the Children's Museum, don't try to cram everything else into half the time. Simply scratch something off the list or reschedule.

 Keep in mind that you won't be the only one who wants to get to the top of the Space Needle on a sunny summer day — so be sure to budget time for waiting in lines at the most popular attractions, or try to get to those places early to beat the crowds.

Give yourself some time to gather yourself and rest up if you have dinner plans. Enjoy a leisurely meal at a fine restaurant. Also, keep in mind that during the summer months, when daylight savings time is in effect, it frequently stays light outside until well after 9 p.m., so you may find that you can still see everything without rushing, even if you have a busy schedule.

Seattle Excursions

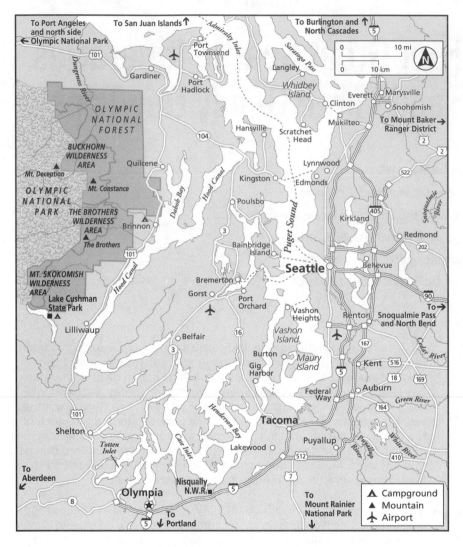

To Port Angeles and north side
← Olympic National Park

To San Juan Islands ↑

Admiralty Inlet

To Burlington and ↑
North Cascades 5

0   10 mi
0   10 km

N

101

Port
Townsend

Saratoga Pass

Langley

Gardiner

Port
Hadlock

Whidbey
Island

Everett Marysville
Clinton Snohomish

Mukilteo

To Mount Baker →
Ranger District
2

OLYMPIC
NATIONAL
FOREST

104

Hansville Scratchet
Head

2

BUCKHORN
WILDERNESS
AREA

Quilcene

Lynnwood

522

Mt. Deception ▲

Mt. Constance ▲

Dabob Bay

Kingston Edmonds

Hood Canal

Snoqualmie River

OLYMPIC
NATIONAL
PARK

THE BROTHERS
WILDERNESS
AREA

Brinnon

Poulsbo

405

Kirkland

The Brothers ▲

101

3

Bainbridge
Island

Puget Sound

Seattle

Bellevue

Redmond

202

MT. SKOKOMISH
WILDERNESS
AREA

Hood Canal

Bremerton

Gorst

90

To →
Snoqualmie Pass
and North Bend

Lake Cushman
State Park ■▲

Lilliwaup

Port
Orchard

Vashon
Heights

Renton

Belfair

16

Vashon
Island

167

Cedar River

3

Burton

Gig
Harbor

Maury
Island

Kent 516

5

To
Aberdeen ↙

101

Shelton

Totten
Inlet

Case Inlet

Henderson Bay

Federal
Way

Auburn

18   169

Green River

164

White River

Tacoma

Puyallup

Puyallup River

Lakewood

512

Nisqually
N.W.R. ■

5

7

410

Olympia ★

8

To
↓ Portland

5

To
Mount Rainier
National Park
↓

▲ Campground
▲ Mountain
✈ Airport

When you're planning your way around the city, remember that it's a lot easier and faster to go north and south in Seattle than it is to go east and west. You can move quickly and smoothly from, say, Pioneer Square to the Pike Place Market to Belltown to Queen Anne, but getting from the waterfront to Madison Park or the eastside communities of Bellevue and Kirkland can be a long, slow journey.

Following are some suggested itineraries for discovering Seattle on your own or with kids in tow. In setting up these routes, I tried to give you a good, overall view of the city and hit the highlights while keeping your travel and transfer time between attractions down to a minimum. For more details on the attractions and top sights listed here, see Chapter 15.

Seattle in Three Days

Three days? Are you kidding? It takes three days for some Seattleites to finish a large cup of latte and eat a bagel! Actually, in three days you can get a good, quick overview of the city's top spots and then spend the rest of your trip either going back for quality time at your favorites or moving in ever-widening circles to see more parts of the city.

Day one

If you stay downtown, leave the car parked and head on foot or by bus to the **Pike Place Market.** If you get there early, you can see the flower vendors setting up blossoms at their stalls and crafts merchants receiving their daily stall assignments for hawking their wares. Have breakfast in one of the Market's many restaurants or take-out vendors and spend some time perusing the unusual shops on the lower levels. Now walk a few blocks south on First Avenue to the **Seattle Art Museum** (except on Mondays, when it's closed) and spend the rest of the morning perusing its galleries and special exhibits. If you prefer street life and art galleries, continue farther south to the **Pioneer Square** district for a wealth of art galleries and shops. For lunch, you can frequent one of the restaurants in the area or head back to the Market, where you can pick up a basket full of goodies and have a picnic overlooking Elliott Bay at **Victor Steinbrueck Park.** Afterward, go down to the waterfront on Alaskan Way and consider taking a ferry ride to **Bainbridge Island** and back, or a cruise on a tour boat. Make your way north to the **Seattle Aquarium** and the adjoining **Seattle IMAX Dome,** and then leisurely stroll alongside Puget Sound at **Myrtle Edwards Park** before heading uphill two blocks to First Avenue for an evening of exploring **Belltown**'s restaurants and pubs.

Day two

Get yourself to **Seattle Center** by either taking a cab, riding the monorail from **Westlake Center,** or heading out on foot, and spend the better part of the morning and early afternoon enjoying the views from atop the **Space Needle** and strolling the Seattle Center grounds. A visit to **Experience Music Project,** the **IMAX theater,** and/or the **Pacific Science Center** would be in order, and you can buy lunch at one of the take-out vendors in the **Seattle Centerhouse** or the many restaurants on nearby Queen Anne Avenue N. Take some time to peruse the **Queen Anne** neighborhood by making the arduous walk halfway up the steep hill to Highland Avenue N., where great views of the city and Mount Rainier are seen from **Kerry Park.** Continue to the top of the hill for more shopping and restaurants, or head back downtown for shopping at **Pacific Place** and the **shopping district** (see Chapter 16 for shopping info).

Day three

Get out of downtown and explore some of the neighborhoods that make Seattle unique. Start with a visit to **Ballard** and the **Ballard Locks,** where salmon might be running and viewable from windows in the fish ladder. Funky **Fremont** is worth several hours of strolling and stopping to shop or have coffee, and **Wallingford** has a lively retail district as well as interesting homes on the streets leading down to **Gasworks Park.** For a uniquely Seattle experience, rent kayaks on **Lake Union** and paddle among the houseboat communities on either shore, or take a sightseeing tour of the city by floatplane.

Seattle for Nature Lovers

This itinerary maximizes the opportunities to see Seattle's marvelous outdoor landscapes, trees, and parks. Start out with a visit to the neighborhood of **Magnolia** and **Discovery Park** for an early hike on the bluffs above Puget Sound. You can walk down the steep trail to a rocky beach or get back in the car and drive to the **Ballard Locks** to see if the salmon are running; then continue west to **Golden Gardens Park** for great views of the Sound, islands, and tidepools. Next stop is **Green Lake,** the manmade lake in the neighborhood of the same name, for a jog or stroll on the paved path that encircles the lake, and then make your way south to **Gasworks Park** for great views of the city and Lake Union. You can rent skates here and navigate the **Burke-Gilman Trail** through the U-District and the University of Washington, or consider crossing the **Fremont Bridge** on foot, walking down the eastern shore of **Lake Union** and renting kayaks at the **Northwest Outdoor Center,** or renting a canoe or sailboat at the **Center for Wooden Boats** to paddle or sail the lake while exploring the communities of dollhouse-like houseboats.

Make sure to include **Volunteer Park** in Capitol Hill and the **Washington Park Arboretum** in your travels, the former for a visit to a greenhouse conservatory with a lovely flower and botanical collection, the latter for walks among themed gardens and towering trees. If you can't get enough of paddling, rent canoes from the **University of Washington Waterfront Activities Center,** and 30-mile-long **Lake Washington** will provide you with all of the watery real estate you could possibly want.

Seattle for Coffee and Snack Lovers

Want to spend most of your time enjoying Seattle's cafe society and lingering over coffee and a newspaper or good book, interspersed with long walks around the city's neighborhoods? Go ahead, I won't tell! Put your finger on the caffeinated pulse of the city at one of these coffee zones.

The **Pike Place Market** is heaven for browsers and snackers. Be sure to check out the coffee bars on **Post Alley** for large, delicious cups of latte and baked goods. You could easily while away a morning moseying through the Market, visiting all of the shops, characters, and vendors and stopping every hour or so to enjoy a cuppa Joe and a snack. Or tear yourself away from the Market and head a few blocks south to **Pioneer Square** for more cafes, as well as great bookstores and art galleries to peruse.

The neighborhoods of **Fremont, Wallingford,** and **Capitol Hill** are also perfectly suited for browsing and sipping. Check out the public art and kitschy antique shops in **Fremont** and take a walk along the quiet, shaded **Ship Canal** in between stops for coffee and homemade cookies at, among others, the **Still Life in Fremont** coffee shop. **Wallingford**'s commercial strip has a wonderful teahouse and bakery to go with the espresso vendors, and handsome houses to line its broad streets. **Capitol Hill**'s Broadway is a lively, ultra-urban thoroughfare where you encounter Seattle's pierced and leather set, but within two blocks you find tree-lined boulevards with some of the oldest and stateliest homes in the city. The coffee shops, particularly in the south part of the neighborhood near Pike and Pine streets, have their own, distinctive qualities that some say are evocative of lower Manhattan.

Seattle for the Tragically Hip

The grunge scene may have long departed the city, but Seattle is still a pretty cool place to be. If art and culture are your thing, try including the following in your schedule.

The hip Seattle neighborhood these days is **Belltown,** that section of upper First through Third avenues that is loaded with new restaurants, clubs, and bars. In summer, the party atmosphere goes up a notch or two when the restaurants open up their sidewalks and patios to diners. **Capitol Hill** is another scenemaker's nabe, with Broadway, the artery that fuels Seattle's gay and alternative scenes and Seattle's hottest dance clubs. **Pioneer Square** has the largest concentration of art galleries in the city, along with fine book and music stores. Venues for live music and concerts are scattered among all three of these neighborhoods.

For culture's sake, don't miss a symphony performance at **Benaroya Hall** and a visit, a few blocks away, to the **Seattle Art Museum.** Combine your trip to Capitol Hill with a stop at the **Seattle Asian Art Museum** in Volunteer Park, and the **Frye Art Museum** for 19th-century American painting. **Dale Chihuly**'s stunning glasswork is on display at the **City Centre** shopping arcade downtown, as well as at **Fuller's** restaurant at the Sheraton and the **Foster/White Gallery,** with outlets in City Centre and Pioneer Square.

Seattle is known in opera circles for its stagings of Wagner's *The Ring* cycle, and tickets sell out as much as a year in advance of a new production. If you can snag tickets to the **Seattle Opera,** you find them performing in **Seattle Center** (in the Mercer Arena until the Opera House is renovated and reopened in 2002). The **Pacific Northwest Ballet** is also based at Seattle Center, as are two of Seattle's biggest and most vital theaters, the **Seattle Repertory Theater** and **Intiman Theatre.** Lovers of the stage should also check out **A Contemporary Theater (ACT)** downtown near the convention center, and Broadway-style shows and musicals are performed at the lavishly renovated **Fifth Avenue Theater** and **Paramount Theater.** For half-price tickets to any of these venues, check out the **Ticket/Ticket** kiosks at the Pike Place Market and in Capitol Hill's Broadway Market.

Exploring Beyond Seattle: Three Dandy Day Trips

After you've had time to explore the city, head out of town to see first-hand why people fall so much in love with the Pacific Northwest. The following day trips, using Seattle as a base, show off some of the marvels of western Washington, from the high mountains that bracket the city, to the water and islands of Puget Sound. If you're heading south to Portland, I also offer some tips on what to see along the way.

Day trip #1: The Mountain Loop: The North Cascades Highway

The North Cascades mountain range provides the spectacular scenery for this driving tour, which begins and ends in Seattle and takes you 6 to 8 hours, depending on how often you stop. Bring lots of film for this trip; the vistas are incredible. This tour is only available from May through the end of September; during winter months the road past Newhalem is generally snowed in and impassible.

Begin by leaving **Seattle** headed north on I-5 through the towns of **Everett** and **Marysville,** which is the home of the **Tulalip** Native American reservation. Exit at **Highway 20** in Burlington, headed east, and make your first stop at the **Mount Baker Ranger District** headquarters and visitor center (2105 Hwy. 20; ☎ 425-775-9702) in nearby Sedro Woolley. Continue east on Hwy. 20, and if you'd like to have an early hike or a dip in a lake on a hot day, take the Baker Lake Highway to lovely **Baker Lake,** with awesome views of looming **Mount Baker** nearby. Return to Hwy. 20 and continue east through the small village of Marblemount to **Newhalem,** where you find the **North Cascades Visitor Center** (☎ 360-856-5700), a handsome, chalet-style lodge with interpretive information on the local forest and great hiking trails to explore, including the **Trail of the Cedars,** a marked trail that winds between towering, old-growth trees.

Continuing east on Hwy. 20, alongside the Skagit River, you pass the three dams that provide the bulk of Seattle's electrical energy. Be sure to stop at the **Diablo Dam,** a cool, Art Deco slab of concrete with street lamps that glow an orange light. You can stop the car and walk across the dam, pausing to stand before an incredible gush of water roaring through its spillway into the twisting river. The **Ross Dam** is a few miles further up the road on **Ross Lake. Seattle City Light** (☎ 206-684-3030) offers guided and self-guided tours of the dams and power plants through September. After passing Ross Lake, you have a long, winding drive on the **North Cascades Scenic Highway,** with gorgeous alpine views, particularly in September when the leaves change. The highway ends in the charming, Old West–style town of **Winthrop** in the rugged Okanogan region of rolling hills and forests. Head south on Rte. 153 and 97 through semi-arid, desertlike terrain to the town of **Wenatchee,** the capital of Washington's apple industry, where you can buy fresh fruit from side-of-the-road stalls. Head west on Hwy. 2 through **Leavenworth,** a tourist village with a Bavarian theme, and then cross back over the mountains over 4,000-foot **Stevens Pass,** rejoining I-5 just north of Everett.

Day trip #2: Bainbridge Island, the Kitsap Peninsula, and Olympic National Park

This trip begins and ends with ferry rides that put you on the water of **Puget Sound,** and then follows the Sound past charming, historic towns on the way to magnificent Olympic National Park. Figure 5 to 7 hours of travel time.

Begin by getting in line for the car ferry at the **Colman Dock** ferry terminal at Pier 52 on the Alaskan Way waterfront. For ferry schedules, contact the **Washington State Ferries** (☎ 800-84-FERRY or 206-464-6400). Plan to wait in the holding area during busy summer months; the earlier you arrive, the better the chance of getting onto the next ferry. Get out of the car and enjoy the breezes from the ferry's upper decks as you cross the Sound to **Bainbridge Island** (a 35-minute passage). As you exit the ferry, head left at the first stop sign to explore the charming town of **Winslow,** the hub of Bainbridge life. Garden lovers should make advance reservations to visit the **Bloedel Reserve** (7571 NE Dolphin Dr.; ☎ 206-842-7631), an elegant private garden with an international selection of plants. Head to the south end of the island to walk alongside Rich Passage at **Fort Ward State Park** (☎ 206-842-4041), or continue to Bainbridge's north side for a walk on the rocky beach of **Fay Bainbridge State Park** (☎ 206-842-3931), which has fine views of the Seattle skyline in the distance.

Cross the small bridge at **Agate Passage** to leave Bainbridge Island, and then take the first right to visit the town of **Suquamish,** a Native American village whose cemetery holds the tomb of Chief Sealth, the chieftain after whom Seattle was named. Nearby **Indianola** is a sleepy little village with a general store where you can buy sandwiches and drinks to consume on an old fishing pier that juts into the sound. Head back to Rte. 305 and continue north to the larger town of **Poulsbo,** which prides itself on its Scandinavian heritage and has Scandinavian-themed shops along broad Front Street. The active set may enjoy a paddle on quiet waters with a kayak rented from the **Olympic Outdoor Center** (18971 Front St.; ☎ 360-697-6095).

Head north on Rte. 3 to reach the long, high **Hood Canal Bridge,** which puts you onto the **Olympic Peninsula.** Hwy. 104 leads into Hwy. 101, the major artery that encircles massive **Olympic National Park,** with its tall range of mountains. A visitor center (☎ 360-452-0330) in the town of **Port Angeles** has maps and information on the myriad hiking trails in the park. Continue west from Port Angeles on Hwy. 101 past pristine **Lake Crescent,** a great spot for a swim or a picnic. Then skirt the ocean near the village of **Kalaloch,** with rugged beaches that are pounded by Pacific waves. Keep going on Hwy. 101 all the way to **Shelton,** which is home to the **Taylor Shellfish Farms** (130 SE Lynch Rd.; ☎ 360-426-6178), where you can watch oysters, clams, and mussels being processed and buy fresh or smoked shellfish. Finish your day by continuing on Hwy. 3 to the town of **Bremerton,** home of a naval base, for the return ferry ride to downtown Seattle.

Day trip #3: The San Juan Islands

The **San Juan Islands** northwest of Seattle are an island-hopper's dream, with ferries or floatplanes connecting a string of peaceful little islands that are wonderful for strolling, biking, or shopping in quaint, small towns. This trip could be done in a long, 8- to 10-hour day or planned for an overnight visit.

Your day should begin very early in the morning with a drive to the town of **Anacortes** in northern Washington, an hour and a quarter's drive from downtown Seattle. Going early gives you a shot at catching an early ferry for this very popular passage, which is often jammed during the summer months. The ferries operated by **Washington State Ferries** (see the preceding section) link four of the hundreds of islands that make up the San Juan chain: **Lopez, Shaw, Orcas,** and **San Juan.** Alternatively, you can catch a passenger-only private ferry operated by **Victoria Clipper** (☎ 800-888-2535 or 206-448-5000) from downtown Seattle to San Juan or Orcas Island.

The San Juan Islands

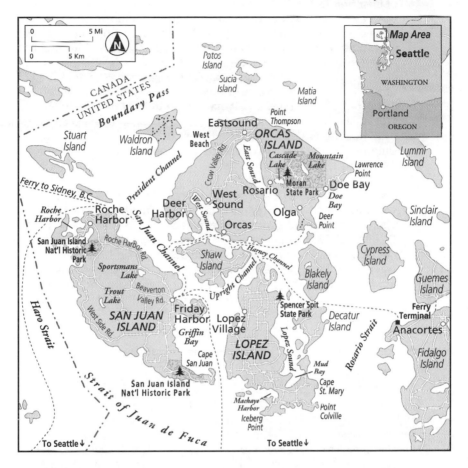

The islands are quiet and peaceful, even during the busy summer months, each with its own character. **Shaw Island** is the smallest and the least commercial, with quiet roads that are ideal for bike rides or long walks. **Lopez Island** is home to many farms and a small retail district in **Lopez Village;** there are nine parks to explore, including **Spencer Spit State Park** (☎ 360-468-2251), where deep woods meet the water on a rustic, rocky beach. The most populous island, and the most welcoming to tourists, is **San Juan Island,** with its bustling town of **Friday Harbor** serving as the county seat for all of the islands. Check out the **Whale Museum** (62 First St. N.; ☎ 360-378-4710) for a look at the history and anatomy of the pods of orca whales that still swim in those waters. **San Juan Excursions** (☎ 800-80-WHALE or 360-378-6636) can take you on a whale-watching cruise that can yield sightings not only of orcas, but of porpoises, minke whales, and sea lions. A walk at waterfront **Lime Kiln State Park** might also reward you a whale sighting. Horseshoe-shaped **Orcas Island,** with its two long inlets (East Sound and West Sound), makes for a nice mix between the totally rustic islands and more commercial San Juan Island. The village of **East Sound** is full of shops and art galleries. Stop by **Orcas Island Pottery** (☎ 360-376-2813) to see beautiful, hand-thrown pieces displayed across the sprawling grounds and studio buildings. Enormous **Moran State Park,** more than 5,000 acres in size, provides plenty of hiking trails and five lakes for swimming or fishing. Campgrounds are also available. For more plush surroundings, consider spending a night or two at the historic **Rosario Resort & Spa** (☎ 800-562-8820 or 360-376-2222), which was originally built in 1904 by shipbuilder Robert Moran and houses a marina, dive shop, pools, and an excellent restaurant. Rosario is also a scheduled stop for floatplane flights from Lake Union in Seattle that are operated by **Kenmore Air** (950 Westlake Ave.; ☎ 800-543-9595 or 425-486-1257).

If you want to splurge and see far more of the San Juan Islands than you could ever see by commercial ferry, consider chartering a floatplane from **Kenmore Air, Seattle Seaplanes** (1325 Fairview Ave. E.; ☎ 800-637-5553 or 206-329-9683), or Lake Washington–based **Sound Flight** (243 W. Perimeter Rd.; ☎ 800-825-0722 or 425-255-8965). The small, 6- to 10-passenger planes are perfect for flying low over the hundreds of islands that constitute the San Juan chain and landing in the water alongside deserted coves of uninhabited islands for beachcombing, swimming, or a solitary picnic.

Sights to see on the drive to Portland

Seattle to Portland is a three-hour drive straight down I-5. If you have some time to spare, though, and would like to see a lovely section of the Washington and Oregon coastlines, consider leaving I-5 in **Olympia** and heading southwest on Hwy. 101 in the direction of **Aberdeen.** You pass through rural areas where logging was king until recently, and pass the Willapa Bay–side towns of **Raymond** and **South Bend,** Washington, where mounds of oyster shells alert you to **shellfish growers** who sell fresh seafood directly to the public. Skirting the shores of tidal Willapa Bay on Hwy. 101 makes for a lovely drive as you make your way to the town of **Ilwaco** on the southern tip of the long, narrow Long Beach Peninsula. The village of **Long Beach** is a tourism haven in the summer, with a wide, sandy beach that is great for kite-flying and sandcastle-building. Make a point of stopping for lunch at the exquisite **Shoalwater** restaurant (4415 Pacific Hwy., Seaview; ☎ 360-642-4142). Nearby **Fort Canby State Park,** just south of Ilwaco, is a great place to view the mouth of the **Columbia River** and tour the **Lewis and Clark Interpretive Center** (☎ 360-642-3029). Crossing a long bridge across the mighty river puts you in the former fishing town of **Astoria.** The windswept sand-dune beaches at **Gearhart** and **Seaside** can give you a taste of the rugged Oregon coast. Head inland on Rte. 26 over **Saddle Mountain** and through farmlands to the strictly limited urban boundaries of **Portland.**

Chapter 18

Living It Up after the Sun Goes Down: Seattle Nightlife

. . . .

In This Chapter

▶ Finding out what's playing, and how to get tickets

▶ Exploring Seattle's vibrant theater scene

▶ Enjoying great classical music, opera, and ballet,

▶ Going into the night: clubs, bars, and hangouts

. . . .

Few groups benefited more from Seattle's technology-fueled prosperity than the city's performing-arts community. The Seattle Symphony moved into gorgeous Benaroya Hall, theater companies flourished and brought expensive new productions to the city, and the Seattle Opera broke ground on a complete renovation of its Opera House. Seattle's cultural scene continues to thrive. Here I give you the lowdown on the local arts-and-entertainment scene, where to find out what's going on, and how to get tickets.

What's Happening: Getting the News

The best sources for finding out what's playing in town are the city's three free weekly newspapers — the **Seattle Weekly, The Stranger,** and **Metropolitan Living** — all of which are distributed in coffee-houses and news boxes around the city. For online information, look to seattle.citysearch.com, or consult the online editions of the **Seattle Times** (www.seattletimes.com) or the **Seattle Post-Intelligencer** (www.seattlep-i.com).

Where to Get Tickets

Most of the big entertainment venues in town, including Benaroya Hall and the theater companies, have their own box offices from which you can procure advance or day-of-show tickets. The major ticket seller in town is **Ticketmaster Northwest** (☎ 206-628-0888), which charges a sliding fee for its services but is frequently the only place in town to obtain tickets for big shows. They also have kiosks in Westlake Center and at Tower Records (5th Avenue and Roy Street), where you can look at seating charts for shows. For discounted tickets, go to the **Ticket/ Ticket** booths (☎ 206-324-2744) at the Pike Place Market or the Broadway Market shopping center on Capitol Hill. They have a list of all shows that offer discounted seats; you pay half-price of the top ticket price plus a small service charge (cash only), receive a voucher, and then pick up your tickets at the event itself.

The Play's the Thing: The Local Theater Scene

Seattle is a great town for live theater. It must be the constant drizzle outside that makes people want to huddle together in cozy theaters and watch live dramas played out before their eyes. Whatever the reason, the city is rewarded for its hearty support of theater with world premieres of new plays that are bound for New York and London, as well as top touring productions of lavish Broadway musicals.

Just as New York has its Broadway, off-Broadway, and off-off-Broadway areas, Seattle's theater tends to break down into similar classifications, with a full range of plays, musicals, and fringe theater to explore.

For Broadway-style shows that are all pomp and music, with dazzling costumes and lively choreography, look to the **Paramount Theatre** (911 Pine St.; ☎ 206-443-1744; box office on the 9th Avenue side of the building), which is housed in a historic old downtown building that received a much-needed major renovation and is now a great venue for big touring productions of Broadway shows. In a similar vein, and located in the center of downtown, is the **5th Avenue Theatre** (1308 Fifth Ave.; ☎ 206-625-1900), another venue that devotes itself to Broadway-style shows in a grand space with a splendid Chinese-themed decor reminiscent of the great theaters of New York and Los Angeles.

Seattle's off-Broadway would be the three major theater companies in town that premiere world-class work and stage top theatrical repertory during their seasons. Actors like Richard Gere and Alan Arkin have put in time on these boards, and it's not unusual to find a star like Lily Tomlin polishing up his or her act in Seattle before taking it to London or New York. The theaters to focus on are the **Intiman Theater** (Intiman Playhouse at Seattle Center; ☎ 206-269-1900), whose season runs from May through October; the **Seattle Repertory Theatre** (Bagley Wright Theatre at Seattle Center; ☎ 206-443-2222), with a season that runs from October through May; and **A Contemporary**

Theater (ACT) (700 Union St.; ☎ 206-292-7676), which offers programs from April to November and usually mounts a splendid production of *A Christmas Carol* to top off the year. The ACT complex also houses a cabaret for late-night music.

You probably won't be too far behind your kids in enjoying the works presented at the **Seattle Children's Theater** (Charlotte Martin Theatre at Seattle Center; ☎ 206-441-3322), which takes its children's theater very seriously. It includes world premieres and specially commissioned works in its repertoire, such as last year's *Mask of the Unicorn Warrior,* which was inspired by the medieval tapestries that hang in the Cluny Museum in Paris. The theater is handsomely supported by the community and returns the favor with shows that are staged during weekdays for school groups, as well as matinees and evening performances for the general public.

For off-off-Broadway-type plays that are simpler in execution and often more daring in theme and content, check out the **Empty Space Theatre** (3509 Fremont Ave. N.; ☎ 206-547-7500) in Fremont. If you love good improvisational comedy, try the shows mounted by Unexpected Productions every weekend at the **Market Theatre** (Post Alley in the Pike Place Market; ☎ 206-781-9273).

Music, Dance, and More: The Performing Arts

Seattle's cultural calendar is filled throughout the year with performances by a top-notch symphony and ballet, as well as an opera company that receives international recognition. Read on to see how you can get your fill of highbrow entertainment in the Emerald City.

The Seattle Symphony

Under the able direction of conductor and musical director Gerard Schwarz, the Seattle Symphony plays its repertoire of classical music in gorgeous new Benaroya Hall, which was largely funded by local philanthropists. With acoustics that have been compared to that of Carnegie Hall, Benaroya is a great place to brush up on your Mozart or Beethoven or, if you're lucky enough to snag a ticket, to catch soloists like violinist Itzhak Perlman on one of his annual visits. Of unusual interest is the addition of a $4-million concert organ, a rarity in most concert halls, which allows for full-throated concerts of baroque organ music that fill every corner of Benaroya Hall with sound (200 University St.; ☎ 206-215-4747).

The Seattle Opera

Opera fans the world over flock to the city every other year to witness the spectacle of Wagner's *Ring Cycle,* the Seattle performances of which set the standard for international productions. Tickets are tough to come by for those shows, but you have a good chance of catching a production of one of the opera's many repertory productions during the August-through-May season. This is grand opera at its best, with lavish sets and costumes to match the big voices. With the Seattle Opera House under renovation until 2002, the company has moved next door into the Mercer Arena, also at Seattle Center, for the short-term future (☎ 206-389-7676).

The Pacific Northwest Ballet

Seattle's resident dance company has been reaching out to the whole family in recent years with productions that are great for introducing kids to classical dance. The company's repertoire has included new works choreographed by co-director Kent Stowell and classical gems like Tchaikovsky's *The Sleeping Beauty.* For many locals, the highlight of the cultural season (September through June) is the ballet's gorgeous production of *The Nutcracker* in December, with Maurice Sendak-designed sets that are one of the ballet's many treasures (Seattle Center; ☎ 206-292-2787).

Hitting the Bars and Clubs

If contemporary live music and making the local nightlife scene are more to your taste, you can find plenty happening in Seattle's bars and clubs, particularly during the summer months and on weekends. Don't come expecting a grunge music scene, however; it left town years ago, but Seattle still has plenty of lively music and dancing to go around.

Live! Music and dancing

For dancing and listening to national touring acts as well as local bands that still prefer their music loud and raw, you have several options in Seattle. Downtown regulars go to the **Showbox** (1426 First Ave., across from the Pike Place Market; ☎ 206-628-3151), a cavernous techno-space that attracts lots of big-name national acts. In Belltown, the **Crocodile Cafe** (2200 2nd Ave.; ☎ 206-441-5611) is a dark, atmospheric room where rock-and-roll is played late into the night. You often find top musicians jamming there in the wee hours after they've played their shows at the mega concert venues such as Key Arena or Memorial Stadium. In the quiet neighborhood of Ballard, two clubs in particular attract dancin' fools: **The Tractor Tavern** (5213 Ballard Ave. NW; ☎ 206-789-3599), which programs everything from good rockabilly bands to swing ensembles, and the **Ballard Firehouse** (5429 Russell Ave. NW; ☎ 206-784-3516), which, true to its name, is an old firehouse that now pulses with r&b-based rock music. Swing dancers do their thing at Capitol Hill's **Century Ballroom** (915 E. Pine St.; ☎ 206-324-7263), an old dowager of a hall where your '50s party dress and dinner jacket fit right in. The most technologically happening club in town has got to be Experience Music Project's **Sky Cathedral** (Seattle Center; ☎ 206-770-2700), where live acts play against the backdrop of an enormous synchronized video screen and a light show that comes straight from the deep pockets of billionaire founder Paul Allen.

Party time: Bars with attitude

College kids and those who like a loud, raucous scene head to the many bars in Pioneer Square, several of which try to schedule music that rises above the din of people slamming beer and shots in ancient drinking establishments like **Doc Maynard's Public House** (610 First Ave. S.; ☎ 206-682-4646) or the **J&M Cafe and Cardroom** (201 First Ave. S.; ☎ 206-292-0663). A few of the clubs and bars in Pioneer Square participate in a joint cover-charge promotion that allows you to access any and all participating places for $8 to $10. More genteel drinkers who like to rub elbows with Seattle's cool set make their way to the **Cyclops** bar (2421 First Ave.; ☎ 206-441-1677), which corners the nightlife scene in Belltown, or **Tini Big's Lounge** (100 Denny Way; ☎ 206-284-0931), which serves outlandishly large and varied martinis. Seattle and the Pacific Northwest have also developed a deserved reputation for their fine microbrews; drink them at the source at the **Trolleyman Pub** (3400 Phinney Ave. N. in Fremont; ☎ 206-548-8000), which pours the wonderfully crafted ales of the Red Hook Brewery, and at the **Pyramid Alehouse & Brewery** (1201 First Ave. S.; ☎ 206-682-3377), which opens an outdoor beer garden before every Mariners game, serving Pyramid's smooth lagers and Hefeweizens to large crowds.

Social magnets: Restaurant and hotel bars

Seattle's restaurant and hotel bars are also magnets for social life. Each has its own crowd, style, and character, and many offer light bites to go with the drinks. Here are a few of the hot spots:

- ✔ **El Gaucho:** For a sophisticated crowd in suits and dresses who sip cocktails before heading off to dinner.

- ✔ **Oliver's:** At the Mayflower Park Hotel. Makes the best martinis in the city and usually proves it every year by winning an impartial Martini Challenge contest.

✔ **Waterfront:** An exciting new venue on Elliott Bay with a long, curving bar that is fast becoming a favorite singles scene.

✔ **Hunt Club:** A dark and atmospheric bar at the Sorrento Hotel that is a great secret getaway for romantics.

✔ **Palace Kitchen:** Lines up a hip Belltown crowd around its horse-shoe-shaped bar for sturdy drinks late at night after the theaters and cultural venues have emptied out.

Seattle's music festivals

For sheer selection and nonstop entertainment, you can't beat Seattle's two big arts festivals, both held every year at Seattle Center. The **Northwest Folklife Festival** (☎ 206-684-7300) brings hundreds of ethnic music, dance, and storytelling acts to the dozens of stages set up on the grounds of Seattle Center. Held over Memorial Day weekend, it makes for a dizzying orgy of entertainment as you careen from an Appalachian fiddle concert to a demonstration of Eastern European line-dancing. Labor Day weekend at the end of the summer brings **Bumbershoot** (☎ 206-281-8111), the extraordinary arts festival that features contemporary entertainment of every stripe and color, from literary readings and modern dance exhibitions to concerts by national touring acts. Be warned: Both of these festivals attract hundreds of thousands of people, so if big crowds are not for you, either go very early in the day or don't go at all.

Part V
Settling in to Portland

The 5th Wave
By Rich Tennant

"As a resident of Portland, Oregon you should know it's illegal to operate a vehicle without a roof rack."

In this part . . .

*H*ere I provide the lowdown on visiting the Rose City, giving you all the information you need to familiarize yourself with the city's different neighborhoods, find the lodging that's just right for you, and choose among Portland's fine assortment of restaurants. I tell you the best ways to get around the city, whether by car, MAX, bus, or bike, and where you can find delicious, inexpensive eats. In the chapter on money matters, I tell you where to get quick cash, what to do if your wallet is stolen, and what to expect in tacked-on taxes.

Chapter 19

Location, Location, Location: Portland

A common misconception about Portland, because it is situated on the Pacific coast, is that if you plan to vacation there you should look for a hotel with an ocean view. That would have to be some hotel, because the coast is actually about 80 miles away due west.

Portland is situated at the confluence of the Columbia and Willamette rivers, which provide the water views and maritime appearance. In this chapter, I provide a quick introduction to the major neighborhoods of the city, particularly those areas where you spend much of your time.

The Downtown Experience

Downtown Portland is where much of the action is and, not coincidentally, where nearly all of the city's major hotels are located. Designated as the **Southwest** portion of Portland's quadrant address system, the downtown area is comprised of several subsections that are easily reached on foot. At the epicenter of the downtown area is **Pioneer Courthouse Square (PCS),** a paved, square-block park in the middle of the shopping district that is often referred to as "Portland's Living Room" for its use as a meeting and gathering place. From there, head east a few blocks to the **Willamette** riverfront and **Tom McCall Waterfront Park,** at the south end of which is the **RiverPlace** hotel, marina, and shopping complex. On the northeastern corner of downtown is the **Skidmore Historic District,** or **Old Town,** with many 19th-century buildings still intact, and next to that is Portland's active **Chinatown.** Heading south a few blocks from Pioneer Courthouse Square brings you to the cool, elegant **South Park Blocks,** on Portland's Park Avenue, a shady oasis in the center of the city and the site of museums and a weekly crafts and food market. The **Pearl District** lies north and west of the PCS; this is the city's arts neighborhood and home to art galleries and hip restaurants, but no lodgings to speak of as yet. Continuing west from the Pearl brings you to the hilly, affluent west side of town and **Nob Hill** (also called **Northwest** by the locals), with its own commercial strip of restaurants and shops.

Greater Portland

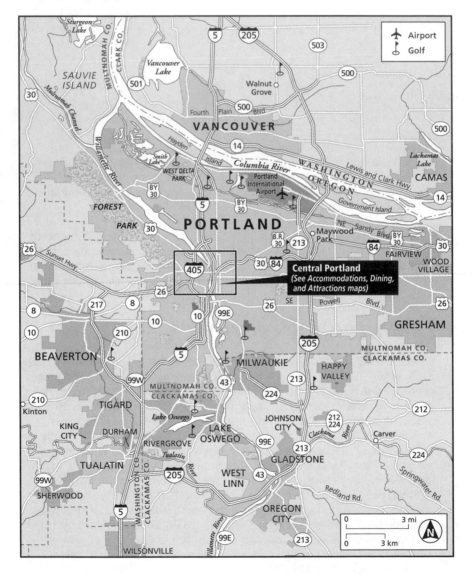

Across the River

Portland's **east side** refers to the burgeoning residential neighborhoods on the east side of the Willamette River, which is easily reached from downtown by a network of bridges and public transportation. Several hotels are located just over the river in **Lloyd Center,** also known as the **Rose Quarter,** which houses the massive Oregon Convention Center, the Rose Garden complex of arenas, and a large indoor shopping mall. Lodgings in this part of town tend to be convention-crowd basic, but they also make for good bargains. You find bed-and-breakfast lodgings nearby in the chic **Irvington** neighborhood and inexpensive airport motels near **PDX airport** in the far, northeast reaches of the city.

Toward the southern end of the east side is **Hawthorne,** a funky neighborhood centered on SE Hawthorne Avenue that is home to several brewpubs, new restaurants, and Portland's youth hostel. Continuing farther south, you come upon the posh **Eastmoreland** and **Westmoreland** sections of town, as well as the **Sellwood** antique district. With no hotels to speak of, these areas are places to visit, not sleep in — not yet, at least.

Portland Neighborhoods

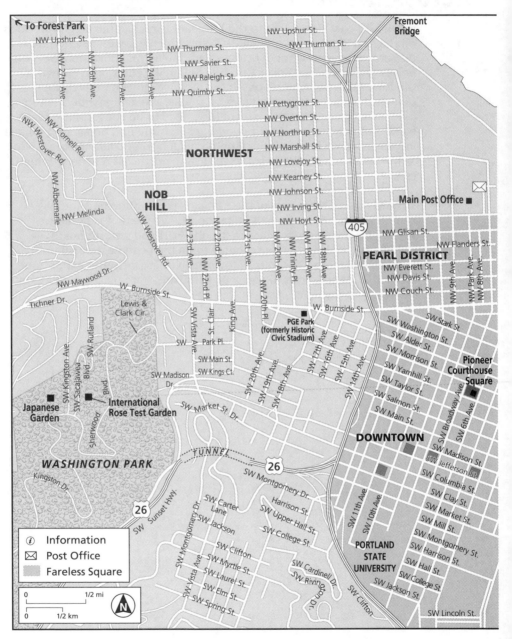

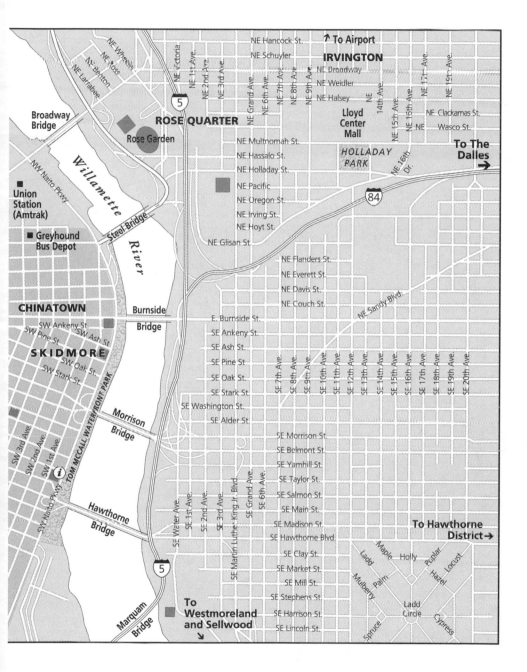

Chapter 20

Portland's Best Hotels

● ●

In This Chapter

▶ Top places to stay in Portland

▶ Runner-up places to stay

● ●

*P*ortland has a lively and competitive hotel scene, which is good news for travelers. Many of the top places have liveried doormen who make you feel as if you're entering a private castle, but even the modestly priced hotels offer worthwhile amenities like in-house restaurants, room service, or parking lots. New, boutique-style properties have made the local competition for your hotel buck even keener — particularly during the long winter months — which ensures that prices stay reasonable and hotels work extra hard to please you.

 Even if you're coming to Portland to attend a convention, you don't have to settle for a nondescript hotel near the convention center. The MAX light-rail line swings right past the center from its downtown route, which means that you can pick just about any downtown hotel that suits your mood and still be just 10 minutes away from the show.

In this chapter I place the hotels in their various locations around the city and try to give you a sense of each property's special qualities. Lodgings that are particularly suited to families are flagged by Kid-Friendly icons. And when there's no room at the inn and all of your top choices are booked solid, look to the list at the end of this chapter for the next tier of recommended hotels.

Portland Hotels from A to Z

The breakdown on hotel prices in Portland is as follows. The dollar signs placed by every listing are based on the hotel's posted rack rates for a standard room. Suites are much more expensive. Keep in mind that rates fluctuate, and rack rates are generally at the top of a hotel's price schedule. You should be able to find considerable discounts during the winter and off-season months.

Portland Accommodations

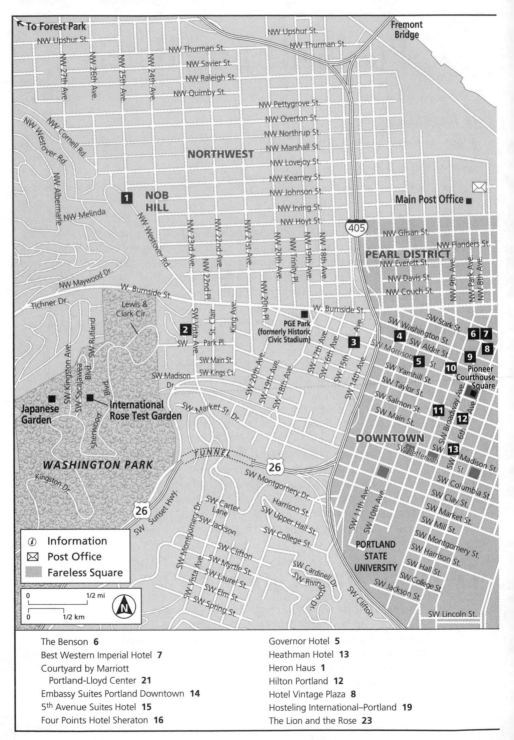

The Benson **6**
Best Western Imperial Hotel **7**
Courtyard by Marriott
  Portland-Lloyd Center **21**
Embassy Suites Portland Downtown **14**
5th Avenue Suites Hotel **15**
Four Points Hotel Sheraton **16**

Governor Hotel **5**
Heathman Hotel **13**
Heron Haus **1**
Hilton Portland **12**
Hotel Vintage Plaza **8**
Hosteling International–Portland **19**
The Lion and the Rose **23**

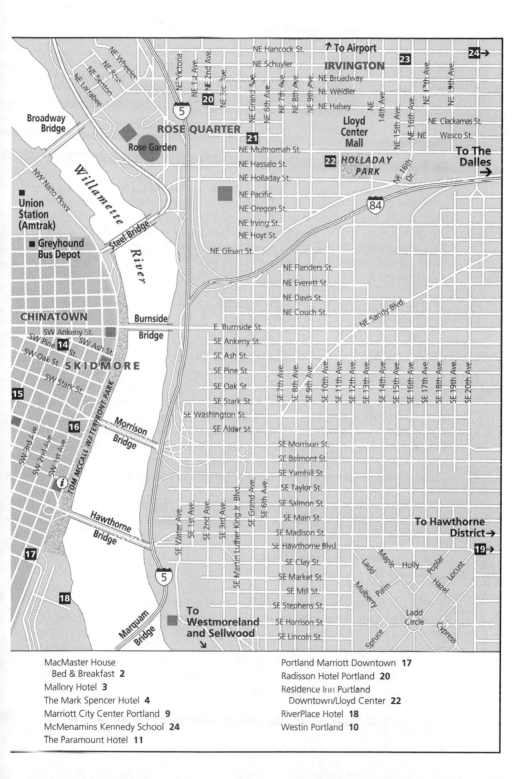

MacMaster House
  Bed & Breakfast **2**
Mallory Hotel **3**
The Mark Spencer Hotel **4**
Marriott City Center Portland **9**
McMenamins Kennedy School **24**
The Paramount Hotel **11**

Portland Marriott Downtown **17**
Radisson Hotel Portland **20**
Residence Inn Portland
  Downtown/Lloyd Center **22**
RiverPlace Hotel **18**
Westin Portland **10**

$	=	$50–$80
$$	=	$80–$125
$$$	=	$125–$175
$$$$	=	$175–$250

The Benson

$$$$ Downtown

Portland's most pedigreed hotel dates back to 1912 and is named for early burgher Simon Benson. The lobby is dazzling, with plush carpets and rare Russian woodwork; it's the poshest place in town to meet for business or drinks. No wonder the Benson is where presidents stay when they visit Portland; they can afford the suites (which start at $275). The other rooms, especially in the original tower, are rather small. Two splendid restaurants keep the place buzzing and produce lots of star sightings.

309 SW Broadway at Stark. ☎ *503-228-2000. Fax: 503-226-2709. Internet:* www. bensonhotel.com. *Rack rates: $225–$800. AE, DC, DISC, MC, V.*

Courtyard by Marriott Portland-Lloyd Center

$$ Lloyd Center

This new property is only a few blocks away from the Convention Center and the Irvington retail district. Standard rooms are spacious and include a queen-size sofa that can easily sleep two additional people. Enjoy the large swimming pool, spa, outdoor sun deck, and well-equipped exercise room. A king suite with a microwave and refrigerator is a huge bargain at $129. A complimentary continental breakfast is included.

435 NE Wasco St. at Grand Avenue. ☎ *503-234-3200. Fax: 503-234-1836. Internet:* www.courtyardlloydcenter.com. *Rack rates: $109–$129. AE, DISC, MC, V.*

Embassy Suites Portland Downtown

$$$ Downtown

It may be unlike any Embassy Suites you've ever seen, set in the grand old Multnomah Hotel with an elegant gingerbread lobby all trimmed in white and a bottom-floor indoor pool and health club. Standard Embassy Suites amenities, like in-room Nintendo and a complimentary breakfast, are part of the package, and the rooms are all suites, if rather cozy ones. Keep in mind that it's located on the fringes of downtown, close to Chinatown and the Saturday market.

319 SW Pine St., at 3rd Avenue. ☎ *800-EMBASSY or 503-279-9000. Fax: 503-497-9051. Internet:* www.embassyportland.com. *Rack rates: $129–$600. AE, DC, DISC, MC, V.*

5th Avenue Suites Hotel

$$$ Downtown

An all-suites hotel that makes an effort to cheer things up a notch or two, with bright rooms that are decorated with yellow-striped wallpaper, French posters, and giant, framed mirrors. Bedrooms are separated from sitting areas by a step and French doors. Business travelers appreciate the larger-than-usual desks and in-room fax machines, but TV buffs decry the small sets tucked away in armoires. It offers a good health club, too, and room service from the Red Star Tavern & Roast House is a huge upgrade from standard hotel fare.

506 SW Washington St. at the 5th Avenue transit mall. ☎ *800-711-2971 or 503-222-0001. Fax: 503-222-0004. Internet:* 5thavenuesuites.com. *Rack rates: $160–$375. AE, DC, DISC, MC, V.*

Governor Hotel

$$$ Downtown

The stage is set when the doorman ushers you into a lobby trimmed in comfortable leather armchairs, with a beautiful sepia mural depicting the Lewis and Clark expedition covering a long wall. Rooms in this handsome old hotel are simple, if on the small side, and bathrooms can be tiny. Corner rooms are the way to go, and the basement houses a lavish health club facility with a pool and running track (extra charge to enter). The location puts you in easy walking distance of the Pearl District.

611 SW 10th Ave. at Alder Street. ☎ *800-554-3456 or 503-224-3400. Fax: 503-241-2122. Internet:* www.govhotel.com. *Rack rates: $165–$240. AE, DC, DISC, MC, V.*

Heathman Hotel

$$$ Downtown

If culture and movies are your thing, this is the place to stay. The location, next door to Portland's symphony hall and arts complex, is perfect for catching shows, and the in-room movie service, whereby hundreds of classic and new movies can be piped into your room, is unparalleled. On top of that, it's a beautifully run boutique hotel with crackerjack service and comfortable, beautifully decorated rooms.

1001 SW Broadway at Salmon Street. ☎ *800-551-0011 or 503-241-4100. Fax: 503-790-7110. Internet:* www.heathmanhotel.com. *Rack rates: $150–$190. AE, DC, DISC, MC, V.*

Hilton Portland

$$ Downtown

Location and price are about the only reasons to recommend this big, convention-style hotel. The lobby is busy and surprisingly unwelcoming, with few places to sit and read the paper (find your way to the mezzanine level for the furniture), and rooms are standard beige with loud floral prints on the bed. With an expansion to nearly twice its current size under way, it's not going to get much quieter anytime soon. An in-house health club has a pool, personal trainers, and massage therapists.

921 SW Sixth Ave. at Salmon Street. ☎ *800-445-8667 or 503-226-1611. Fax: 503-220-2565. Internet:* www.hilton.com. *Rack rates: $125–$205. AE, DC, DISC, MC, V.*

Hosteling International–Portland

$ Hawthorne

Portland's youth hostel is anything but a cheerless dormitory building. It's actually housed in a large, sunny house in the middle of the funky and fun Hawthorne strip of shops and bars, with dormitory beds and a private room in the attic for couples. You can't beat the price, and you share kitchen facilities and a roomy, wraparound porch.

3031 SE Hawthorne Blvd. ☎ *503-236-3380. Fax: 503-236-7940. Internet:* www.teleport.com/~hip. *Rack rates: $15–$42. MC, V.*

Hotel Vintage Plaza

$$ Downtown

From the Kimpton Hotel group, which sets the standard for boutique hotels, comes this cozy business hotel in the heart of downtown, with rooms that are named after Oregon wineries. The grape colors and motif might grate after awhile, but the service is exceptional, the rooms are roomy and comfortable, and the suites are an upstairs/downstairs design that are perfect for meetings. Complimentary wine is served in the evening in the lobby, and room service is provided by the excellent Pazzo Ristorante.

422 SW Broadway at Washington. ☎ *800-243-0555 or 503-228-1212. Fax: 503-228-3598. Internet:* www.vintageplaza.com. *Rack rates: $99–$400. AE, DC, DISC, MC, V.*

The Lion and the Rose

$$ Irvington

This lovely Victorian B&B in the up-and-coming Northeast neighborhood makes for a cozy stay, particularly if romance is on your agenda. Within quick walking distance are plenty of new shops and restaurants, and even the convention center isn't too far to hoof it. The public areas are beautifully done in period antiques, and the rooms all have individual color schemes and styles. Don't plan to dash out the door in the morning, because breakfasts, taken around a large, communal dining table, are huge and memorable.

1810 NE 15th Ave. ☎ *800-955-1647 or 503-287-9245. Fax: 503 287 9247. Internet:* www.lionrose.com. *Rack rates: $95–$140. AE, DISC, MC, V.*

Mallory Hotel

$$ Downtown

For a truly retro experience without a shred of pretension, you'll love this aging dowager on the western fringes of downtown. The green lobby is a grandma's sitting room of gilt-trimmed coved ceilings and faded furniture. The restaurant is simply called the Mallory Hotel Dining Room, and it still serves calves liver and onions. Upstairs, the tiny rooms have burgundy carpets and small bathrooms with even smaller tubs, but, really, who cares? If it was good enough for your grandparents' honeymoon, Mallory-lovers insist, it's good enough for you.

729 SW 15th Ave. at Yamhill. ☎ *800-228-8657 or 503-223-6311. Fax: 503-223-0522. Internet:* www.malloryhotel.com. *Rack rates: $90–$150. AE, DC, DISC, MC, V.*

Marriott City Center Portland

$$$ Downtown

It may not look like much from the entrance and lobby, but this convention/business hotel has nice, spacious rooms trimmed in dark wood, each with free Internet access. The hotel doesn't have a pool, but a modest on-site exercise facility has a large indoor tub, and the roomy suites are a bargain, with free parking and breakfast included in the price. Don't confuse this with the Marriott Downtown, a high-rise a few blocks away that offers less charm and a longer hike to downtown attractions.

520 SW Broadway at 5th Avenue. ☎ *800-228-9290 or 503-226-6300. Fax: 503-227-7515. Internet:* www.marriotthotels.com. *Rack rates: $149–$189. AE, DC, DISC, MC, V.*

McMenamins Kennedy School

$$ NE Portland

This place must be seen to be believed. It's a vacated elementary school that has been restored and refurbished into a wonderfully unique bed-and-breakfast inn, with classrooms — their chalkboards and cloakrooms still intact — serving as spacious bedrooms. The place is also a center for the residential neighborhood, as movies are shown in the former auditorium, meals are served in the old cafeteria, and drinks are offered in two bars: Honors and Detention. After a day of touring, take a soak in the small, outdoor hot tub. Just a delightful place, if somewhat removed from the more lively parts of town. A car is definitely necessary if you stay here, but parking is free (just don't park in the Principal's space).

*5736 NE 33rd Ave. ☎ **888-249-3983** or 503-249-3983. Fax: 503-288-6559. Internet:* www.mcmenamins.com. *Rack rates: $99–$109. AE, DISC, MC, V.*

The Paramount Hotel

$$$ Downtown

One of Portland's newest properties is this elegant boutique property near the South Park Blocks, a sister to Seattle's Paramount. It strives to be posh and upscale and largely succeeds, with its elegant marble lobby with wrought-iron chandeliers and extra-large guestrooms trimmed in stripes. Bathrooms are roomy and done in marble. The fitness center is comparatively undersized, and the in-house restaurant was still under construction as of this writing, so I can't vouch for the food.

*808 SW Taylor at Park Avenue. ☎ **800-426-0670** or 503-223-9900. Fax: 503-223-7900. Internet:* www.portlandparamount.com. *Rack rates: $124–$199. AE, DC, DISC, MC, V.*

RiverPlace Hotel

$$$$ Downtown

You'd think that with all its water views Portland would have more lodging properties on the waterfront, but this is it for now. This handsome, small hotel in the RiverPlace complex has large rooms done in teal accents, with botanical prints on the walls and wonderful views of the Willamette flowing by, which is at its heartwarming best when brightly decorated Christmas ships float past in December. Guests have access to a private room with a sauna and whirlpool tub, and free passes are available to the fancy RiverPlace Athletic Club. Meals at the Esplanade restaurant are expensive, but good, with more of those excellent views.

*1510 SW Harbor Way, just south of Tom McCall Waterfront Park. ☎ **800-227-1333** or 503-228-3233. Fax: 503-295-6161. Internet:* www.riverplacehotel.com. *Rack rates: $219–$769. AE, DC, MC, V.*

Westin Portland

$$ Downtown

Westin's attempt at a cross between a business hotel and a boutique is this new-ish property in the heart of downtown, with sitting areas in the lobby that are done living-room style with leather furniture and newspaper racks. The rooms are surprisingly small, and some corner rooms only have showers in the bathrooms. Westin's "heavenly beds" are indeed terrific, and every room has a CD player and Internet access; upgrade to a Guest Office Suite for a working nook with a larger desk than usual and a fax machine.

750 SW Alder St. at Park Avenue. ☎ *503-294-9000. Fax: 503-241-9565. Internet:* www.westinportland.com. *Rack rates: $190–$295. AE, DC, DISC, MC, V.*

Index of Accommodations by Price

$
Hosteling International–Portland

$$
Courtyard by Marriott Portland-Lloyd
  Center
Hilton Portland
Hotel Vintage Plaza
The Lion and the Rose
Mallory Hotel
McMenamins Kennedy School
Westin Portland

$$$
Embassy Suites Portland Downtown
5th Avenue Suites Hotel
Governor Hotel
Heathman Hotel
Marriott City Center Portland
The Paramount Hotel

$$$$
The Benson
RiverPlace Hotel

Index of Accommodations by Neighborhood

Downtown
The Benson
Embassy Suites Portland Downtown
5th Avenue Suites Hotel
Governor Hotel
Heathman Hotel
Hilton Portland
Hotel Vintage Plaza
Mallory Hotel
Marriott City Center Portland
The Paramount Hotel
RiverPlace Hotel
Westin Portland

Lloyd Center, Irvington, and NE Portland
Courtyard by Marriott Portland-Lloyd
  Center
The Lion and the Rose
McMenamins Kennedy School

SE Portland/Hawthorne
Hosteling International–Portland

No Room at the Inn?

Space limitations prevent me from listing all the recommended hotels and lodging in Portland. If you find that my favorites are booked solid, the following accommodations are perfectly fine alternatives. Don't forget to inquire about special packages or discounted weekend and off-peak rates.

Four Points Hotel Sheraton

$$ Downtown

50 SW Morrison St. ☎ 800-899-0247 or 503-221-0711. Fax: 503-274-0312. Rack rates: $99–$134. AE, DC, DISC, MC, V.

Best Western Imperial Hotel

$$–$$$ Downtown

400 SW Broadway. ☎ 800-243-0555 or 503-228-7221. Fax: 503-223-4551. Rack rates: $120–$140. AE, DC, DISC, MC, V.

Heron Haus

$$$–$$$$ Nob Hill

2545 NW Westover Rd. ☎ 503-274-1846. Fax: 503-243-1075. Internet: www.europa.com/~hhaus. *Rack rates: $135–$350. MC, V.*

MacMaster House Bed and Breakfast Inn

$$–$$$ Nob Hill

1041 SW Vista Ave. ☎ 800-774-9523 or 503-223-7362. Internet: www.macmaster.com. *Rack rates: $85–$130. AE, DISC, MC, V.*

The Mark Spencer Hotel

$–$$ Downtown

409 SW 11th Ave. ☎ 800-548-3934 or 503-224-3293. Fax: 503-223-7848. Rack rates: $89–$109. AE, DC, DISC, MC, V.

Portland Marriott Downtown

$$$ Downtown

1401 SW Naito Pkwy. ☎ 800-228-9290 or 503-226-7600. Fax: 503-221-1789. Rack rates: $159–$179. AE, DC, DISC, MC, V.

Radisson Hotel Portland

$$ Downtown

1441 NE 2nd Ave. ☎ 503-233-2401. Fax: 503-233-0498. Rack rates: $119–$139. AE, DC, DISC, MC, V.

Residence Inn Portland Downtown/Lloyd Center

$$–$$$ Downtown/Lloyd Center

1710 NE Multnomah St. ☎ 800-331-3131 or 503-288-1400. Fax: 503-288-0241. Rack rates: $99–$189. AE, DC, DISC, MC, V.

Chapter 21

Orienting Yourself in Portland and Getting Around

•••

In This Chapter

▶ Portland or bust: by air, car, or train

▶ Portland's marvelous MAX

▶ Rose City buses: Follow that deer!

▶ Portland behind the wheel

▶ The trouble with taxis

▶ The city on foot or by bike

•••

*L*ewis and Clark paddled past the site of Portland in hand-hewn canoes, but you'll probably want to arrive in the Rose City by less strenuous means of transportation. Chances are that you're driving down from Seattle, arriving by train, or flying in. Here, I cover all the options of getting to Portland, navigating your way through Portland's airport, and getting around in the city after you arrive. If you do decide to come by dugout canoe, however, you're on your own.

Navigating Portland International Airport

Portland International Airport (PDX) is located alongside the Columbia River, about 10 miles northeast of the downtown area. The airport has undergone a great deal of construction and renovation in recent years, including roadwork on the access roads leading in and out and an expansion of the parking facilities. If you arrive on Alaska or Horizon Airlines, or have a connection on those airlines, you may have to take a temporary shuttle that connects the A and C concourses while construction is under way; signs point you in the right direction. An information booth with maps and transportation information into the city is located at the baggage claim area.

Do you need a rental car in Portland?

Downtown Portland is so manageable and connected with public transportation that you probably don't need a car for much of your trip, unless you have kids and strollers and things to carry, in which cases you do need a car for the sake of sheer convenience. Outlying parts of the city, like Sellwood's Antiques Row (see Chapter 26 on shopping) and Mount Tabor, can be tough to reach on public transportation, and if you want to explore Mount Hood and the Columbia River Gorge, you need your own wheels. Consider renting a car after you've seen all of the downtown attractions and are ready to explore more far-flung places. Keep in mind that renting a car downtown comes with a 12.5 percent sales tax, a savings of 10 percent from the 22.5 percent they charge at the airport. Most of the major car-rental agencies have downtown locations, including **Avis** (330 SW Washington; ☎ **503-227-0220**), **Enterprise** (611 E. Burnside; ☎ **503-230-1212**), **Hertz** (1009 SW 6th Ave.; ☎ **503-249-5727**) and **Thrifty** (632 SW Pine; ☎ **503-227-6587**).

Getting from the Airport to Your Hotel

From the airport you have several options for getting into town. The quickest and easiest is to grab a taxi located outside the baggage claim in the center part of the arrivals access road. A cab ride runs you about $25 to a downtown location. A cheaper alternative is the **Gray Line Airport Shuttle** (☎ **800-422-7042** or 503-285-9845), which departs every 45 minutes from 5 a.m. until midnight, costs $15, and stops at most major downtown hotels. If your hotel is not one of the stops, you probably have a quick and easy walk to wherever you're staying (this is not an option if you have more bags than you can comfortably carry a block or two). A third option is to take **Tri-Met bus #12,** which runs from 5:30 a.m. to 11:30 p.m. and makes its way slowly through the northeast neighborhood to downtown. At $1.15, it's certainly cheap, but it takes twice as long to get where you're going.

Portland's wonderful **MAX light-rail train** is scheduled to open at the airport in September 2001, with new tracks and a new station under construction at press time. When it opens, it will provide the fastest and most cost-effective way into the city.

Rental-car companies are found in the rental-car center on the first floor of the parking garage (which is now connected to the terminal by a covered walkway, PDX's first concession to the fact that it rains occasionally in Portland). To get to the city, follow signs leading downtown, first on I-205 south (you know you're going the wrong way if you cross the Columbia River), and then on I-84 west. Take the Morrison Bridge exit over the Willamette River, and you'll be in the heart of downtown Portland.

Arriving by Car

The Columbia River makes for a grand entrance when you arrive from the north by car, as I-5 crosses the mighty river over a high, steel-trussed bridge, marking the crossing of the Washington/Oregon border, and puts you into the northern section of the city. Use the I-405 bypass over the Fremont Bridge to reach the downtown area quickly. From the east, I-84 runs directly into the city, with the Morrison Bridge acting as access into downtown. For directions to Portland from the airport, see the preceding section.

Arriving by Train

Amtrak trains from Seattle and points south arrive in Portland's elderly **Union Station** (800 NW Sixth Ave.; ☎ **503-273-4866**), which is perched on the northern edge of downtown on the west side of the river. Taxis are usually waiting in front of the station for quick rides to nearby hotels for under $10; if they're not, wait a few minutes for some to arrive, or call from a station telephone. You can even walk into the heart of downtown in less than 15 minutes if you don't have too much to carry, but don't do it late at night, when the streets can get pretty dark and seedy. City buses are also available a few blocks away at the transit mall on NW 6th and 5th avenues, and many hotels and down-town car-rental companies can send a van or shuttle to pick you up if you give them a call.

Street smarts: Where to pick up information

The large, efficient **Portland Oregon Visitors Association (POVA)** has its main infor-mation center downtown at the World Trade Center complex (25 SW Salmon St., at Naito Pky; ☎ **877-678-5263** or 503-275-9750; Internet: www.pova.com). They can supply you with tons of brochures, maps of the immediate downtown area (but not of outlying sections like the Hawthorne and Sellwood districts), and information on lodging and events. You may find their "Hot Sheet" extremely handy; it's published weekly and lists that week's major events around town, and is available in most hotels. Note: For some reason that only the phone gods are privy to, you need to dial 10 digits when making local phone calls in Portland, which means that you always have to dial the 503 area code, even if you're calling from across the street.

Getting Around Once You're Here

Portland is a very easy city to navigate, particularly in the downtown area, where the streets are, for the most part, flat and walkable, and good public transit links major sites for free. Following are some tips for getting around the city, whether by light rail, taxi, car, bus, bike, or on foot.

Using the light rail to the MAX

Portland tries very, very hard to relieve congestion in its city core, and the best thing the city ever did was to plan and build an excellent light-rail system that winds its way through the downtown corridor. **MAX** (the common name for Metropolitan Area Express) was built to help deliver workers into the downtown core from far-flung neighborhoods, but this comfortable and convenient system is a boon to visitors as well. MAX can swing you through large sections of downtown for free in a generous ride-free zone (called the Fareless Square; keep reading for more information), or get you across the river to Lloyds Center and the Rose Quarter for just over a dollar. Use it to go from Chinatown or Pioneer Courthouse Square, to ballgames at PGE Stadium, and all the way up to the zoo at Washington Park. MAX is operated by **Tri-Met,** the city's transportation agency (☎ **503-238-7433;** Internet: `www.tri-met.org`); guides to routes and schedules are available from the POVA information kiosk at the World Trade Center (25 SW Salmon St. at Naito Pkwy.; ☎ **877-678-5263** or 503-275-9750) or from the Tri-Met kiosk at Pioneer Courthouse Square.

The **Fareless Square** extends throughout most of downtown, but if you travel out of it, do the right thing and buy a ticket. MAX operates largely on the honor system: You buy your ticket from a machine at the stop and validate it by punching it in the adjacent machine. Conductors and train personnel can't sell you tickets, and inspectors come by periodically to check for validated tickets outside the Fareless Square.

Look for a new extension to MAX, called the Portland Streetcar, to navigate west-side streets from downtown to the Pearl District and Nob Hill by the fall of 2001. Another MAX extension, to Portland International Airport, is scheduled to open by the end of 2001.

Beavers and deer: Traveling the Portland bus system

Portland's bus system is concentrated in the transit mall downtown on NW 5th and NW 6th avenues (for south- and north-bound traffic, respectively). There, you find bus stops that are coded with a number of icons, including deer, beavers, and roses, among others, each of which represents a different area of the city. Buses to the southeast section of the city, for example, all stop at the Brown Beaver-coded stops. Buses are free in the Fareless Square downtown, and then begin to charge based on the length of your trip, from $1.20 to $1.50. Single day passes for $4 are available, as are three-day visitor's passes for $10, all of which can be purchased from the bus driver with exact change. Ask the driver for a transfer if you want to change to another bus or to the MAX. For information on routes and schedules, contact Tri-Met (☎ **503-238-7433;** Internet: www.tri-met.org).

Tri-Met also operates **ART,** the Cultural Bus (Route #63), a vibrantly painted city bus whose route includes the city's main attractions, including the International Rose Test Garden, the Oregon Museum of Science and Industry (OMSI), and the Oregon Convention Center.

Getting around by car

If you drive into Portland, keep in mind that parking downtown is congested, and a hotel usually charges up to $18 per day to park your car for you. You can try to find spaces with parking meters on downtown streets, but they are filled up quickly and early by office workers — and if you *do* find a space, you have to go back again and again to feed the meter with quarters. The best deal for parking is at **Smart Park garages** (several locations, including SW Third Avenue and SW Alder Street), which are identified by red, white, and black signs. They charge just 95 cents an hour for the first four hours and have low evening rates. Most downtown merchants validate your Smart Park tickets if you spend more than $25 at their stores.

If you can live without your car for a portion of your trip, think about parking it for free on the street in a safe residential neighborhood in the northeast section of the city and using MAX to take you downtown, only returning to your car when you need to make a trip that isn't covered by public transportation.

Getting around by taxi

There are cabs in Portland; they're just not where you want them to be most of the time. You find them queued at most of the big hotels, at the airport, and (usually) at the train station, but they generally aren't available to hail on the street. If you need one, call in advance. Try **Broadway Cab** (☎ **503-227-1234**) or **Radio Cab** (☎ **503-227-1212**). Fares are $2 to $2.50 for the first mile and $1.50 for each additional mile — generally a good bargain in the downtown area, but expensive if you need to cross the river.

Getting around on foot and by bike

Walking is a pleasure in Portland: The downtown city blocks are shorter than most and the sidewalks are wide, encouraging a nice, pedestrian flow. Benches and small parks can be found on many streets, and the city prides itself on its fountains and public art, a walking tour of which is available from POVA. Best of all, the terrain is fairly flat, thanks to the topography of the Willamette River Valley.

Cyclists appreciate the city's commitment to bicycle travel, including bike lanes on most major streets and bridges, municipal bike racks, and bike racks on most city buses. You can also carry a bike on board a MAX train without paying extra charges. Bikes are available to rent downtown at the **Bike Central Co-Op** (732 SW 1st Ave.; ☎ **503-227-4439**) for about $35 per day.

Chapter 22

Money Matters

● ●

In This Chapter

▶ Accessing your cash on the road

▶ Salvaging your vacation if your wallet is stolen

▶ Taxing tourists, the Portland way

● ●

*H*ere's where I discuss how to get your hands on plenty of cash in Portland (short of winning the Oregon State Lottery). Why? Because I have some very good news concerning the state income tax.

Where to Get Cash in Portland

You find plenty of bank ATMs scattered around downtown Portland, but keep in mind that most of them charge service fees of $1 to $2 for withdrawals if you're not their customer. Look for ATMs belonging to the local credit unions, which don't charge service fees for cash withdrawals. Inquire about machines affiliated with the **Portland Teachers Credit Union** (☎ 800-527-3932 or 503-228-7077) at 1720 NE 9th Ave. in Lloyd Center, or the **Multco Credit Union** (☎ 503-248-3076) at 408 SW 5th Ave., near the Fifth Avenue Suites Hotel.

The major banks in town are **Wells Fargo Bank** (☎ 800-869-3557), with locations at SW 5th Avenue and Salmon Street and SW 6th Avenue at Morrison, among many others downtown, and **Bank of the West** (☎ 800-488-2265), another big local player with locations in Lloyd Center (905 NE Halsey St.) and Old Town (223 NW 1st Ave.).

Your hotel can usually cash a personal check if they have your credit card on file as security.

What to Do If Your Wallet Gets Stolen

Almost every credit card company has an emergency 800-number you can call if your wallet or purse is stolen. They may be able to wire you a cash advance off your credit card immediately; in many places, they can get you an emergency credit card within a day or two. The issuing bank's 800-number is usually on the back of the credit card, but that won't help you much if the card was stolen. Copy the number on the back of your card onto another piece of paper before you leave, and keep it in a safe place just in case. **Citicorp Visa's** U.S. emergency number is ☎ **800-645-6556. American Express** cardholders and traveler's check holders should call ☎ **800-221-7282** for all money emergencies. **MasterCard** holders should call ☎ **800-307-7309.**

If you opt to carry traveler's checks, be sure to keep a record of their serial numbers so you can handle just such an emergency. You should always keep a list of the traveler's checks numbers in a safe and separate place, so that you're ensured a refund if checks are lost or stolen. Also, dual checks are available for traveling couples, and either person can sign for them.

If you need quick cash, you can always have someone wire you money from home through **Western Union,** which has several locations in Portland. Among them are offices at 418 SW 2nd Ave. (☎ **206-324-8740**) and at the Greyhound Bus Lines station at 550 NW 6th Ave. (☎ **503-243-2361**).

Odds are that if your wallet is gone, you've seen the last of it, and the police aren't likely to recover it for you. However, after you realize it's gone and you cancel your credit cards, you should call to inform the police. You may need the police report number for credit card or insurance purposes later.

Taxing Matters

Here's the great news from Portland: Oregon has no sales tax. That's why you see so many Washington residents crossing the border a few weeks before Christmas to load up on gift purchases. Which is not to say that you never get taxed: Your hotel bill is marked up 11.5 percent, and car rentals get hit with a 12.5 percent tax in the city and a hefty 22.5 percent if you rent at the airport.

Chapter 23

The Lowdown on the Portland Dining Scene

● ●

In This Chapter

▶ What's happening on Portland's restaurant scene

▶ Local favorites

▶ Tips on reserving a table

▶ How to eat well on the cheap

● ●

*P*ortland's thriving food scene has gotten even hotter in recent years, with new restaurants opening not only downtown but in the city's neighborhoods, and talented chefs are making names for themselves with their own distinctive cooking. In this chapter, I run you through some of the local trends and points of interest around the food and dining scene; for a complete listing of restaurants, see Chapter 24.

Discovering What's New, What's Hot, and Who's in the Kitchen

What's new on the Portland food scene? In a word, flavor. Portland diners are embracing a wider range of foods and tastes as local chefs experiment with cuisines from all over the world. It may have started with **¡Oba!,** the lively Latin restaurant in the Pearl District that packs people in for spicy foods from South America and the Caribbean, but it has continued with **Saucebox**'s simple Asian flavors, the Japanese delicacies served at **Terra, Typhoon's** bold Thai dishes, and the Mediterranean/Asian fusion that colors the menu of **Oritalia.** Even high-end, sophisticated new restaurants like **Castagna** and **Bluehour** are bringing new tastes and combinations to their French-inspired menus.

Upscale branded restaurants are also staking their claims in the Rose City. The **McCormick & Schmick's** chain started here and continues to run several successful restaurants, but they are now joined by

Morton's of Chicago steakhouse, **Ruth's Chris Steak House,** and a splendid, updated version of Seattle's **El Gaucho,** a sophisticated steakhouse with terrific tableside service in the Benson Hotel.

With the exception of **Atwater's,** which lost its lease last year along with the best views in town, the city's tried-and-true restaurants continue to thrive, and Portland's culinary stars are handsomely supported by the community. **Huber's,** Portland's oldest restaurant, continues to pack in visitors and locals for simple dinners and exotic flaming-coffee presentations, and the venerable old **Genoa** still gets raves for its simple, family-style Italian dinners. Star chefs Cory Schreiber (**Wildwood**) and Caprial Pence (**Caprial's Bistro**) continue to solidify their reputations as interpreters of fine, Northwest cuisine, and Philippe Boulot of the **Heathman Restaurant** and Greg Higgins of **Higgins** bring their elegant fares to the south end of Broadway. In 2000, Schreiber produced what may well be the definitive cookbook on the subject with *Wildwood: Cooking from the Source in the Pacific Northwest.* The talented chef Kenny Giambalvo moved from **Pazzo** to **Bluehour,** where he dazzles with a broader menu, and Rob Pando of the **Red Star Tavern & Roast House** continues to explore fine American regional cooking with his characteristic flare. Restaurateur Bruce Carey, who may have started the whole upscale restaurant craze in Portland with the now-defunct Zefiro, is busier than ever with **Bluehour** and **Saucebox.**

Eating Like a Local

Portlanders are fiercely supportive of the foods that are grown, raised, or caught in Oregon, and you would do well to follow their lead. Don't miss out on the local favorites: hazelnuts, used in salads or to encrust fish; excellent pinot noir wines from the Willamette Valley; fresh mushrooms and berries that are gathered by foragers and sold directly to restaurants; fresh seafood, sold in restaurants like Jake's Famous Crawfish and McCormick & Schmick's Harborside Restaurant, which pride themselves on serving a wide variety of fish that have never have been (and never will be) frozen. Aside from typical Northwest favorites like salmon, halibut, and oysters, add Columbia River sturgeon to the list of local delicacies to sample. Portland also has terrific pub food, such as excellent, chewy pizza, served alongside delicious local microbrews, making for fun, inexpensive nights out at thriving brewpubs that serve as community gathering places.

Dressing to Dine, Portland Style

A word to the wise: Don't do it. If Seattle is an utterly casual place where almost nobody dresses up to go out, it looks like New York or Paris compared with Portland, where jeans and casual clothes are the norm at even the fancier places.

Making Reservations

Securing a table for dinner — even at the city's hottest restaurants — is generally not a problem in Portland, although I definitely advise making a reservation if you have limited options for choosing dates. It's entirely possible that the restaurant of your choice may be closed for a private party on the night you wish to go, particularly hotel restaurants like **El Gaucho** or **Pazzo.** In the Pearl District, restaurants like ¡**Oba!** and **Bluehour** are usually packed during First Thursday art-walk nights, and the popular **Genoa,** with its limited seating, is rarely available on short notice. If you get shut out of a restaurant that you're dying to try for dinner, see if a lunch seating is offered.

Cost-Cutting Tips for Dining Out

It's very easy to keep your food costs down in Portland. The city offers plenty of good, inexpensive dining options, allowing you to save up for a big splurge on a fancy restaurant meal. Here are a few ways to keep food costs down in Portland:

✔ Breakfast is big in the Rose City. Fill up on a big, satisfying breakfast that won't cost you a fortune, and you can make it all the way to dinner with only a snack to get you through the afternoon; Chapter 24 has some tips for great breakfast places. Let your kids fill up on breakfast cereals and juices at your hotel's continental breakfast, if offered.

✔ For light breakfasts on the go, Portland has a thriving coffee-shop scene that nearly rivals Seattle's for sheer number of places that serve espresso along with baked goods like muffins and scones.

✔ To save money on lunches, eat where the locals eat. The food carts downtown serve delicious sandwiches and unusual items like crepes. You can also eat well at teriyaki and fast-food Asian outlets or inexpensive local chains that sell submarine sandwiches and pizza.

✔ If you love pizza, you can fit right in with the locals and eat very cheaply at the same time. Don't bother with the national chains; head instead to a local pizza joint or brewpub (many of which have seating areas that can accommodate children) for excellent pizza with all the traditional toppings, and then some (like goat cheese or salmon).

Chapter 24

Portland's Best: Dining and Snacking

● ●

In This Chapter

▶ Where to find the best meals in Portland

▶ The lighter side of Portland

● ●

*H*ere's a rundown of Portland's top restaurants, followed by indices with at-a-glance breakdowns on price, cuisine, and location. Most of Portland's finest dining rooms are located in the vibrant downtown area, but as you move into the neighborhoods, particularly on the east side of the river, you find some interesting new choices. Then I offer tips on finding lighter fare and good street food.

Each listing in this chapter includes typical prices for standard entrees. The "$" category for each restaurant refers to prices for a three-course meal of appetizer, entree, dessert, a beverage, and a tip (from 15 to 20 percent of the total check), per person.

$	under $20	
$$	$20–$30	
$$$	$30–$40	
$$$$	over $40	

Portland Dining

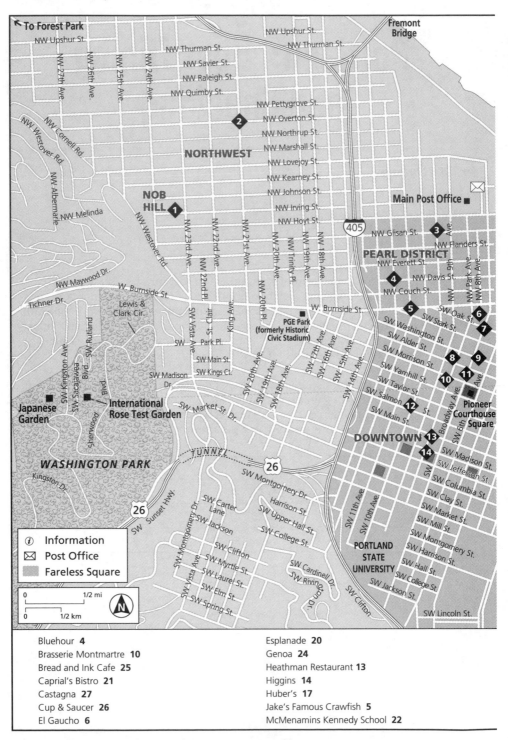

Bluehour **4**
Brasserie Montmartre **10**
Bread and Ink Cafe **25**
Caprial's Bistro **21**
Castagna **27**
Cup & Saucer **26**
El Gaucho **6**

Esplanade **20**
Genoa **24**
Heathman Restaurant **13**
Higgins **14**
Huber's **17**
Jake's Famous Crawfish **5**
McMenamins Kennedy School **22**

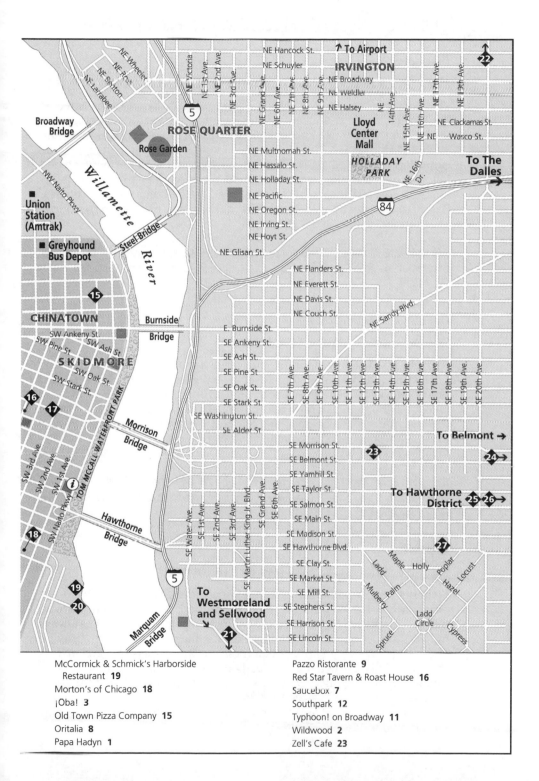

McCormick & Schmick's Harborside
  Restaurant **19**
Morton's of Chicago **18**
¡Oba! **3**
Old Town Pizza Company **15**
Oritalia **8**
Papa Hadyn **1**

Pazzo Ristorante **9**
Red Star Tavern & Roast House **16**
Saucebox **7**
Southpark **12**
Typhoon! on Broadway **11**
Wildwood **2**
Zell's Cafe **23**

Portland's Restaurants from A to Z

Bluehour

$$$$ Pearl District NORTHWEST/CONTINENTAL

The newest venture by restaurateur extraordinaire Bruce Carey and chef Kenny Giambalvo is unlike anything else in Portland. It's a cavernous, ultra-urban warehouse space adorned with flowing purple drapes and leather dining chairs. The food easily matches the grand concept — the exquisitely prepared, expensive fare might begin with perfectly seared foie gras or sea scallops wrapped in bacon and proceed to risottos, gnocchis, or roasted meats and fish served with delicious side dishes. Desserts are a cut above as well, and the daily menus post up to a dozen international wines by the glass.

250 NW 13th Ave. near Davis Street. ☎ *503-226-3394. Reservations suggested. Main courses: $19–$32. Open: Mon–Sat, 11:30 a.m.–2:30 p.m. and 6–10:30 p.m. AE, DC, MC, V.*

Brasserie Montmartre

$$ Downtown FRENCH/AMERICAN

A lively late-night restaurant that, true to its name, delivers basic brasserie food in a noisy, somewhat crowded space with checkerboard floors and walls covered with framed prints. Dinner choices include chicken Dijon or a seafood crepe, but most customers are happy grazing their way through dinner, noshing on the baked camembert cheese appetizer, onion soup, or a leg of lamb sandwich. Good desserts, too, for late-night sweet cravings.

626 SW Park Ave. near Morrison Street. ☎ *503-224-5552. Main courses: $8.25–$11.25. Open: Sun–Thurs, 7:30–11:30 p.m.; Fri and Sat, 8:30 p.m.–12:30 a.m. AE, DC, DISC, MC, V.*

Caprial's Bistro

$$$ Westmoreland NORTHWEST REGIONAL

Star chef and TV personality Caprial Pence gets it just right in this open, airy space in the Westmoreland neighborhood, far from the downtown bustle. The menus for lunch and dinner change monthly and are always full of interesting combinations, like a salmon stuffed with Gruyère cheese or a velvety smoked-sturgeon chowder. Desserts are just as thoughtfully constructed and equally captivating, and the wine presentation is unlike anything I've ever seen, with bottles lined up on shelves, wine-store-style, and prices that are very similar to what you pay in a store. Lunches are just as popular as dinners here; book well in advance.

7015 SE Milwaukie Ave. ☎ *503-236-6457. Reservations suggested. Main courses: $18–$22. Open: Tues–Fri, 11 a.m.–3 p.m. and 5–9 p.m. (Fri to 9:30 p.m.); Sat. 11:30 a.m.–3 p.m. and 5–9:30 p.m. MC, V.*

Castagna

$$$ Hawthorne   MEDITERRANEAN

This elegant, spare space in a quiet block of the Hawthorne strip is a perfect example of a fine-dining restaurant moving into a neighborhood where no fine dining has gone before. The decor, from the varnished cork floors to the tall, nearly bare white walls, is restrained, leaving you to focus on bright, vibrant foods in exciting combinations, such as a fettucine with roasted beets and ricotta, a satisfying bouillabaise, or fennel shaved into fine strips with tiny julienned carrots in a blood-orange vinaigrette. Next door is Café Castagna, which serves a lighter bistro menu. At either place, order the mountain of crispy, perfect fries.

1752 SE Hawthorne Blvd. at 17th Avenue. ☎ *503-231-7373. Reservations suggested for restaurant; not necessary for cafe. Main courses: $14–$24. Open: Tues–Fri, 6–10 p.m. (Fri to 10:30 p.m.); Sat 5:30–10:30 p.m. AE, DC, MC, V.*

El Gaucho

$$$$ Downtown   STEAK

Seattle's favorite steakhouse opened its second location in a smaller, more intimate setting at the Benson Hotel in Portland, with the same menu of superb, dry-aged beef in several cuts, rich appetizers such as oysters Rockefeller or escargot, and hardly a vegetable in sight. With the meat (and heavenly prices to match) comes top-notch tableside service, including kabobs that arrive at the table with flames shooting off the skewers and a fiery dessert of bananas Foster that is a bona fide crowd-pleaser.

319 SW Broadway at the Benson Hotel. ☎ *503-227-8794. Reservations suggested. Main courses: $30–$42. Open: Daily 5 p.m.–2 a.m. (Sun to 11 p.m.). AE, DC, DISC, MC, V.*

Esplanade

$$$ RiverPlace   CONTINENTAL

This has become one of the premier restaurants for views in town, thanks to its location in the RiverPlace complex alongside the Willamette River. All eyes are on the river and marina while the kitchen turns out elegant and expensive preparations of imported lamb, medallions of beef in a pinot noir sauce, or a superb steelhead served with a tangy fruit reduction. It's a bit of a hike from central downtown and across busy Naito Parkway, so take a cab or drive. This is a good place to meet for business breakfasts.

1510 SW Harbor Way at the RiverPlace Hotel. ☎ 503- 295-6166. Reservations suggested. Main courses: $16.50–$28. Open: Mon–Fri, 6:30 a.m.–2 p.m. and 5–10 p.m. Sat and Sun, 6:30–11 a.m. and 5–10 p.m. (Sun to 9 p.m.). AE, DISC, MC, V.

Genoa

$$$$ Hawthorne/Belmont ITALIAN

This is one of the toughest tables to get in town, because there are only ten of them in this small, atmospheric family restaurant in the Belmont neighborhood, and people have been coming back for years for the strictly prix-fixe menus of four or seven courses. Everything is fresh and homemade, from the breads and pastas to the luscious desserts, and the service is attentive and good. The pan-Italian food is hearty and simple, but lovingly prepared.

2832 SE Belmont St., over the Morrison Bridge from downtown. ☎ 503-238-1464. Prix-fixe menus: $45 and $55. Open: Mon–Sat, 5:30–9:30 p.m. AE, DC, DISC, MC, V.

Heathman Restaurant

$$$ Downtown FRENCH CONTINENTAL

This very stylish and elegant French restaurant is the perfect spot for a night out at the theater or symphony, with its location in the Heathman Hotel next door to Portland's performing-arts complex. French chef Philippe Boulot does a star turn dressing up Northwest specialties with complex French sauces, and his wife, Susan, does a wonderful job with the varied dessert menu. Keep an eye out for promotions where Boulot brings in visiting chefs for special menus that make for memorable meals.

1001 SW Broadway at the Heathman Hotel. ☎ 503-241-4100. Pioneer Square South MAX stop. Reservations suggested. Main courses: $13–$24. Open: Breakfast daily, 6:30–10:30 a.m. (Sat and Sun to 2 p.m.); lunch Mon–Fri, 11:30 a.m.–2:30 p.m.; dinner Sun–Sat, 5–10 p.m. (Fri and Sat to 11 p.m.). AE, DC, MC, V.

Higgins

$$$$ Downtown NORTHWEST

A favorite of theater-goers and the downtown business community is this quiet, elegant restaurant of chef/owner Greg Higgins. The multileveled dining room is peaceful and calming, and Higgins and his staff apply fine French shadings to fresh Northwest ingredients, starting with his signature chilled oysters on the half shell with a peppery *mignotte* spiced with *habaneros* (hot peppers). Crab-and-shrimp cakes are another big hit, but really, you can't go wrong putting yourself into Higgins' capable hands *whatever* you order. Next door is a bistro with a more casual atmosphere and lower prices.

1239 SW Broadway at Jefferson Street. ☎ 503-222-9070. Reservations suggested. Main courses: $15.75–$26.50. Open: Lunch Mon–Fri, 11:30 a.m.–2 p.m.; dinner daily 5–10:30 p.m. AE, DC, DISC, MC, V.

Huber's

$$ **Downtown AMERICAN**

Portland's oldest restaurant (it originally opened in 1879) is set deep inside a downtown office building, with an old-world ambience of dark woods and a vaulted ceiling decorated in cut-glass. The menu is strictly old-fashioned as well, consisting almost exclusively of inexpensive turkey dishes. No, the real reason to come to Huber's is for the extravagant cocktail presentations, including a tableside Spanish coffee service that is all flaming brandy and three kinds of liqueurs, served by wizened waiters who seem to have been there forever. It's great fun, appealing to college students and old-timers alike.

411 SW Third Ave. near Washington Street. ☎ 503-228-5686. Main courses: $8–$19. Open: Mon–Sat, 11:30 a.m.–4 p.m. (Sat from noon) and 4–10 p.m. (Fri and Sat to 11 p.m.). AE, DC, DISC, MC, V.

Jake's Famous Crawfish

$$ **Downtown SEAFOOD**

An urban gem of dark wood paneling and a saloon-style bar, Jake's has been at it for over a century and still brings in big crowds for its excellent seafood preparations. The crawfish are a special treat and well worth trying, but you can also try items from the daily fresh sheet that hail from all over the world, like a California abalone steak or ahi tuna prepared Hawaiian-style. Well-worn and venerable, Jake's has atmosphere that many new restaurants would kill for.

401 SW 12th Ave. at Washington Street. Galleria/SW 10th Ave. MAX stop. ☎ 503-226-1419. Main courses: $9–$25. Open: Mon–Fri, 11:30 a.m.–11 p.m. (Fri to midnight); Sat and Sun, 4–10 p.m. (Sat to midnight). AE, DISC, MC, V.

McCormick & Schmick's Harborside Restaurant

$$ **RiverPlace SEAFOOD**

Views of the Willamette River and the RiverPlace Marina are maximized here, with four dining rooms stacked vertically from the ground up, each offering good views from long windows. On sunny days, sidewalk tables fill up quickly. A daily fresh sheet points you to different varieties of seafood, both local and international, many of which you may never have tried before, such as a Hawaiian ono whitefish or an Oregon lingcod. But fish isn't the only thing on the long menu, which ventures off into meat, chicken, and pasta dishes to satisfy everyone. Kids and anglers alike enjoy the stuffed and mounted fish displayed on the walls, from big trout to sailfish.

309 SW Montgomery St. at the RiverPlace complex. ☎ 503-220-1865. Main courses: $14–$24. Open: Mon–Fri, 11:30 a.m.–11 p.m.; Sat 11:30 a.m.–3 p.m. and 4–11p.m.; Sun 10 a.m.–3 p.m. and 4–10 p.m. AE, DISC, MC, V.

McMenamins Kennedy School

$ NE Portland PIZZA AND BURGERS

This distinctive complex, built in a decommissioned grade school, will have your family clamoring to go to school for dinner. Movies are shown in the old auditorium, and the school cafeteria is now a restaurant that serves excellent pizza, sandwiches, and thick hamburgers in booths or in an outside courtyard. Afterward, wander the halls to find the Honor Bar and Detention Bar, as well as loads of fascinating artwork that now adorns the walls and former classrooms, which serve as bed-and-breakfast rooms.

5736 NE 33rd Ave. in the Concordia section of NE Portland. ☎ 503-228-2192. Main courses: $5–$9.50. Open: Breakfast daily 7–10:30 a.m. (Sat and Sun to 11:30 a.m.); lunch and dinner daily 11 a.m.–1 a.m. (Sat. from noon; Sun noon–midnight). AE, DISC, MC, V.

Morton's of Chicago

$$$$ Downtown STEAK

The venerable Chicago steakhouse chain set up its Portland shop (the 43rd Morton's, if you're keeping score) in the KOIN Tower complex in a clubby room of dark wood and leather booths. The fare is steak and more steak, and the beef is done to perfection; you can also order lamb, veal, chicken, or lobster if you want something different. Topped off with big slabs of cheesecake, this thoroughly rich, indulgent feast is practically guaranteed to fend off the business traveler's homesick blues.

213 SW Clay St. at 2nd Avenue. ☎ 503-248-2100. Reservations suggested. Main courses: $19.95–$33.95. Open: Mon–Sat, 5:30–11 p.m. (Sat from 5); Sun 5–10 p.m. AE, DC, MC, V.

¡Oba!

$$$ Pearl District LATIN

A long bar packed with trendsetters greets you as you enter this exuberant spot in the hip Pearl District. The restaurant is broken up into a series of bright, lively dining rooms that complement the pan-Caribbean and Latino menu of jerked Jamaican chicken, peppery tuna, and salmon finished with a banana-lime sauce, all served with interesting side dishes like yellow Cuban rice and beans, or a corn salsa. A big hit ever since it opened, it still draws crowds on weekends and First Thursday art-walk nights.

555 NW 12th Ave. at Hoyt Street. ☎ *503-228-6161. Reservations suggested. Main courses: $14–$22. Open: Daily 5:30–10 p.m. (Sun and Mon to 9 p.m., Fri and Sat to 10:30 p.m.). DISC, MC, V.*

Oritalia

$$$ Downtown   ASIAN FUSION

The Westin Hotel's hip new restaurant is fusion all the way, right down to the batik booths, bamboo menu boards, and black-lacquered chopsticks on the table. The menu tries to bridge the gap between Asia and Europe with a few pasta dishes and lots of unusual flavor combinations, such as a Szechuan pork chop with pancetta-onion marmalade on the side, or a lamb shank that is spiced with ginger and served with fennel and tomatoes. It's definitely new and unusual for Portland, and quite a twist from standard hotel-dining fare.

750 SW Alder St. at Park. Pioneer Courthouse Square stop on MAX. ☎ *503-295-0680. Main courses: $16–$24. Open: Breakfast daily 6:30–11 a.m.; lunch daily 11 a.m.– 5 p.m.; dinner daily 5–11 p.m. AE, DC, DISC, MC, V.*

Pazzo Ristorante

$$$ Downtown   ITALIAN

From the hanging hams over the bar to the cellar-style decor of rough, redbrick walls and arched doorways, this hotel restaurant succeeds in creating a convivial, ultra-Italian bistro setting. I've eaten often and well here over such upscale Northern Italian offerings as the exquisite, paper-thin tuna carpaccio on a parsley sauce or rich, flavorful risottos. The casual bar area serves oversize drinks and is a fine place to mingle with the sports celebrities who bunk in the adjoining Hotel Vintage Plaza. A wine cellar room is available for private parties of ten or more.

627 SW Washington St. at Broadway. Mall/SW 5th Ave. MAX stop. ☎ *503-228-1515. Reservations suggested. Main courses: $9.50–$23. Open: Daily breakfast 7–10:30 a.m. (Sat from 8 a.m., Sun 8–11 a.m.); lunch Mon–Sat, 11:30 a.m.–2:30 p.m.; dinner Mon–Fri, 5–10 p.m., Sat 4:30–11 p.m., Sun noon–10 p.m. AE, DC, DISC, MC, V.*

Red Star Tavern & Roast House

$$$ Downtown   AMERICAN REGIONAL

The theme here is the celebration of regional American cooking, and the execution is awfully good as the kitchen spins out big, hearty platters of Virginia ham, Cajun jambalayas, and Northwest seafood. Here's a restaurant where even the kids know what's on the menu, and the adults have plenty of fine dishes to choose from, too. You can't go wrong with the grilled and rotisserie meats, and side dishes of garlic mashed potatoes and cornbread cooked in an iron skillet and served with lavender honey are the ultimate comfort foods.

503 SW Alder at the 5th Avenue Suites Hotel. Mall/SW 5th Avenue MAX stop.
☎ *503-222-0005. Main courses: $14–$23. Open: Breakfast Mon–Fri, 6:30–10:30 a.m.;*
Sat and Sun, 8:30 a.m.–3 p.m. (brunch); lunch Mon–Fri, 11:30 a.m.–2:30 p.m.; dinner
daily 5–9:30 p.m. (Fri and Sat to 10:30p.m.). AE, DC, DISC, MC, V.

Saucebox

$$ Downtown   ASIAN

This spare, industrial space at the northern end of Broadway is a favorite
meeting spot for drinks and light bites, as well as a fine place to sample
Asian specialties, from appetizers of steamed edamame soybeans to rich
Thai crab cakes or Korean-style ribs. Owner Bruce Carey moved his
crowd-pleasing Zefiro ahi and avocado dish to this restaurant, and it con-
tinues to be a hit. The cocktails at the long, dark bar are sensational. If
sweet mixed drinks are your favorite way to start out an evening, try a
coconut lime rickey or a blood-orange drop.

214 SW Broadway at Oak Street. ☎ *503-241-3393. Main courses: $12–$19. Open:*
Lunch Tues–Fri, 11:30 a.m.–2:30 p.m.; dinner Tues–Sat, 6–10:30 p.m.; bar menu 10:30
p.m.–2 a.m. AE, MC, V.

Southpark

$$$ Downtown   SEAFOOD

It aims to be as classy and elegant as the South Park blocks from which
it draws its name, and it succeeds with a very handsome design of par-
quet floors, burgundy booths, and a long, stainless-steel wine bar from
which you can sample dozens of wines by the glass. The food is simple
and delicious, leaning heavily toward seafoods that are grilled in a wood
oven and delicately sauced, often with a light, Mediterranean flavor.

901 SW Salmon St. at 9th Avenue. Library/SW 9th Avenue MAX stop. ☎ *503-*
326-1300. Reservations suggested. Main courses: $8–$20. Open: Daily lunch
11:30 a.m.–3 p.m. (Sat from 11 a.m., Sun from 10:30 a.m.); dinner daily 5:30–1 p.m.
(Fri and Sat. to 11 p.m.). AE, MC, V.

Typhoon! on Broadway

$$ Downtown   THAI

Thai food in all its glory is the attraction here, in a bustling restaurant
that pulls in a big, downtown lunch and dinner crowd. They come for
"Bags of Gold," an appetizer of shrimp wrapped in a wonton skin and
sealed with a chewy leaf, the spicy green papaya salad, and sumptuous
noodle dishes. To get the lively room even more energized, order the
"Fish on Fire," and the waiter rings a brass gong as a flaming halibut is
carried to your table.

400 SW Broadway at the Imperial Hotel. ☎ 503-224-8285. Main courses: $8.95–$14.95. Open: Lunch Mon–Fri, 11:30 a.m.–2:30 p.m.; dinner daily 5–9 p.m. (Fri and Sat to 10 p.m., Sun 4:30–9 p.m.). AE, DC, DISC, MC, V.

Wildwood

$$$ Nob Hill   NORTHWEST

Star chef Corey Schreiber literally wrote the (cook)book on Northwest cooking. His imaginative use of local ingredients gets him international recognition, and this lively, pleasant bistro allows you to watch Schreiber and his team prepare seasonal foods from an open kitchen with a wood-fired oven. Be sure to try the buttery, cornmeal-encrusted razor clams if they're in season, or mussels roasted in a skillet and kissed with saffron. This can be a tough reservation to get, so book well in advance for either lunch or dinner.

1221 NW 21st Ave. on Nob Hill. ☎ 503-248-WOOD. Reservations suggested. Main courses: $18–$23. Open: lunch Mon–Sat, 11:30 a.m.–2:30 p.m.; Sun brunch 10 a.m.– 2 p.m.; dinner Mon–Sat, 5:30–10 p.m (Fri and Sat to 11 p.m.), Sun 5–9:30m p.m. AE, MC, V.

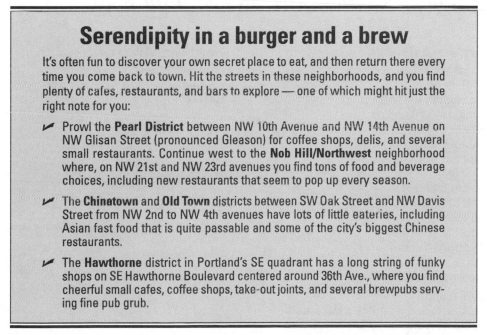

Serendipity in a burger and a brew

It's often fun to discover your own secret place to eat, and then return there every time you come back to town. Hit the streets in these neighborhoods, and you find plenty of cafes, restaurants, and bars to explore — one of which might hit just the right note for you:

- Prowl the **Pearl District** between NW 10th Avenue and NW 14th Avenue on NW Glisan Street (pronounced Gleason) for coffee shops, delis, and several small restaurants. Continue west to the **Nob Hill/Northwest** neighborhood where, on NW 21st and NW 23rd avenues you find tons of food and beverage choices, including new restaurants that seem to pop up every season.

- The **Chinatown** and **Old Town** districts between SW Oak Street and NW Davis Street from NW 2nd to NW 4th avenues have lots of little eateries, including Asian fast food that is quite passable and some of the city's biggest Chinese restaurants.

- The **Hawthorne** district in Portland's SE quadrant has a long string of funky shops on SE Hawthorne Boulevard centered around 36th Ave., where you find cheerful small cafes, coffee shops, take-out joints, and several brewpubs serving fine pub grub.

Index of Restaurants by Price

$
McMenamins Kennedy School

$$
Brasserie Montmartre
Huber's
Jake's Famous Crawfish
McCormick & Schmick's Harborside
    Restaurant
Saucebox
Typhoon! on Broadway

$$$
Caprial's Bistro
Castagna

Esplanade
Heathman Restaurant
¡Oba!
Oritalia
Pazzo Ristorante
Red Star Tavern & Roast House
Southpark
Wildwood

$$$$
Bluehour
El Gaucho
Genoa
Higgins
Morton's of Chicago

Index of Restaurants by Neighborhood

Downtown/Broadway
Brasserie Montmartre
El Gaucho
Heathman Restaurant
Higgins
Huber's
Jake's Famous Crawfish
Morton's of Chicago
Oritalia
Pazzo Ristorante
Red Star Tavern & Roast House
Saucebox
Southpark
Typhoon! on Broadway

Downtown/RiverPlace
Esplanade
McCormick & Schmick's Harborside
    Restaurant

Hawthorne/Westmoreland
Caprial's Bistro
Castagna
Genoa

NE Portland
McMenamins Kennedy School

Pearl District/Nob Hill
Bluehour
¡Oba!
Wildwood

Index of Restaurants by Cuisine

American Regional
Huber's
McMenamins Kennedy School
Red Star Tavern & Roast House

Asian/Fusion
Oritalia
Saucebox
Typhoon! on Broadway

Continental
Bluehour
Esplanade

French/Mediterranean
Brasserie Montmartre
Castagna
Heathman Restaurant

Italian
Genoa
Pazzo Ristorante

Latin
¡Oba!

Northwest
Bluehour
Caprial's Bistro
Higgins
Wildwood

Seafood
Jake's Famous Crawfish
McCormick & Schmick's Harborside
  Restaurant
Southpark

Steak
El Gaucho
Morton's of Chicago

On the Lighter Side: Top Picks for Snacks and Meals on the Go

Portland is a great town for inexpensive dining. Pizza is practically a civic treasure, and you can find good variations of the classic thin-crust pie in every neighborhood. The downtown streets are dotted with sandwich shops and take-out restaurants, and you can even eat well in the area's parking lots, which are occupied by lunch-wagon trucks out-fitted to serve everything from hot dogs to ethnic fare. Coffee is nearly as popular here as it is in Seattle; you won't have to look very hard to find a good cuppa Joe. Following are some tips on dining quickly and cheaply as you explore the city.

Breakfast in Portland: Sunny side up

The morning meal is a favorite of Portlanders, who stake out tables at neighborhood hangouts and order great piles of meat, eggs and potatoes, fluffy pancakes, or salmon and eggs. In the Hawthorne neighborhood, check out **Cup & Saucer** (3566 SE Hawthorne Blvd.; ☎ **503-236-6001**), a comfortable bistro with local art on the walls that serves breakfast all day long. Down the street a block is the **Bread and Ink Cafe** (3610 SE Hawthorne Blvd.; ☎ **503-239-4756),** which takes breakfast to another level with such offerings as polenta, oyster frittata, and smoked trout. In the Belmont neighborhood, stake out a table early at **Zell's Cafe** (1300 SE Morrison St.; ☎ **503-239-0196**), and watch the locals arrive throughout the morning for wonderful baked goods like an orange-fennel pancake or waffles served with a homemade pear and ginger sauce. The **Red Star Tavern & Roast House** at the 5th Avenue Suites Hotel (see Chapter 20) makes a wondrous corned beef hash with chunks, not slivers, of beef and sweet potatoes.

Where to take a coffee break

For great cups of the local brew, look to one of the numerous locations of **Coffee People** (including downtown at SW Salmon and Park Avenue or SW 6th Avenue and Washington Street), which serve lattes and cappuccinos along with the admirable slogan, "Great coffee and no backtalk." **Peet's Coffee and Tea** is another local favorite; its store in Irvington (1441 NE Broadway) is roomy and designed for lingering over a hot drink while you read the paper or catch up with friends. If you're still stuck on a Seattle brew, **Seattle's Best Coffee** has its foot in the Portland door downtown (1001 SW 5th Ave.). For an exquisite and very unusual selection of fine teas in a gorgeous garden setting, go to the teahouse in the new **Classical Chinese Garden** (NW Third Avenue and Everett Street).

Quick eats on the street

Food vendors operating out of parked lunch wagons do a brisk business with Portland's downtown office workers, and the variety of foods available is pretty amazing. Walk past parking lots on the northern blocks of SW 4th Avenue or the streets surrounding Pioneer Courthouse Square, and you see vendors hawking Mexican food, Indian cuisine, hot dogs, and Greek sandwiches. One even extols its "Honkin' Huge Burritos." Some favorites include the **Snow White House** and **Bad Kitty Koffee,** both of which occupy a lot on SW 9th Avenue at Yamhill Street; the former makes excellent fresh crepes, both sweet and savory, that I say rival Parisian street crepes, and the latter serves coffee and baked goods.

The best of good and cheap

Look for some of the following restaurants and stores for good, filling, inexpensive food.

Pizza

Portland's brewpubs pride themselves on their excellent pizza and compete for the business of locals by piling on the toppings and serving nothing but fresh-baked pies. On the edge of the Pearl District, look for the ivy covered walls of the **Bridgeport Brew Pub** (1318 NW Marshall St.; ☎ 503-241-7179), which puts some of the malty mash from the brewing process into the pizza dough. At three of the several **McMenamins Pubs,** you can take your crispy-crust pizza into an attached movie theater and munch while you watch a second-run movie from the comfort of old sofas and lounge chairs. Look for more pizza at the **Bagdad Theater & Pub** (3702 SE Hawthorne Blvd.; ☎ 503-236-9234), the **Mission Theater & Pub** (1624 NW Glisan St.; ☎ 503-225-5555) or the **Kennedy School** (5736 NE 33rd St.; ☎ 503-249-3983). Another great setting for eating pizza is among the antiques and knick-knacks that decorate the popular **Old Town Pizza Company** downtown (226 NW Davis; ☎ 503-222-9999); among the more unusual ingredients here are fresh zucchini, roasted yellow peppers, and fontina cheese.

Burgers and sandwiches

Portland's best sandwiches are borrowed from New York delis and served at **Kornblatt's** on Nob Hill (628 NW 23rd Ave.; ☎ 503-242-0055), where you can get a thick Reuben or corned-beef sandwich with a cream soda chaser. **Big Town Hero** is a local submarine sandwich shop that serves long, cold and hot subs (412 SW 2nd Ave.; ☎ 503-243-1909; call for other locations). For burgers, any of the brewpubs will produce a fine one, including the **Blue Moon Tavern & Grill** on Nob Hill (432 NW 21st Ave.; ☎ 503-223-3184).

Desserts

For a slice of heaven, get yourself to one of the two locations of **Papa Haydn** (701 NW 23rd Ave.; ☎ 503- 228-7317, or 5829 SE Milwaukie Ave.; ☎ 503-232-9440). These cafes sell sandwiches and salads but specialize in exquisite, freshly made desserts. There are never fewer than a dozen desserts on the menu, ranging from the simplest pies and cakes to sublime French-inspired confections. On NE Broadway, **Helen Bernhard's Bakery** (1717 NE Broadway; ☎ 503-287-1251) is a homey, old-style place with a broad selection of cookies, rolls, and cakes. Downtown visitors with late-night cravings frequently find their way to the **Brasserie Montmartre** (626 SW Park Ave.; ☎ 503-224-5552) for apple tarts or a rich, tall, and satisfying Chocolate Bonbon Dome Cake. If you can get into the popular **Bluehour** restaurant (250 NW 13th Ave.; ☎ 503-226-3394,) look forward to one of pastry chef Mandy Groom's upscale concoctions, such as a maple crème brûlée or a Bartlett pear tart that is served with sensational house-made ice creams of port and star anise.

Picnic picks in Portland

Portland has plenty of green space in which to spread a blanket and enjoy a meal in the open air. The city is dotted with parks that are great for enjoying the great outdoors, especially Tom McCall Waterfront Park downtown and Washington Park on the west side. To gather items for a picnic, make your way to **City Market** (735 NW 2st Ave.; ☎ **503-221-3004**) for everything from breads and cheeses to prepared salads. On the east side, **Pastaworks** (3731 SE Hawthorne Blvd.; ☎ **503-232-1010**) is a full-service Italian supermarket and deli with imported items and lots of lovingly made foods that are perfect for a take-out lunch or dinner.

Part VI
Exploring Portland

"Don't worry Louise. I'll replace them with salmon sticky notes."

In this part . . .

You've arrived in Portland, you've settled in to your hotel, and you're ready to see the sights. Here I describe the city's top attractions — giving advice on what to see and what to avoid — and offer an insider's look at other cool things to see and do. I give advice on the best places to take kids and teens, and where to go to enjoy Portland's glorious natural spaces. In addition, I outline several specific city itineraries as well as day trips to the surrounding rivers, coastline, and mountains. For shoppers, I give a breakdown of Portland's great shopping neighborhoods and where to find items that are uniquely Pacific Northwest. Finally, the nightcrawler in you can appreciate the chapter on Portland nightlife, from performing arts to theater to bars and clubs with attitude.

Chapter 25

Portland's Top Sights and Cool Things to Do

· ·

In This Chapter

▶ The best things to see and do in Portland

▶ Guided tours of Portland: On foot or by bus, rail, or boat

· ·

*P*ortlanders love their mountain and river views, expansive city parks, and public art, and they enjoy some of the prettiest themed gardens on the planet. Here are the city's top sights and cool things to do, as well as my personal favorite guided tours.

The Top Attractions from A to Z

Classical Chinese Garden

Chinatown

Sixty artisans from the city of Suzhou in China came to Portland equipped with everything from hand-carved wood to stones and volcanic rock to create this astonishing walled garden, which occupies an entire city block in Chinatown. Inside are hand-laid stone paths that wind around a central pond and a series of pagoda-roofed structures that contain simple benches for peaceful reflection. The grounds, planted with dozens of trees, orchids, and Chinese plants, are decorated with a gentle waterfall, and the "Tower of Cosmic Reflections" teahouse is a wonderful place to meet friends over a cup of imported jasmine tea.

W. 3rd Avenue and NW Everett Street. ☎ *503-228-8131. Open: 9 a.m.–6 p.m. April–Oct; 10 a.m.–5 p.m. Nov–March. Admission: $6 adults, $5 seniors and children over 6, children under 5 free.*

Portland Attractions

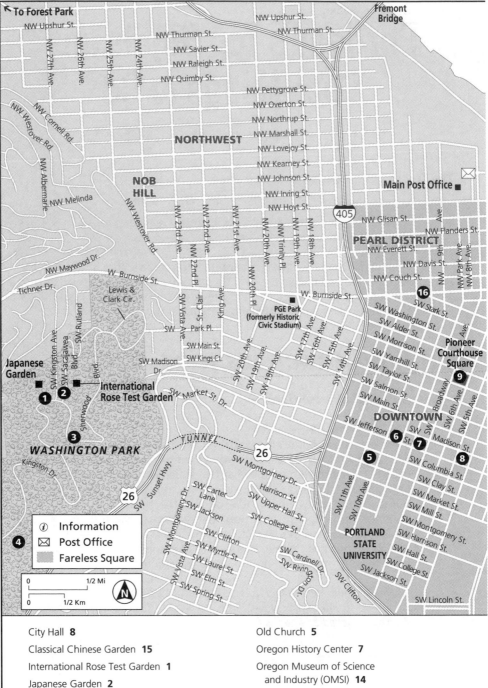

City Hall **8**

Classical Chinese Garden **15**

International Rose Test Garden **1**

Japanese Garden **2**

Mill Ends Park **12**

Old Church **5**

Oregon History Center **7**

Oregon Museum of Science
  and Industry (OMSI) **14**

Oregon Zoo **4**

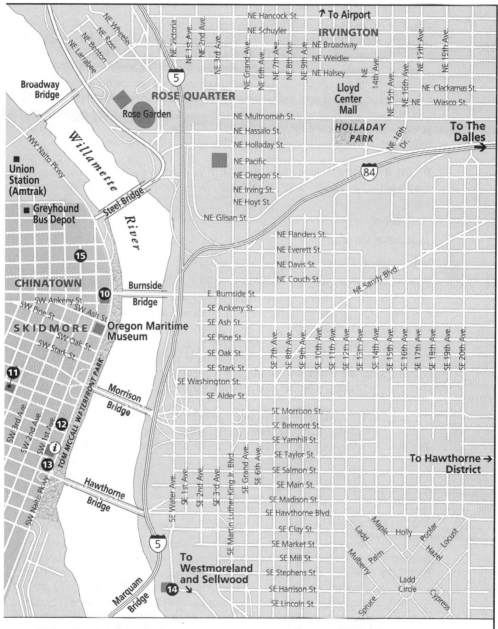

Pioneer Courthouse Square **9**

Pioneer Place **11**

Portland Art Museum **6**

Portlandia and the Portland Building **8**

Portland Saturday Market **10**

Powell's City of Books **16**

Washington Park **3**

World Trade Center **13**

International Rose Test Garden

Washington Park

The Rose City gets its nickname from this rosy site located high above the city, with panoramic views of downtown Portland and Mount Hood in the distance. Begun in 1917, the test garden is a great place to learn about hundreds of rose varietals and drink in the sights and fragrances of some 8,000 individual plants. They keep it moving with winding paths through the garden and few places to sit, and in summertime the crowds can outnumber the petals, so come early or late. *Note:* Don't confuse the garden with the Rose Quarter or Rose Garden Arena, which are entertainment and sports complexes on the other side of town.

400 SW Kingston Ave. in Washington Park. Take MAX to the zoo and then board a shuttle to the Rose Garden. ☎ *503-823-3636. Open: Daily, dawn to dusk. Admission: Free.*

Japanese Garden

Washington Park

The Rose Garden gets more ink, but this peaceful, authentically Japanese site across the street from the roses gets my vote as the top garden in the city. The hilly topography allows for several isolated pockets where koi ponds flow, waterfalls gurgle, and benches are used for relaxing and drinking in the scene. Gardens of smooth black stones glisten in the Portland mist, and other stone gardens are raked in concentric arcs. Guided tours are available, but this is one place where wandering on your own can capture the spirit of the place better than a wordy description.

611 SW Kingston Ave. in Washington Park. Take MAX to the zoo exit, and then a shuttle to the garden. ☎ *503-223-0913. Open: 9 a.m.–8 p.m. during summer months, 10 a.m.–6 p.m. in spring and fall, and 10 a.m.–4 p.m. in winter. Admission: $6 adults, $3.50 students, and children,under 6 free.*

Mount Hood

East of the city

Portland's most picturesque views are provided courtesy of this beautifully sculpted mountain in the Cascade range, with an elevation of 11,235 feet. Like Seattle's Mount Rainier, Mount Hood comes out on clear days to provide a rocky, snowcapped backdrop to the city. You can drive there in about an hour to explore the alpine wilderness (see Chapter 27 for daytrip information and directions), but for the best views of downtown Portland with the big mountain in the background, go to vantage points in Washington Park at the International Rose Test Garden or the Japanese Garden.

Oregon History Center

Downtown

Oregon's early history is told in this handsome brick building, which has an incredible trompe l'oeil mural painted on its exterior, facing SW Park Avenue, that shouldn't be missed. Inside are galleries with covered wagons, American Indian artifacts, and exhibits that document places and events important to Oregon's history, including the Lewis and Clark Expedition and the Oregon Trail, which brought so many families westward to settle in the state's fertile valleys. If you really want to dig deep, a research library has many original documents and diaries from early settlers. And while you're on a history kick, walk the four or so blocks to 1422 SW 11th Avenue to see Old Church, a Gothic landmark built in 1883. You can take a self-guided tour of Old Church between 11 a.m. and 3 p.m. Tuesdays through Saturdays (free admission).

1200 SW Park Ave. at Madison Street ☎ *503-222-1741. Open: Tues–Sun, 10 a.m.–5 p.m. (noon–5 p.m. on Sun and to 8 p.m. on Thurs). Admission: $6 adults, $1.50 children 6–12, free to children under 5.*

Oregon Zoo

Washington Park

Portland's zoo occupies a rolling site high up in Washington Park, with an underground MAX stop that practically puts you at the entry gate after an elevator ride to the surface. The elephant breeding program has garnered world renown for the zoo, and an authentic African savanna comfortably houses lions, giraffes, and zebras. The first stages of a major Northwest exhibit have been completed, with a mountain-zone climate meant to simulate the Cascades range where mountain goats and other alpine creatures dwell, and a coastal zone that simulates the Oregon coast. Subsequent phases will bring a family farm environment and forest habitats.

4001 SW Canyon Rd. in Washington Park. MAX stop at Zoo Station. ☎ *503-226-1561. Open: Daily 9 a.m.–6 p.m. April–Sept, and 9 a.m.–4 p.m. Oct–March. Admission: $6.50 adults, $4 children 3–11, under 3 free.*

Pioneer Courthouse Square

Downtown

Portland's "living room" and central meeting place is a redbrick square and urban park in the middle of downtown on Broadway. It's worth strolling by if for no other reason than to take in a daily performance of the Weather Machine, a sculpture that pops open at noon and displays a forecast for the day's weather. An espresso shop and a bookstore lie within the boundaries of PCS, and special events are programmed throughout the year, such as jazz music on summer weekdays, a Christmas tree in December, and dozens of potted flowers to celebrate Rose Festival.

SW Broadway and Morrison Street MAX stop at Pioneer Courthouse Square. Open: Always. Admission: Free.

Portland Art Museum

Downtown

The major art museum in town has been busily expanding in recent years, to the point where, in square-footage at least, it's now among the top-25 largest museums in the country. This means that it can attract bigger and better touring exhibits, such as recent shows that displayed rare treasures from Russia and China's Imperial Tombs. A new outdoor sculpture garden is a treat, as is a gallery devoted to Northwest American Indian art, and the setting on the peaceful South Park Blocks is cool and inviting.

1219 SW Park Ave. at Madison Street. ☎ **503-226-2811.** Open: Tues–Sun, 10 a.m.– 5 p.m. (noon–5 p.m. on Sun and to 9 p.m. first Thurs). Admission: $7.50 adults, $4 ages 5–18, under 5 free.

Tom McCall Waterfront Park

Downtown

This long expanse of green grass alongside the Willamette River is a great place for long walks or a jog or for kids to burn up excess energy. Big carnivals draw thousands of people here during the Rose Festival with rides and music, and in the winter the park is a wonderful place to stop and watch colorfully lit "Christmas ships" move slowly down the river at night. Bring the young ones to see the tile maze installed in the ground at the northern end of the park near the Burnside Bridge or to play in the computerized fountain opposite Salmon Street.

Willamette riverfront from Burnside Street to the RiverPlace Marina. ☎ **503-823- 5122.** Open: Daily. Admission: Free.

More Cool Things to Do and See

In this section I sort out the best attractions for different age groups and interests. You don't, of course, have to be a kid to enjoy the interactive features of the OMSI museum, and you don't have to be a major hiker to take in the views of Mount Tabor — in other words, don't feel as if the attractions are only suitable for the group under which they're listed. Go to the end of the chapter for organized tours the whole family can enjoy.

Portland just for kids

Aside from the **Zoo** and **Tom McCall Waterfront Park,** listed earlier in the chapter, there are loads of things for kids to do in Portland. Adults also enjoy participating in some of the following activities.

Oaks Park Amusement Center

Sellwood

This old-style amusement park has basic, reasonably priced thrill rides and carnival attractions. Kids and grown-ups alike are enchanted with the old wooden-floored rollerskating pavilion, where you can rent skates and glide along on the huge floor. Buy some cotton candy and hot dogs, and enjoy a fun family outing on a hot summer's day. Also, during summer months, the open-air Samtrak excursion train (☎ **503-659-5452**) connects the park to the OMSI museum, a few miles north.

East end of the Sellwood bridge. ☎ 503-233-5777. Open: Summer Tues–Sun, noon–9 p.m. (to 10p.m. Fri and Sat, to 7p.m. Sun). Limited hours in May and Sept. Admission: Free, with rides charged on a per-ticket basis.

Oregon Museum of Science and Industry (OMSI)

Willamette River Waterfront

Just across the river from downtown Portland rises the high-rise OMSI (Oregon Museum of Science and Industry), inside of which is a whirlwind of hands-on activities that demonstrate scientific principles and really do make science fun for all ages. Try building bridges out of blocks to see how forces interact, or sign up for sessions in the new Science Lab, where kids get to schmooze with real scientists. In all, the museum has six big halls to explore, with something for every age group. The submarine used in the movie *The Hunt for Red October* is docked at the river and gives tours, and an OMNIMAX movie screen provides a domed movie experience.

1945 SE Water Ave. (between the Ross Island and Hawthorne bridges). ☎ 503-797-4537. Open: Tues–Sat, 9:30 a.m.–7 p.m. in summer, to 5:30 p.m. the rest of the year. Admission: $6.50 adults, $4.50 children 4–13; additional fees for submarine tours and OMNIMAX movies.

Portland Children's Museum

Washington Park

At presstime, this interactive museum aimed for younger children was planning to move to a spacious facility next to the Oregon Zoo in Washington Park. Check before you go to see if the move was accomplished, but at either location, you find bubble-blowing stations, seashells to listen to, and a clay-sculpting area where kids create fanciful designs that they can take home.

3037 SW Second Ave., or Washington Park (move was planned for July 2001).
☎ *503-823-2227. Open: Tues–Sun, 9 a.m.–5 p.m. Admission: $4 adults and children, under 1 year free.*

Washington Park and Zoo Railway

This replica steam train that runs on a narrow 30-inch gauge track is a big favorite of train buffs and families visiting the Oregon Zoo and Washington Park. It chugs along through the forests of the park, with great views below of downtown Portland between its two stations at the International Rose Test Garden and the Zoo. You can even have your mail franked on board the train with a distinctive cancellation stamp, the last such railroad mail-service in the country.

4001 SW Canyon Rd. at the Oregon Zoo. Take MAX to the Zoo Station exit. ☎ *503-226-1561. Open: Hourly runs during summer months from 11 a.m.–4:15 p.m. daily. Available weekends only in April, May, and Oct. Admission: $2.75 adults, $2 children 3–11 with paid Zoo admission.*

Portland just for teens

Teens may find their favorite part of Portland at a pizza parlor, an outdoor concert, a stroll through a cool neighborhood, or at one of these attractions.

The Grotto

Northeast Portland

Teens with a spiritual bent appreciate this Catholic retreat in a corner of northeast Portland on the grounds of the National Sanctuary of Our Sorrowful Mother. The grounds are lovely, with gardens and tall trees and a cliff that you can ascend by elevator for sweeping regional views. In winter, the place is ablaze with holiday lights and music.

NE 85th Ave. and Sandy Boulevard. ☎ *503-261-2404. Open: Daily 9 a.m.–8 p.m. (to 5:30 p.m. in winter). Admission: Free.*

McMenamins movie theaters

By any chance, does your teen enjoy lounging around on sofas or easy chairs, eating popcorn, and watching movies all day? If so, then you've got a winner with these three ultra-casual theaters operated by the McMenamins brewpub chain. Seating is in big, old, thrift-store-style sofas and chairs, or at tables where you can scarf pizza while watching second-run movies at bargain prices. Note that minors (under 21) are not allowed into all shows, because the theaters double as brewpubs, so check to see which matinees and early-evening shows are available for kids and teens.

Bagdad Theater & Pub, *3702 SE Hawthorne Blvd.,* ☎ *503-236-9234;* **Mission Theater & Pub,** *1624 NW Glisan St.,* ☎ *503-225-5555;* **Kennedy School,** *5736 NE 33rd St.,* ☎ *503-249-3983. Open: Daily. Admission: $2–$3.*

Mountain biking in Forest Park

Forest Park, Portland's enormous, 4,900-acre urban wilderness, is a great, safe place to explore, especially on mountain bikes that can be rented by the day at nearby Fat Tire Farm (2714 NW Thurman St.; ☎ 503-222-3276), which, as the name suggests, offers bikes for the trails and off-road areas of the park, as well as maps and information on where to go. A nearby trailhead leads to the Leif Erickson Trail, a 12-mile-long path that is closed to traffic. Avid mountain bikers head to the fire trails that lead up and over hills through the park.

Access point at end of NW Thurman Street. Portland Parks & Recreation (☎ *503-823-5122). Open: Daily, dawn to dusk. Admission: Free.*

Portland Saturday Market

Skidmore

A cool place to hang out and browse the many creations of Portland's craftsmen is this long-standing weekend market that sets up shop in a funky area of the Old Town/Skidmore district under the Burnside Bridge. Booths sell clothing, hand-carved musical instruments, jewelry, and knick-knacks, and you can get a snack at one of the market's food trucks and carts. The market folds up its tents in the evenings and then vanishes altogether on Sunday night.

Market begins at SW Ankeny Street at First Avenue. ☎ *503-222-6072. Open: Weekends March–Dec on Sat 10 a.m.–5 p.m., and Sun 11 a.m.–4:30 p.m. Admission: Free.*

Portland TrailBlazers and other sports events

Rose Quarter and Downtown

Even if you don't know much about the teams or the game, sporting events are fun places to hang out and surefire entertainment for the older kids. The NBA's **Portland TrailBlazers** (☎ 503-234-9291) are the biggest game in town, and tickets can be tough to come by, but winter months also bring the exciting junior-hockey of the **Portland Winter Hawks** (☎ 503-238-6366), with games played at the Rose Quarter's Memorial Coliseum and Rose Garden arena. In summer, the **Portland Timbers** (☎ 503-553-5555) men's professional soccer team will set up shop at the newly revamped PGE Park (formerly Civic Stadium, on the western edges of downtown; 1844 SW Morrison St.), as will the **Portland Beavers,** the city's brand-new minor-league triple-A affiliate of the San Diego Padres baseball team (☎ 503-553-5555). Women's professional basketball comes to Rose Garden arena in the spring and summer with games by the **Portland Fire** (☎ 503-234-9291). Call these numbers for ticket information. Tickets to many of these events are also sold at the POVA Visitor Information and Services Center (25 SW Salmon St.), which operates the excellent **Ticket Central** service, a one-stop clearinghouse that consolidates **Ticketmaster** (☎ 503-224-4400), **Fastixx** (☎ 800-922-8499), and **Artistix** (☎ 503-275-8352) services into one location.

Portland for nature lovers

The quality of Portland's parks and outdoor environment is a big reason why people who live here would never leave. The city takes extraordinary measures to preserve its green heritage, including the establishment of a large greenbelt on the outskirts of town to combat urban sprawl. Check out the following urban parks, gardens, and activities to get a taste of the great outdoors, Portland-style. For more information on Portland's parks, contact **Parks and Recreation** (☎ 503-823-5132).

Bike and jogging trails

Cycling and running are very big in Portland (and a certain local shoe company hopes to keep it that way), and the city is full of trails dedicated to joggers and cyclists. **Forest Park** has the best off-road trails, but the city is also full of paved paths. Closer to the center of downtown, the **Bike Central Co-op** (732 SW 1st Ave. and Yamhill; ☎ 503-227-4439) has day rentals of bikes. Take a bike to the **Tom McCall Waterfront Park,** the long swath of green grass with a paved path alongside the Willamette River. Lunchtime joggers come here for their runs, and cyclists (and marathoners) continue south to Willamette Park for an additional three miles or so of continuous, traffic-free pavement. The toughest bike path in town is the **Terwilliger Path,** which starts near Portland State University and heads into the west-side hills to **Tryon Creek State Park.** For a long ride on a former railroad bed, now paved over, get directions to the **Springwater Corridor** from any bike shop; it runs roughly from the Westmoreland neighborhood to distant Gresham.

The littlest park: Mill Ends

It's barely the length of a yardstick, but this 452-square-inch space epitomizes the city's passion for green. Mill Ends Park, the world's smallest dedicated public park, was but an empy telephone-pole hole when *Oregon Journal* columnist Dick Fagan planted a few flowers and declared the space a city park. It was deemed officially so on St. Patrick's Day 1948, and since then has been the site of weddings, concerts, and other various and sundry mini-events.

Crystal Springs Rhododendron Garden

Hawthorne

Rhodie lovers head to this lovely garden in the southeast district, particularly when the signature rhododendrons are in full bloom (generally from March to June). You also find peaceful paths, a waterfall, and a lake.

SE 28th Ave. (just north of SE Woodstock Boulevard). ☎ 503-777-1734. Open: Daily, dawn to dusk. Admission: $3, charged from March 1 to Labor Day.

Hoyt Arboretum and Forest Park

Washington Park

For peaceful hikes among hundreds of trees, head to the Hoyt Arboretum in Washington Park, next door to the zoo. The 10 miles of hiking trails wind through splendid stands of trees and plants that have been imported from each of the seven continents. From the Arboretum, you can continue your explorations into enormous Forest Park, one of the largest urban parks in the nation, with more than 60 miles of trails through dense woods.

Arboretum: 4000 SW Fairview Blvd. in Washington Park; MAX stop at Zoo Station. ☎ 503-228-8733. Open: Daily. Admission: Free. Forest Park trail access at the end of NW Thurman Street.

Kayaking

For a unique Pacific Northwest experience, take to the water in a self-powered craft. In Portland, you can run the gentle Willamette or Columbia rivers with kayaks rented from the **Portland River Company** (315 SW Montgomery St.; ☎ 503-229-0551), headquartered at the RiverPlace complex just south of Tom McCall Waterfront Park. The company offers guided tours of the Willamette south to Ross Island or among small islets in the Columbia that are havens for wildlife. Experienced paddlers can just rent kayaks by the hour, launch right there at the RiverPlace Marina, and head south for their own tours of Ross Island (look for the single resident bald eagle).

Mount Tabor Park

Southeast Portland

It's not every metropolitan area that has an active volcano inside its city limits. The upper reaches of Mount Tabor have been turned into a park, with several paths for hiking and biking, stands of tall Douglas firs, and great views of the territory. On weekends, the whole place is closed to vehicular traffic, and it becomes a favorite, if somewhat uphill, jog for dozens of runners.

Mount Tabor is located in a southeastern neighborhood near Reed College; entrance at SE 60th Ave. and Salmon Street.

Oaks Bottom Wildlife Refuge

Sellwood

On the eastern shore of the Willamette River, near the Oaks Bottom Amusement Park, lies a bird-watcher's haven — some 160 acres of woodsy riverfront land that is home to dozens of species of birds. Trailheads are on SE Milwaukie Boulevard at Mitchell Street or at Sellwood Park on SE 7th Avenue.

Portland for book and art lovers

Portland has one of the greatest bookstores in the country, along with an active and lively local art scene. You could pass many a misty Northwest day in the following locales.

Pearl District

The Pearl, just over Burnside St. in the NW district of downtown, is the neighborhood of choice for art lovers and the place to be, especially on the first Thursdays of every month, when the streets get crowded and galleries entertain a nonstop stream of visitors. Stop at the **Margo Jacobsen Gallery** (1039 NW Glisan St.; ☎ **503-224-7287**) to find ceramics and glass pieces, as well as contemporary paintings. Photography lovers browse the works at the **Blue Sky Gallery** (1231 NW Hoyt St.; ☎ **503-225-0210**), and the **SK Josefsberg Gallery** (403 NW 11th Ave.; ☎ **503-241-9112**). Interspersed among the galleries are restaurants with lively bar scenes, where you can revel in your shopping finds over glasses of an Oregon pinot noir.

Powell's City of Books

They don't call this enormous repository of new and used books the "City of Books" for nothing. Many people come to Portland just to spend hours and days browsing Powell's main store, which occupies a solid block between downtown and the Pearl District and is said to hold over 750,000 titles. You pick up a map at the front door and then head off to huge rooms coded by colors (the Gold Room for science-fiction and children's books, for example), and you'd better make sure you have a rendezvous point if you're with kids or companions who scatter to find their favorites. The large cafe is a good place to have a cup of coffee and take a break from book-browsing. You could make a pretty comprehensive tour of the city just by seeking out Powell's satellite stores, each with its own specialty. **Powell's Travel Store** (SW Sixth Ave. at Yamhill Street; ☎ **503-228-1108**) is located in the middle of downtown at Pioneer Courthouse Square. In the Hawthorne district you can browse cookbooks and seed books to your heart's delight at **Powell's Books for Cooks and Gardeners** (3747 SE Hawthorne Blvd; ☎ **503-235-3802**), and techies shuffle off to **Powell's Technical Bookstore** downtown (33 NW Park St.; ☎ **503-228-3906**). Fittingly, for book lovers at least, Powell's may be the first and last thing you see when you come to Portland — it even has a location at the Portland airport, **Powell's Books at PDX** (☎ 503-240-1950).

Main store: 1005 W. Burnside St. ☎ 503-228-4651. Open: Daily 9 a.m.–11 p.m. Admission: Free.

Public art

Thanks to a civic ordinance that requires new building projects to earmark 1 percent of their budgets to public art, Portland's streets, particularly in the downtown and Old Town districts, are chock-a-block with whimsical fountains, bold statues, and other art projects that are well worth visiting. A walking-tour map of public art is available from **POVA** (25 SW Salmon St; ☎ **877-678-5263** or 503-275-9750). Make your first stop at **Portlandia,** the kneeling brass giantess who greets visitors to Michael Graves' postmodern **Portland Building** (1120 SW 5th Ave. at Main Street). Alongside **Pioneer Courthouse Square** (home to the **Weather Station** sculpture), you find bronzed **"Animals in Pools"** on the Yamhill Street side, including a bear and her cubs and curious river otters. On SW Main Street near 4th Avenue resides a life-size **bronze elk** standing alongside a pool, and up the street at SW 4th and Yamhill, look down to find **"Street Wise,"** a collection of quotations engraved in the granite paving stones. Wind up in Old Town at the **Skidmore Fountain** (NW First Ave. and Ash Street), which dates back to 1888, making it one of the oldest pieces of art in the city. It still gushes water from its decorative bronze and granite fixtures.

If This Is Tuesday, That Must Be the International Rose Test Garden: Seeing Portland by Guided Tour

Many good guided tours of Portland's sights and attractions are available, from walking tours to coach (bus) jaunts around the city to watery excursions on the city's rivers.

Touring Portland by bus

The major bus tour operator in the city is **Gray Line** (☎ 800-422-7042 or 503-285-9845), which, like its Seattle counterpart, offers several options for half- or full-day tours in comfortable buses. The tours take you to all of the usual suspects — the **International Rose Test Garden,** for example, and the **Japanese Garden** — on rather brisk schedules, with the driver providing narration and information. Gray Line also offers longer tours to some of the sights outside of Portland, such as the **Columbia River Gorge** and **Mount St. Helens.**

Keep in mind that for the price of a regular bus fare ($1.20, with two-hour free transfers) you can visit most of the same places (without the narration) on **Tri-Met's ART, the Cultural Bus** (Rte. #63), a vibrantly painted city bus that goes to the city's main attractions, including the International Rose Test Garden, the Oregon Museum of Science and Industry (OMSI), and the Oregon Convention Center. The bus travels in a loop, letting you get on and off where you want. At press time, however, the bus was running only once an hour.

Hoofing it!

Downtown Portland is especially conducive to walking tours, with its wide, flat streets and major points of interest clustered within a few blocks. Local historian Gary Ripley leads a lively tour of the streets around Pioneer Courthouse Square, with lots of anecdotal information on how Portland became what it is today. His **Personalized Tours & Travel** (☎ 503-248-0414) can meet your group at your hotel and travel at your pace. A similar service is offered by university instructor Peter Chausse, who leads **Peter's Walking Tours of Portland** (☎ 503-665-2558), which take in the downtown sights in a brisk, 2- to 4-hour stroll.

If you prefer a self-guided tour of downtown art, the Pearl District, or Nob Hill, you can pick up a brochure from **POVA** at its visitor headquarters (25 SW Salmon St.; ☎ 877-678-5263 or 503-275-9750).

Touring Portland by water

Getting onto the water on Portland's two rivers is a fine way to see the city from afar, especially on a warm summer day when open-air tour boats provide the coolest seats in town. You have several options to consider. The most popular boat in town is the **Sternwheeler Columbia Gorge** (☎ 503-223-3928), a Mississippi River–style touring boat with a working paddlewheel mounted on the back and indoor and outdoor viewing decks. From October through June the boat is based in downtown Portland, operating cruises up and down the Willamette, but the real fun comes during the summer months when it moves to the Columbia River and offers incredibly scenic rides through the Columbia River Gorge. Two-hour cruises begin at $12.95 for adults, $7.95 for children, and lunch, brunch, and dinner cruises are also offered throughout the year.

Another sternwheel paddleboat, the **Sternwheeler Rose** (☎ 503-286-7673) plies the Willamette from Portland harbor throughout the year, with options that range from a one-hour harbor cruise for $12 to a two-hour dinner cruise ($35). For more lavish settings and an upgrade in food service, the **Portland Spirit** (☎ **800-224-3901** or 503-224-3900) is a sleek, 75-foot yacht that specializes in meal-service cruises that pack in as many as 350 people onto two decks crammed with tables set with white linens. Cruises board from the spirit's dock at Tom McCall Waterfront Park near SW Salmon Street and include dinner cruises ($52 adults, $47 children), two-hour lunch tours ($28 adults, $10 children), and Sunday champagne brunch cruises ($36 adults, $10 children).

Not sure if you want to eat a meal on a moving ship? Portland's tour boats are big and stable, and the rivers don't offer much in the way of waves or movement, but if you have any doubts about your ability to handle the motion of a ship, particularly during a meal, it would be wise to try out a short sightseeing cruise before you commit to the time and expense of a meal cruise.

Seeing Portland by jetboat

For a unique ride aboard a boat that was first designed to navigate rivers, book a tour on a Willamette Falls Jetboat (☎ **888-JETBOAT** or 503-231-1532). These open-air launches sound powerful and fast, and they are, thanks to the jet-powered propulsion system that allows them to lift off the surface of the water and skim along. The boats dock at OMSI, but you can also have them cross the river and pick you up at the RiverPlace Marina. From there they head south past elegant mansions all the way to the base of lovely Willamette Falls on 2-hour tours that cost $22 for adults, and $14 for children ages 4 to 11. Although the drivers helming the boat never really push the limits of speed or the unique handling capabilities of the jetboats, they may spin a few doughnuts in the water on the way home, which is great fun for kids and people who don't mind a lively ride.

Chapter 26

A Shopper's Guide to Portland

- -

In This Chapter

▶ Getting in tune with the local shopping scene

▶ Browsing the big names in Portland retailing

▶ Enjoying Portland's outdoor markets

▶ Discovering Portland shopping from A to Z

- -

*W*hat is it about Portland that makes it such a fun place to shop? Is it that the city's shopping zones are concentrated, with lots of stores close together? Is it because the city continues to have a strong presence of locally-owned shops and few of the fast-food outlets or nationally-branded stores that make many shopping areas look the same? Do shoppers flock to Portland for the treasure trove of unique finds at local street markets and bookstores?

Certainly, all of the above help make Portland's a great shopping scene. But the big reason that shopping in Portland is the cat's meow is the *complete and utter absence of a local or state sales tax,* which automatically makes your purchases nearly 10 percent cheaper than they would be in Seattle. Come to Portland and experience it for yourself: Paying the sticker price — and *only* the sticker price — for purchases can be extremely satisfying.

How to Make the Shopping Scene

To find the heart of Portland shopping, head downtown to the blocks surrounding Pioneer Courthouse Square and the big hotels. It's here that you find the big department stores, such as **Nordstrom** and **Meier & Frank,** as well as major specialty shops like the original **NIKETOWN** and Portland's most upscale shopping mall, the burgeoning **Pioneer Place,** which doubled in size in 2000 with the opening of a second retail pavilion. Other neighborhoods and parts of town are known for their specialty items, which I detail in this chapter.

Store hours are usually set from 9 or 10 a.m. to 5 or 6 p.m., Monday through Saturday, and from noon to 5 p.m. on Sunday. The malls have slightly longer hours: **Pioneer Place** keeps its doors open from 9:30 a.m. to 9 p.m., Monday to Friday, from 9:30 a.m. to 7 p.m. on Saturday, and from 11 a.m. to 6 p.m. on Sunday. Many art galleries and smaller shops are closed on Monday. In the **Pearl District,** shops and galleries are generally open from 11 a.m. to 5 p.m., staying open until 9 p.m. on first Thursdays.

The Big Boys (and Girls) of Portland Retailing

Portland has its own local stars in the shopping sector, many of which were created to clothe, shoe, or outfit the outdoor lifestyles that the locals love to lead, including the following:

- ✔ **Columbia Sportswear:** 911 SW Broadway Ave. at Taylor Street (☎ 503-226-6800). The flagship store for the Portland-based maker of lightweight outdoor sportswear is a warm, welcoming space of natural wood beams.

- ✔ **Meier & Frank:** 621 SW Fifth Ave. at Morrison Street (☎ 503-223-0512). This Portland institution, which goes back over 100 years, remains a major department store, with ten floors' worth of consumer goods to browse and purchase.

- ✔ **NIKETOWN:** 930 SW 6th Ave. at Salmon Street (☎ 503-221-6453). The local shoe company changed brand-name retailing forever when it opened this flashy shrine to the swoosh, with small, boutique rooms separated by catwalks and flashing video screens everywhere. It still carries top-of-the-line shoes at top-of-the-line prices.

- ✔ **Nordstrom:** 701 SW Broadway at Yamhill Street (☎ 503-224-6666); second location in Lloyd Center Shopping Mall. Located directly across from Pioneer Courthouse Square, this Seattle import was embraced by Portlanders and serves as a cornerstone of the downtown shopping scene.

- ✔ **Pioneer Place:** 700 SW Fifth Ave. at Morrison Street (☎ 503-228-5800). Portland's most upscale shopping mall represented a major upgrading of the local retail scene when it opened, and has attracted national brands like Saks Fifth Avenue and a new Tiffany & Co. to Portland.

- ✔ **Powell's Acres of Books:** 1005 W. Burnside Street (☎ 503-228-4651). Some three-quarters of a million new and used books are on the shelves at any one time in Portland's much-beloved local bookstore, and the selection is so great that satellite stores have popped up around the city to accommodate specific tastes.

Two Street Markets That Portlanders Love

Portland's Saturday Market (☎ 503-222-6072), which sets up on weekends in the lots and alleys around the Skidmore Fountain, is a much-beloved local institution. Craftspeople display their wares in simple, basic stalls, and you find everything from household goods to fine jewelry and casual clothes, nearly all of it with a artful touch. It spills from the street into the **Skidmore Fountain Building,** where more shops sell interesting stuff, much of it with a counter-cultural twist. Food vendors operating out of trucks complete the scene, and frequently street musicians show up to entertain the browsers. The Market shuts down from Christmas day to early March and then resumes in earnest, open every weekend, rain or shine.

On the genteel South Park Blocks, just north of Portland State University, a **Farmer's Market** sets up shop every Wednesday and Saturday morning from May through October. This is a great place to find Oregon produce and agricultural products, as vendors arrive from surrounding farm areas with the freshest fruits and vegetables, as well as home-baked bread and artisan cheeses. People sell out of the back of their trucks, giving the market a charming, impromptu feel. Get there by mid-morning if you hope to stock your picnic basket with the choicest picks.

Portland's Great Shopping Neighborhoods

Downtown is where most of the major shopping action in Portland takes place, and SW Broadway and SW Fifth Avenue are the major shopping thoroughfares. But you can also snap up some great deals and unique finds by venturing out into the city's other neighborhoods.

Downtown

You'll undoubtedly find your way to **Nordstrom, Meier & Frank, NIKE-TOWN,** and **Pioneer Place** (see information earlier in the chapter) during your downtown ramblings, but also look to the following stores for specialty items. In the blocks surrounding **Powell's Acres of Books** (1005 W. Burnside St.; ☎ 503-228-4651) you also find several of Portland's hippest music stores. **Django's** (1111 SW Stark St.; ☎ 503-227-4381) is a cavernous space that sells used records and CDs, with an emphasis on classic rock from the 1960s. **Music Millennium** (3158 E. Burnside St.; ☎ 503-231-8926) has a comprehensive stock of popular music from the modern era, and the edgy **Ozone** (1036 W. Burnside St.; ☎ **503-227-1975**) offers rap, metal, and alternative choices from small labels. For unusual crafts, head to **Quintana Gallery** (501 SW Broadway; ☎ **503-223-1729**) for the best selection of American Indian arts and crafts in the city; **The Real Mother Goose** (901 SW Yamhill St.; ☎ **503-223-9510**) has an extensive collection of craftsy furniture, jewelry, and household items assembled from artisans throughout the country. For climbing and hiking gear, the locals head to **Oregon Mountain Community** (60 NW Davis; ☎ **503-227-1038**). The **U.S. Outdoor Store** (219 SW Broadway; ☎ **503-223-5937**) adds gear and outerwear for snowboarders, skiers, and campers to its selection.

Pearl District

The Pearl is Portland's hippest neighborhood, and aside from the art galleries that do a brisk business at nearly every corner, the streets are studded with specialty shops selling high-end clothing, home furnishings, furniture, and accessories. It's the corporate home of **Hanna Andersson** (1010 NW Flanders St.; ☎ **503-242-0920**), which manufactures and sells bright, indestructible children's clothes. The **Portland Antique Company** (1211 NW Glisan St.; ☎ **503-223-0999**) is an enormous warehouse with home furnishings culled from sources in Asia and Europe. Italian dinnerware and linens are the stock-in-trade of **dieci soli** (304 NW 11th Ave.; ☎ **503-222-4221**). Head to **Aubergine LLC** (1100 NW Glisan St.; ☎ **503-228-7313**) for specialty women's clothing from international designers, and **A Place in Time** (526 NW 13th Ave.; ☎ **503-227-5223**) for stylish urban decor items.

Nob Hill

Nob Hill, also called "Northwest" by locals, is one of Portland's more affluent neighborhoods, and the boutiques and restaurants centered on NW 23rd and NW 21st avenues cater to a fashion-conscious crowd. For clothing, European-based **Red/Green of Scandinavia** (437 NW 23rd Ave.; ☎ **503-552-9130**) has made Nob Hill the site of its first U.S. retail store, selling fine, comfortable European sportswear for men and women. Also on the clothing front is **Dakota** (2285 NW Johnson St.; ☎ **503-243-4468**), with sophisticated fashions and accessories for women from European and American designers, and **Girlfriends** (904 NW 23rd Ave.; ☎ **503-294-0488**), which carries contemporary women's clothing, pajamas, and gifts. More casual styles are offered by **CP Shades** (513 NW 23rd Ave.; ☎ **503-241-7838**), with comfortable clothing in natural fibers, and **Monkey Wear** (811 NW 23rd Ave.; ☎ **503-222-5160**), which is fun and funky, and adds wigs, jewelry, and tiaras to the mix. For crafts and gifts, head to **Gilt** (720 NW 23rd Ave.; ☎ **503-226-0629**), which specializes in vintage and local artisan jewelry, and **3 Monkeys** (803 NW 23rd Ave.; ☎ **503-222-9894**), with books, toys, and jewelry. **Twist** (30 NW 23rd Place; ☎ **503-224-0334**; another location in

Pioneer Place) carries fantastic, whimsical furniture and accessories from craftsmen who have a uniquely American style. **The Compleat Bed & Breakfast** (615 NW 23rd Ave.; ☎ 503-221-0193) can outfit your bedroom and kitchen to look like a stylish B&B. Kids enjoy **Child's Play** (907 NW 23rd Ave.; ☎ 503-224-5586) for toys, games, and plush animals, as well as **Christmas at the Zoo** (118 NW 23rd Ave.; ☎ 503-223-4048), which carries stuffed animals and a wide range of Christmas ornaments year-round.

Hawthorne Boulevard and the East Side

Crossing the Willamette River on the Burnside, Hawthorne, and Morrison bridges to Portland's east side puts you into neighborhoods of more modest means, with retail corridors that are great for finding small, funky shops. On Hawthorne Boulevard, look for **Crossroads Music** (3130 SE Hawthorne Blvd.; ☎ 503-232-1767), a browser's paradise and cooperative of record dealers who specialize in classic rock albums. Powell's bookstore has its **Powell's for Cooks & Gardeners** (3747 SE Hawthorne Blvd.; ☎ 503-235-3802) here, with a huge assortment of cookbooks and gardening tomes, both new and used, to sort through. If you can do without the flashy displays at the downtown store, the **Nike Factory Store** (2650 NE Martin Luther King Jr. Blvd.; ☎ 503-281-5901) can save you a bundle on athletic shoes, cutting prices by 50 to 80 percent in some cases. **The Mountain Shop** (628 NE Broadway; ☎ 503-288-6768) can hook you up with crampons and ice axes for mountain climbing, as well as ski and snowboard equipment and outerwear. To dress up your old home, check out the incredible **Rejuvenation House Parts** (1100 SE Grand Ave.; ☎ 503-238-1900), which carries practically everything you need to restore an older home, from rare fixtures to salvaged doors. They have a good selection of books on restoration, too.

Westmoreland and the Sellwood Antiques Row

The distant southeast reaches of the city are home to Portland's major antiques dealers, and even if you're not in the mood to purchase, you'll love the neighborhood ambience. Treat yourself to a very pleasant afternoon by making your way to Westmoreland, having lunch, and browsing the antiques shops. From there, drive a mile or two to Sellwood, where the shops are located in restored homes that proudly display their heritage on large signs, and then head back downtown in time for the cocktail hour. From downtown, take the Ross Island Bridge and head south on SE Milwaukie Avenue.

In the **Westmoreland** neighborhood, a lively retail corridor on Milwaukie includes two locations of **Stars Antiques Mall** (7027 SE Milwaukie Ave. and 7030 SE Milwaukie; ☎ **503-239-0346** and **503-235-5990,** respectively), big, open spaces crammed with tables and shelves holding every kind of knick-knack and collectible imaginable. The malls have a kind of indoor garage-sale feel to them, and if you rummage around long enough, you're sure to find a treasure. Moving into the **Sellwood** strip of blocks on SE 13th Ave., you find house after restored house that has been transformed into an antiques store, offering some aspect of collectible furniture, memorabilia, or household goods. **Cabbages and Kings Collections** (8017 SE 13th Ave.; ☎ 503-235-5688) has a dazzling display of collectible windup toys, including European models and vintage tin toys. For lacy furnishings and hand-sewn lamp-shades to decorate your Victorian sitting room, look to **Satin and Old Lace Shades** (8079 SE 13th Ave.; ☎ 503-234-2650). Across the street is **Southern Accents** (7718 SE 13th Ave.; ☎ 503-231-5508), which carries handcrafted furniture, including rocking chairs that would look just fine on your Auntie Bellum's broad porch.

Portland Shopping A to Z

Here is a breakdown of stores sorted by the types of merchandise carried.

Antiques

Portland Antique Company: 1211 NW Glisan St.; ☎ 503-223-0999.

Satin and Old Lace Shades: 8079 SE 13th Ave.; ☎ 503-234-2650.

Southern Accents: 7718 SE 13th Ave.; ☎ 503-231-5508.

Stars Antiques Mall: 7027 SE Milwaukie Ave. and 7030 SE Milwaukie; ☎ 503-239-0346 and 503-235-5990, respectively.

Books and music

Crossroads Music: 3130 SE Hawthorne Blvd.; ☎ 503-232-1767.

Django's: 1111 SW Stark St.; ☎ 503-227-4381.

Music Millennium: 3158 E. Burnside St.; ☎ 503-231-8926.

Ozone: 1036 W. Burnside St.; ☎ 503-227-1975.

Powell's Acres of Books: 1005 W. Burnside St.; ☎ 503-228-4651.

Powell's for Cooks & Gardeners: 3747 SE Hawthorne Blvd.; ☎ 503-235-3802.

Crafts and gifts

Gilt: 720 NW 23rd Ave.; ☎ 503-226-0629.

Quintana Gallery: 501 SW Broadway; ☎ 503-223-1729.

The Real Mother Goose: 901 SW Yamhill St.; ☎ 503-223-9510.

3 Monkeys: 803 NW 23rd Ave.; ☎ 503-222-9894.

Twist: 30 NW 23rd Place; ☎ 503-224-0334.

Department stores

Meier & Frank: 621 SW Fifth Ave. at Morrison Street; ☎ 503-223-0512.

Nordstrom: 701 SW Broadway at Yamhill Street; ☎ 503-224-6666. (Second location in Lloyd Center Shopping Mall.)

Saks Fifth Avenue: Pioneer Place; ☎ 503-226-3200.

Fashion

Aubergine LLC: 1100 NW Glisan St.; ☎ 503-228-7313.

CP Shades: 513 NW 23rd Ave.; ☎ 503-241-7838.

Dakota: 2285 NW Johnson St.; ☎ 503-243-4468.

Girlfriends: 904 NW 23rd Ave.; ☎ 503-294-0488.

Monkey Wear: 811 NW 23rd Ave.; ☎ 503-222-5160.

Red/Green of Scandinavia: 437 NW 23rd Ave.; ☎ 503-552-9130.

Home decor

A Place in Time: 526 NW 13th Ave.; ☎ 503-227-5223.

The Compleat Bed & Breakfast: 615 NW 23rd Ave.; ☎ 503-221-0193.

dieci soli: 304 NW 11th Ave.; ☎ 503-222-4221.

Rejuvenation House Parts: 1100 SE Grand Ave.; ☎ 503-238-1900.

Outdoor clothing and gear

Columbia Sportswear: 911 SW Broadway Ave. at Taylor Street; ☎ 503-226-6800.

The Mountain Shop: 628 NE Broadway; ☎ 503-288-6768.

Nike Factory Store: 2650 NE Martin Luther King Jr. Blvd.; ☎ 503-281-5901.

NIKETOWN: 930 SW 6th Ave. at Salmon Street; ☎ 503-221-6453.

Oregon Mountain Community: 60 NW Davis; ☎ 503-227-1038.

U.S. Outdoor Store: 219 SW Broadway; ☎ 503-223-5937.

Toys and children's clothing

Cabbages and Kings Collections: 8017 SE 13th Ave.; ☎ 503-235-5688.

Child's Play: 907 NW 23rd Ave.; ☎ 503-224-5586.

Christmas at the Zoo: 118 NW 23rd Ave.; ☎ 503-223-4048.

Hanna Andersson: 1010 NW Flanders St.; ☎ 503-242-0920.

Chapter 27

Five Great Portland Itineraries and Three Dandy Day Trips

● ●

In This Chapter

▶ How to manage your time in Portland

▶ Itineraries for those in a hurry, nature lovers, athletes, families with kids, and shopaholics

● ●

*S*o you've read about all there is to do and see in Portland, but you'd like a little more advice on managing your time to maximize your visit. Here I offer a few planned itineraries to help you group activities so that you use your precious vacation time wisely. These are by no means hard-and-fast rules — in fact, feel free to mix and match from the different itineraries as your interests dictate. For more details on the attractions and places listed here, see the in-depth write-ups in Chapter 25.

Before you plan your itinerary, write down all the things you want to see *and* all those you don't. You can spend a lot of time crossing the river to the eastside or hopping on the freeways to explore distant corners of the city. If you plan to do either, try to schedule your day so that you see everything you want to see before returning downtown, and then stay put.

When you're downtown shopping or sightseeing, use the MAX trains to get from east to west (the river to Washington Park) quickly, and use the buses on the transit malls of SW 5th and 6th avenues to travel north and south. Most trips are within the ride-free area and can get you within a few blocks of where you're headed. The Pearl District and Nob Hill are tougher to reach on public transportation (at least, until the Portland Streetcar begins operation) and are a long walk from downtown. Try to concentrate your sightseeing time in those neighborhoods so that you don't have to go back and forth to your downtown hotel several times in a day. Plan to wind up at a restaurant or bar for a meal or drinks so that you can comfortably wait for a cab to take you back to your hotel.

Portland in a Day and a Half

So you wound up spending more time in Seattle than you thought, huh? And suddenly you've got to see all of Portland before your flight leaves tomorrow night? Well relax, because it ain't gonna happen, but you *can* maximize your time with the following itinerary.

The afternoon

Check into your hotel, dump your bags, and get the heck out onto the streets — you can study the toiletries in your bathroom later. Head directly to **Pioneer Courthouse Square** in the heart of downtown, and look at the street sculptures and fountains along the way. From there, board the MAX train headed toward the river (it's a free ride) or walk to **Tom McCall Waterfront Park** to take in the views of the river and Portland's famous bridges. Walk north on the broad green lawn. If it's a weekend, the **Portland Saturday Market** is open at the very north end of the park for shopping and perusing the local crafts. If it's closed when you get there, check out the turn-of-the-century buildings of **Old Town** and the venerable **Skidmore Fountain.** In either case, walk a few blocks farther north into Chinatown and enjoy the **Classical Chinese Garden,** Portland's newest attraction. Then walk or take a cab north on Burnside Street until you reach **Powell's Acres of Books,** Portland's famous bookstore. Even if you don't have the time or inclination to shop, you can stop at the store's coffee shop for a restorative latte before continuing.

Twilight and evening

From Powell's, walk to the **Pearl District,** which is centered on NW 12th Avenue, north of Burnside. If it's the first Thursday night of the month, the streets will be buzzing with **art gallery** openings. On any other night, you can window-shop and choose one of several cool restaurants and bars for cocktails and dinner. Your walk might continue west to the **Nob Hill** district of shops centered on NW 21st and NW 23rd avenues. Enjoy a nightcap at any one of the fine hotel bars downtown on Broadway.

The next morning

Pack your things, check out of the hotel, and have them store your bags. Jump on the MAX and head directly to **Washington Park** and the Zoo Station. Awaiting you there as you ascend the deep elevator shaft are the **Oregon Zoo,** the **Hoyt Arboretum,** and **Washington Park**'s hiking trails. A shuttle takes you from there to the **International Rose Test Garden** and, if you still have time, the **Japanese Garden,** both of which overlook downtown Portland; don't forget your camera. Grab a cab and beat it back downtown, get fast food from a sidewalk vendor or take-out place, grab your stuff, and get to the airport or train station. Breathe out.

Seeing Portland in Three Days

This itinerary includes most of the major sights of the city and still allows time for lingering in cool neighborhoods, taking in some of the local nightlife, and planning meals at restaurants.

Day one

Explore **downtown** on your first day, with stops at the **Pioneer Courthouse Square** and the shops and department stores along Broadway and the central shopping district. Heading south on SW Park Avenue leads to the peaceful **South Park Blocks** and the **Portland Art Museum** and the **Oregon History Center.** Walk or take a bus due east from there to have lunch at the **RiverPlace Marina,** which overlooks the Willamette River, or hook up a ride on a guided tourboat. Walking north from RiverPlace puts you at the broad swath of **Tom McCall Waterfront Park,** which has a number of built-in attractions, including the computerized fountain at the foot of SW Salmon Street called **Salmon Street Springs.** Across the street, on Salmon and Naito Parkway, is the **POVA visitor center,** where you can get maps, suggested walking tours of public art, or info on the local scene. After leaving the park at its northern end, take in the public art in **Old Town** and the **Skidmore Fountain,** and, if you still have time and your legs are holding up, visit the **Classical Chinese Garden** nearby in Chinatown. Give yourself time to relax and catch your breath before heading out to dinner at a fine downtown restaurant or in the **Pearl District,** or check with **Ticket Central** to see which shows are playing at the local clubs and theaters. Wind up your night drinking flaming Spanish coffees at **Huber's** or bar-hopping the fine hotel bars downtown.

Day two

This is your park day. After a leisurely breakfast, catch the MAX train west to Zoo Station and **Washington Park.** Take as much time as you like — the whole day, if necessary — exploring one or all of the many attractions in the park, including the **Oregon Zoo, Hoyt Arboretum,** the **International Rose Test Garden,** and the **Japanese Garden.** Get away from the crowds by walking through the park and adjacent **Forest Park.** A ballgame at **PGE Park** isn't far away if you'd like a low-key evening activity, or you could take a cab to the **Nob Hill** neighborhood for evening shopping, cocktails, and dinner, perhaps at a trademark Portland brewpub that serves great pizza and burgers.

Day three

Spend your third day exploring Portland's east-side neighborhoods, starting with breakfast at a lively cafe in the **Belmont** or **Hawthorne districts,** just east of the river. You're close to the **OMSI** museum and its interactive science exhibits, as well as the **Oaks Bottom Wildlife Refuge** for bird-watching. Stroll **SE Hawthorne Avenue** to see the shops and street life, then head south to the **Westmoreland district** for lunch at a bistro and antiquing. Continue to the strip of antiques merchants housed in restored homes in **Sellwood.** Spend your last night in the neighborhood or restaurant you've enjoyed most.

Portland for Outdoor Lovers and Athletes

The Rose City's civic landscape is dotted with wonderful parks and recreational opportunities. Following are suggestions for getting out and keeping active.

Portland runners begin their day (or their lunch hours) with a jog alongside the **Willamette River** at **Tom McCall Waterfront Park.** From there, you can rent kayaks at the **RiverPlace Marina** for paddles on the river or sign up for a guided tour that takes you up to the **Columbia River** for a half-day paddle. At some point, you may want to head to the west side and take in the trails and scenery of **Forest Park,** which has miles of hiking trails in thick woods, as well as mountain-bike trails. Nearby in **Washington Park** is the **Hoyt Arboretum** and its many species of introduced and native trees and plants. On the east side of the city, a long drive from downtown, is **Mount Tabor,** an active (though dormant) volcano with good trails for running and biking and long views of the city. On your way back, think about meeting the **Willamette Falls Jetboat** at **OMSI** for a fast spin south on the river on a racy jetboat.

Portland for Families with Kids

If you're traveling with children, make sure to pace yourself and set aside some time for them simply to blow off steam. Don't overload them with a schedule that packs in one museum or attraction after another — the kids will be just as happy spending a couple of hours a day at the hotel pool. Remember that in the summer months it gets dark very late in the Northwest, and if you try to keep things moving all day long, you wind up with some very pooped campers. Build in time for naps and use the long afternoons to fill in the sights that you want to see.

The **Oregon Zoo** is a great place to start: From downtown you travel to the zoo on the MAX light-rail train, a guaranteed great adventure for kids, and **Washington Park** is perfect for the younger set. From there, board the **Washington Park and Zoo Railway** for an enjoyable spin through the park that winds up at the **International Rose Test Garden** and the **Japanese Garden** (tell the kids that if they behave themselves long enough for you to enjoy the two gardens, they get to ride the train back to the zoo). Downtown, **Pioneer Courthouse Square** is a nice, paved block where they can run around a bit. **Tom McCall Waterfront Park** has wide green lawns and views of the river, plus lots of interactive entertainments for kids, including a **tile maze** at the north end and the **Salmon Street Springs** computerized fountain. The park also houses a big **carnival** during the summer **Rose Festival,** with rides and music. From the park, you can also book guided tours and boat rides on big paddlewheelers.

Another day can be spent on the east side of the river, where you can occupy yourself at the **OMSI** museum, with its fun interactive exhibits, taking tours of a real **submarine,** or seeing a movie in the **OMNIMAX** theater. Head south from OMSI to the **Oaks Bottom Amusement Park,** a cheerful old park with thrill rides and a terrific **roller-skating pavilion** that you're sure to enjoy as much as the kids. For a very unusual entertainment, particularly in the middle of the summer, the **Lloyd Center** indoor shopping mall (which, incidentally, has a Toys 'R Us), houses an **ice-skating rink** where the kids can rent skates while you relax with a coffee from the adjacent food court.

Portland for Shopaholics

The absence of a state sales tax and the presence of a vibrant shopping scene, much of it locally-owned and distinctly-regional, makes a visit to the Rose City a shopper's dream, especially in the fall months when the shopping districts are decorated for the holidays, hotel rooms are discounted, and the sales are on.

Plot your shopping strategy as you fuel yourself with a morning latte at the coffee shop at **Pioneer Courthouse Square.** Directly behind you is **Nordstrom** and its fine selection of clothing and shoes. To your left is **Meier & Frank,** the venerable department store, and in front of you is **Pioneer Place,** with its upscale shops, **Tiffany & Co.** and **Saks Fifth Avenue.** Within several blocks, in fact, are all of Portland's major retailers, including **NIKETOWN** and **Columbia Sportswear,** and by the end of the day you may find that you've made more than one return trip to your hotel room to drop off bags full of goodies. If you have time, make a quick dash across the river on the MAX train to the shopping mall at **Lloyd Center,** which contains the standard national outlets found at most urban malls.

Portland Excursions

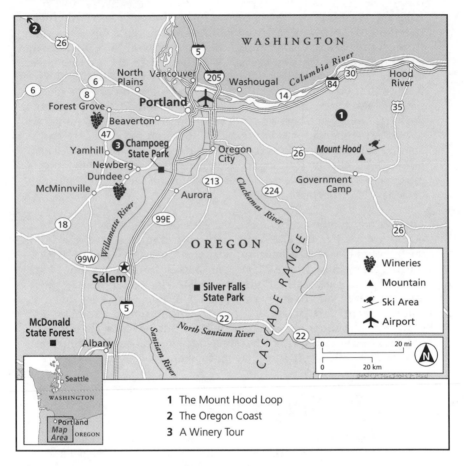

1 The Mount Hood Loop
2 The Oregon Coast
3 A Winery Tour

On another day, head to the **Northwest** part of town to shop the art
and home-decor boutiques in the **Pearl District.** Book lunch at a restaurant in the Pearl or on **Nob Hill,** and then continue your shopping at
the stores that line **NW 23rd Avenue,** which sell clothing, jewelry, and
precious items for the home.

If antiques are your passion, spend a day browsing the antiques stores
on the **Sellwood** strip of **SE 13th Avenue,** and then head to **SE
Milwaukie Avenue** and the **Westmoreland** neighborhood for lunch and
more shopping before returning downtown and scouring the streets
you might have missed before. Book lovers can lose themselves in the
labyrinthine rooms of **Powell's Acres of Books** until nearly midnight.

Exploring Beyond Portland: Three Dandy Day Trips

Portland is nicely situated for day trips that can quickly take you into some remarkable Northwest terrain. Head due west for the ocean, east to set out for the striking Columbia River Gorge and Cascade Mountains, and south in the fertile Willamette River Valley to tour Oregon's delightful wineries. Following are suggestions for doing each of the trips as one-day excursions that begin and end in Portland.

The Columbia River and Mount Hood Loop

This is an all-day trip, so get up early, pack a breakfast, and make sure the car is gassed up. You can do the trip in either direction, but I like seeing the river in the morning hours. Head east out of Portland and travel alongside the Columbia River for jaw-dropping scenery of the **Columbia River Gorge;** returning via **Mount Hood** gives you access to one of Oregon's great recreational areas.

Begin by taking I-84 east out of Portland, and picking up U.S. 30 at **Troutdale.** For the next 40 miles or so, you have a front-row seat to spectacular views offered up by the high cliffs that border the Columbia as the road climbs up and through thick woods and opens to vistas of cliffs and the river. **Multnomah Falls,** at 620 feet the highest cascade in Oregon, is a must-see stop. A bit farther up the road you find the **Bonneville Dam and Locks,** with fish ladders and viewing windows to see salmon fighting their way upstream, as well as the **Bridge of the Gods,** which crosses the river at a point where American Indians claim a natural rock bridge once stood. For information and more details on the area, stop at the **Columbia Gorge Interpretive Center** (990 SW Rock Creek Dr., Stevenson; ☎ **509-427-8211**), on the Washington side of the bridge, before returning to the Oregon side and pressing on to **Hood River,** which is the epicenter of the famous **Columbia Gorge windsurfing** scene. This is not the place for beginners to learn the sport — high winds whipping through the gorge are best handled by experienced riders — but you can have a great time watching the pros dip, swoop, and fly across the river.

From here, head inland on Hwy. 35 farmland where roadside stands sell fresh fruit and produce. You're bound for **Mount Hood,** which looms ahead. A good stop is at 6,000-foot **Timberline,** just after the juncture with Hwy. 26, where the W.P.A.-built **Timberline Lodge,** all heavy wooden beams and stone, has withstood the mountain's weather since its construction in the 1930s. Trails lead through meadows that bloom with wildflowers in July and August. Above is the awesome **Palmer Snowfield,** a year-round blanket of ice and snow that can be visited via chairlifts. Serious hikers might consider tackling the **Timberline Trail,** which extends some 40 miles. An easier hike is the path around pretty **Trillium Lake** near **Government Camp,** the site of two of the mountain's three winter ski areas. To return to Portland, put the mountain in your rear-view mirror as you continue on Hwy. 26 all the way back into town.

Oregon's ocean highways

Oregon's rugged beaches may be too cold for swimming (although your kids might argue that point), but the beachcombing amid piles of driftwood is amazing, as are the views of wind-and-water-battered offshore islets. The nearest beach to Portland is about an hour-and-a-half drive; after that you have a number of options, from a half-day to a full day, for exploring the coast before returning to the city.

Begin by taking Hwy. 26, known as the **Sunset Highway,** west from the city. You travel over a low coastal mountain range before reaching **Hwy. 101**, the coastal strip that hugs the shoreline (as best it can with all the cliffs and promontories) all the way down to California. First stop is **Ecola Beach State Park,** just after the 101 juncture, with gorgeous views of the ocean and trails that lead through thick forests of old-growth trees. The town and shoreline of **Cannon Beach** is next, with the much-photographed **Haystack Rock** formation just offshore and an artsy town to explore. Like most of Oregon's beaches, Cannon is a great place to build sandcastles and fly kites. Head south for the next 60 miles or so up high cliffs bordering the ocean, through thick forests, and down to quiet little bays and towns like **Manzanita;** you can do a little beachcombing at **Newhalem Bay State Park** while you're here. **Tillamook,** which sits at the head of the bay of the same name, is a major dairy-producing area with a popular cheese factory that receives scores of visitors throughout the year. From here, Hwy. 101 remains inland for 30 miles or so; continue south on the highway for more ocean and beach views and to poke around in the lively tourist centers at **Lincoln City** and **Depoe Bay.** Or simply head back over the mountains to Portland via Hwy. 6 or Hwy. 18.

The Pacific Ocean can be treacherous on these beaches, with multiple breaks and undertows, and unlike anything you or your kids may have experienced in more placid ocean destinations like Florida, California, or Hawaii. There are no lifeguards on Oregon's beaches, either. If your kids are anything like my kids, they may want to play in the water anyway, but be sure to keep an eye on them and make them stay in the shallowest parts of the water.

Mount Hood

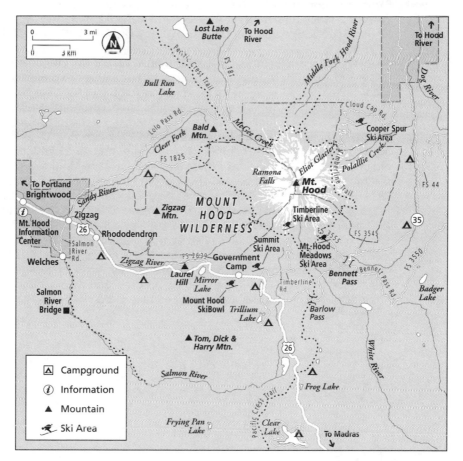

The Willamette Wineries Loop

In recent years, local wines have caught up with — and maybe even passed — microbrews as the beverage of choice among Portland's sipping set. The fertile **Willamette Valley,** whose farmland attracted settlers to the region in the first place, has become the home of a thriving wine industry. Even French vintners like **Joseph Drouhin,** who compares the Oregon climate to that of his local Burgundy, have begun to open farms in the area to get in on the grape-growing action. A variety of grapes are grown here, including chardonnays and rieslings, but the star of the Oregon wine scene is pinot noir, a flavorful, light-bodied red wine that is a staple in local restaurants. With 97 of Oregon's 166 wineries located in the rural areas south and west of the city, a winemaking tour is a fine way to see some countryside, enjoy a picnic (tables are available at most wineries), and acquaint yourself with local wines. The area begins within 20 miles of downtown Portland, so you can easily do this tour in a half-day. Most wineries are open daily, from 11 a.m. to 5 p.m. For more information and detailed maps, contact the **Oregon Wine Advisory Board** (offices in Portland at 1200 NW Naito Pkwy; ☎ 503-228-8336) or get the **Oregon Winery Guide** (☎ 800-242-2363).

Many wineries are located in the rolling hills west of the city near the villages of **Yamhill, Dundee,** and **Newberg.** For a nice drive on rural roads, take Hwy. 26 west out of Portland, switching to Rte. 6 at North Plains, and then south on Rte. 8 a few miles later. Turn right on Rte. 47 at Forest Grove and look for signs on the road as you head south toward Yamhill. **Montinore Vineyards** (3663 SW Dilley Rd.; ☎ 503-259-5012) has its headquarters here, with a tasting room in a handsome old mansion and nice views of the valley and Cascade Mountains in the distance. Alternatively, you can shoot down I-5 south, getting off at Exit 283 bound for Newberg. Between Newberg and Dundee, you find the **Erath Winery** (☎ 800-539-WINE), **Duck Pond** (☎ 503-538-3199), and the **Sokol Blosser Winery** (☎ 800-582-6668 or 503-864-2282), each of which offers tastings and sells directly to the public. The latter, at 24 years old, is one of Oregon's oldest wineries, which gives you an idea of how fresh this industry is. **Sokol Blosser**'s vineyards are posted for self-guided tours that explain the grape process, and the spacious grounds have green lawns, tall trees, and nice views of the valley.

Chapter 28

Living It Up after the Sun Goes Down: Portland Nightlife

. . . .

In This Chapter

▶ Sources for entertainment listings

▶ How to find tickets quickly and easily

▶ The Portland performing-arts scene

▶ Great music clubs and lively bars

. . . .

*P*ortland has all the big cultural attractions that you'd expect of a large metropolis, but it also has a cheerful, intimate tavern scene that's fun to explore. Portland enjoys an energetic blues and jazz scene as well, and top touring acts come to town throughout the year. Thanks to their proximity, Seattle and Portland are frequently on the same schedule for major performers, so if you miss a band one night in Seattle, chances are good that you can catch it the next in Portland.

What's Happening: Getting the News

Portland's lively weekly newspaper, the **Willamette Week,** offers extensive guides to what's playing in town. You can find it for free throughout the city at most convenience stores, bars, and coffee shops. **The Oregonian** daily newspaper publishes a calendar every Friday and Sunday. The best online source is **portland.citysearch.com,** which offers up-to-the-minute information on shows and ticket availability around town. Your hotel should also have copies of the weekly **"Hot Sheet,"** a publication distributed by the Portland Oregon Visitors Association (POVA) that lists everything playing in town that week at the major theaters and auditoriums (but not at the bars and smaller clubs), as well as festivals and special events.

Where to Get Tickets

POVA operates the excellent **Ticket Central** service, a one-stop clear-inghouse that consolidates **Ticketmaster** (☎ 503-224-4400), **Fastixx** (☎ 800-922-8499), and **Artistix** (☎ 503-275-8352) services into one location. They also have information on half-price tickets on the day of a show, as well as tickets to local sporting events, such as a Portland Trail Blazers basketball game in the Rose Garden or an afternoon of baseball in the newly refurbished PGE Park (formerly Historic Civic Stadium), home of the Portland Beavers, the city's new Triple A franchise (see Chapter 25 for more information). They're presently located at the POVA headquarters at Naito Pkwy and SW Salmon Street, but they will move into a kiosk at Pioneer Courthouse Square in the summer of 2001. The half-price hotline is ☎ 503-275-8358; for other information, call the ticket services directly. Students and seniors should keep in mind that many venues can sell them discounted, day-of-show tickets; go straight to the box office to see if any are available.

The Play's the Thing: The Local Theater Scene

The modern building of glass and brick next door to the Arlene Schnitzer Concert Hall (see later in the chapter) is the **New Theater Building,** which houses Portland's main theatrical companies and touring productions. Much of the cultural life of the city takes place in these two buildings, as well as at **Keller Auditorium** (SW Third Avenue and SW Clay Street; formerly known as Civic Auditorium), with smaller theaters dotted around the city, such as the Belmont district's **Theatre! Theatre!** (3430 SE Belmont), which hosts avant-garde theater works throughout the year.

Portland Center Stage (☎ 503-274-6588), the city's largest profes-sional company, has been upping the ante in recent years by adding edgier productions to their six-play season. Last year, a riveting pro-duction of Patrick Marber's *Closer* stirred things up a bit with the kind of adult themes and language rarely seen on Portland's main stage in the New Theater Building. Oregon has a long and distinguished history of mounting the plays of the Bard, the singular mission of the **Tygres Heart Shakespeare Company** (☎ 503-288-8400), which puts on its very professional shows at the New Theater Buildings' Winningstad Theatre. Look for big touring productions of Broadway shows at the **Keller Auditorium** (☎ 503-274-6560). Among the many smaller theater companies around town that stage original shows as well as fringe and avant-garde plays and musicals are **Artists Repertory Theatre** (☎ 503-294-7373), **Imago Theatre** (☎ 503-231-3959), **Miracle Theatre/Tea Milagro** (☎ 503-236-7253), the **Musical Theatre Company** (☎ 503-224-8730), and **Triangle Productions** (☎ 503-223-6790).

For theater specifically geared to kids, look for shows by the **Oregon Children's Theatre** (☎ 503-224-4400), which stages big, professional productions with great sets, costumes, and acting.

Music, Dance, and More: The Performing Arts

A lovingly restored 1920s movie palace on SW Broadway is the epicenter of Portland's current cultural scene. Known affectionately as "The Schnitz," the **Arlene Schnitzer Concert Hall** (SW Broadway at SW Main Street) is home of the Oregon Symphony. Look for the antique PORTLAND sign above the Broadway marquee.

The **Oregon Symphony** (☎ 800-229-7243 or 503-228-1353) is a local institution that dates back over a hundred years, making it the oldest symphony orchestra on the West Coast. Conductor James de Preist ably handles the music, which ranges from big, orchestral productions to pops concerts and shows with guest artists (Ray Charles returns nearly every year for popular shows). In August the Symphony performs concerts outdoors at Tom McCall Waterfront Park. For the kids, the symphony has Sunday matinees and children's concerts. Look for tickets early in your visit, and book in advance. During the summer, Portland hosts dozens of great chamber musicians for its annual, five-week **Chamber Music Northwest** series (☎ 503-294-6400), with performances at Reed College on the eastern edge of the city and at the Catlin Gable School in the far reaches of the southwest district.

The **Portland Opera** (Keller Auditorium; SW Third Avenue. and SW Clay; ☎ 503-241-1802) offers five-show seasons that intersperse lighter fare with serious opera. The 2001-2002 season, for example, included works by Verdi and Mozart, as well as Georges Bizet and Leonard Bernstein. Every now and then they throw in a performance of Broadway show tunes.

The resident dance company is the **Oregon Ballet Theatre** (☎ 503-222-5538), whose season runs from March to December and culminates in a much-beloved production of *The Nutcracker* (which sells out early, so buy tickets in advance if you hope to include a show in your trip to Portland). Staged at the Keller Auditorium, the season consists of classical dances, such as *Romeo and Juliet,* as well as showcases of work by American choreographers.

The Club and Bar Scene

Portland's lively nightlife scene has something for every taste: College students from Portland State, Lewis & Clark, and Reed head to the dance clubs; Goths dressed in black seek out dark spaces playing pounding music; neighbors meet over pizza and beer; and attorneys and artistes mingle at wine bars. Here are a few recommended spots to see the city's populace in play mode.

Brewpubs to know and love

Microbrews continue to be a popular beverage in Portland, and the locals are loyal to their favorite locally-made lagers, ales, porters, and stouts. One name you're sure to see around town is **McMenamins,** the trademark of a pair of Portland brothers who have done awfully well with hand-crafted beers served in wildly eclectic settings. Their **McMenamin Ringlers Pub** (1332 W. Burnside St.; ☎ 503-225-0543) is actually three spaces within a block of one another, the main room being a huge, friendly spot decorated with Indonesian antiques and mosaics. The **Blue Moon Tavern** (432 NW 21st Ave.; ☎ 503-223-3184) is a McMenamins in the trendy Nob Hill district that recently reopened after a fire; it stands in counterpoint to the fashionable surroundings by offering pool tables and simple wooden booths. The **Kennedy School** (5736 NE 33rd Ave.; ☎ 503-228-2192) is a typically over-the-top McMenamins venture. It's a converted grade school with an "Honors Bar" and "Detention Baro," movie theater, and a cafeteria/restaurant. McMenamins also pioneered the wildly successful concept of opening second-run movie theaters where you buy pitchers of beer and slices of pizza and watch movies from comfortable old lounge chairs and sofas. You find them at the **Bagdad Theater & Pub** (3702 SE Hawthorne Blvd.; ☎ 503-236-9234), the **Mission Theater & Pub** (1624 NW Glisan St.; ☎ 503-225-5555), and the **Kennedy School.** All McMenamins serve distinctive microbrews in many varieties (Hammerhead Ale and Terminator Stout are especially good), along with seasonal specials.

Other brewpubs of note include the **Bridgeport Brew Pub** (1318 NW Marshall St.; ☎ 503-241-7179) at the far northern edge of the Pearl District in an old brick building covered in ivy, with a taproom and restaurant alongside the big brewery spaces. The beers are smooth and distinctive and the house-made pizza is especially good. If you really like the beer, you can also find it in the Hawthorne retail strip at the **Hawthorne Street Ale House** (3632 SE Hawthorne Blvd.; ☎ 503-233-6540). That gives you two stops on Hawthorne (including the **Bagdad**) for microbrew; a third is farther west at a cozy neighborhood place called the **Lucky Labrador Brewing Co.** (915 SE Hawthorne Blvd.; ☎ 503-236-3555) where the regulars bring their dogs to the covered outdoor patio, and the inside is decorated with those famous paintings of dogs playing pool. Downtown, the **Tug Boat Brewing Co.** (711 SW Ankeny St.; ☎ 503-226-2508) is an unpretentious little place where the lagers are especially bitter and locals gather to hear music played on a small stage.

Cool and jazzy: Portland's best music clubs

From jazz in Old Town and blues in the Pearl District to folk music at small clubs and national touring acts playing the big concert halls, Portland offers a rich and varied live-music scene.

The biggest venue in town for seeing major acts is the **Roseland Theater & Grill** (8 NW 6th Ave., just across West Burnside Street; ☎ 503-219-9929), which draws artists like Little Feat and Coolio on national tours. The adjoining cafe has posters of former acts that comprise a who's who of popular music over the last 25 years. Over the Ross Island Bridge is the **Aladdin Theater** (3017 SE Milwaukie Ave.; ☎ 503-233-1994), with local and national acts that tend more toward folk, blues, and classic rock. If you like to dance, or if you just like classic ballrooms, check out the **Crystal Ballroom** (1332 Burnside St.; ☎ 503-778-5625), another McMenamins venture, wherein a dowager ballroom was restored, right down to the unique ball-bearing-supported dance floor that bounces underfoot. They showcase a variety of live-music acts and offer weekly ballroom dancing.

Jazz lovers flock to **Jimmy Mak's** (305 NW 10th Ave.; ☎ 503-295-6542), a hotspot in the Pearl District, as well as the venerable **Jazz de Opus** in Old Town (33 NW 2nd Ave.; ☎ 503-222-6077), one of Portland's older clubs. Jazz favorites play on the jukebox when the stage isn't being used. Live jazz is also performed most nights downtown at the very Parisian **Brasserie Montmartre** (626 SW Park Ave.; ☎ 503-224-5552). Jazz-piano lovers who enjoyed going to **Atwater's** restaurant will, alas, be disappointed to learn that the space lost its lease and has shut down.

Bottom's up: Portland's favorite bars

For general scene-making fun, you can join Portland's regulars who head to one (or several, on a particularly lively night) of these drinking establishments from happy hour until last call.

The elegant lobby in the **Benson Hotel** (309 SW Broadway; ☎ 503-228-2000) is trimmed in a rare Russian walnut, making it an elegant place to meet (especially for business) for martinis and cocktails in a lounge where soft music is performed. Across the street on the following block is **Pazzo,** the in-house restaurant of the Hotel Vintage Plaza (627 SW Washington St.; ☎ 503-228-1515), which brings its Italian cheer (and food) to a lively bar area. Also on Broadway, you find **Saucebox** (214 SW Broadway; ☎ 503-241-3393), a hip, dark space that offers food with an Asian flair and tasty, exotic cocktails (like a coconut lime-rickey or a blood-orange drop) to sip alongside an artsy crowd late into the night.

Still ticking for late-night drinks is **Huber's** (411 SW Third Ave.; ☎ 503-228-5686), Portland's oldest restaurant, which draws a touristy and suburban crowd to enjoy its trademark flaming Spanish coffees, prepared tableside. The chic and sophisticated **El Gaucho** (319 SW Broadway; ☎ 503-227-8794) also makes dazzling flaming coffees at its location back at the Benson Hotel, which is where, you might note, this particular binge began.

Another jaunt might begin in Chinatown at **Hung Far Low** (112 NW 4th Ave.; ☎ 503-223-8686), a dingy but atmospheric dive where the waitresses are renowned for barking at customers and the drinks are cheap. Moving west (and upscaling in a hurry), stop at **¡Oba!** (555 NW 12th Ave.; ☎ 503-228-6161), a Latin bar/restaurant in the Pearl District that attracts a fashionable, lively crowd to its long bar. Even farther west in the Nob Hill neighborhood is **Gypsy** (625 NW 21st Ave.; ☎ 503-796-1859), a stylish lounge of dark velvet booths next door to a diner, with enormous drinks that are meant to be shared.

Wine lovers can enjoy the offerings at Portland's wine bars, which offer tastings of expensive wines that are usually only served by the bottle. In Nob Hill, check out the **Blue Tango Bistro & Wine Bar** (930 NW 23rd Ave.; ☎ 503-221-1466), a classy place with upholstered furniture and art on the walls, and a nice selection of Northwest wines to sample. **Southpark** (901 SW Salmon St.; ☎ 503-326-1300) devotes a large part of its space to a stainless steel bar and booths from which you can try whole flights of wines from specific regions. They specialize in Mediterranean foods and wines. A great place to really learn about your Oregon pinot noirs is **Oregon Wines on Broadway** (515 SW Broadway; ☎ 503-228-4655), where you can pull up a stool at the small bar and sample the wines of as many as 30 different Oregon wineries.

Part VII
The Part of Tens

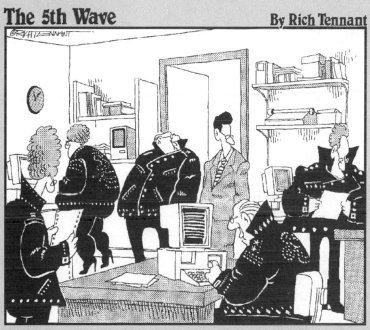

"Being in Seattle, we had the first grunge IS dept. Then we were a techno-Pop dept., and now we're sort of a neo-50's- Lou Reed IS dept."

In this part . . .

*H*ere I provide fun, quirky tips on visiting Seattle and Portland that are guaranteed to make your visit all the richer — and separate you from all the other dummies who don't know a geoduck from a Quilcene oyster.

Chapter 29

Ten Northwest Taste Treats You Simply Can't Miss

· ·

In This Chapter

▶ Local treats that are indigenous to the Northwest

▶ Sampling Seattle and Portland's tastiest dishes

· ·

1 don't know about you, but I get hungry — *every day.* And I find
that when I travel, a great way to get into the local scene quickly is
through my palate. I review and discuss Seattle and Portland's restaurants elsewhere in this book; here's where I get down to the specifics
and write about ten things I could eat over and over, and the best
places to get them.

Pie at the Dahlia Lounge

For those of us who have scoured the world for coconut-cream pie, it
may come as a surprise that the best one ever doesn't come from a
fancy restaurant in Hawaii, but from Tom Douglas's **Dahlia Lounge**
(2001 Fourth Ave. at Virginia Street; ☎ 206-682-4142) in Seattle. This is
a pie to be reckoned with, a pile of rich coconut cream on a flaky crust,
with shavings of white chocolate cascading over the top. It's also available by the whole pie at the restaurant's take-out bakery.

The Fries at Castagna

Portland's **Castagna** (1752 SE Hawthorne Blvd. at 17th Avenue; ☎ 503-
231-7373) is an elegant, urban restaurant that serves fine French and
Mediterranean foods, but don't think that just because it has fine-dining
items on the menu you can't order a plate of perfect french fries. Here
they ascend to the level of *pommes frites,* a crispy pile of julienned
potatoes that are crunchy and flavorful. They're practically a meal in
themselves and make a perfect late-night nosh at the adjoining Café
Castagna.

Crab Cocktails

Shrimp cocktail might be good, exotic even, but it pales in comparison to a Northwest Dungeness crab cocktail, which consists of chunks of sweet, fresh crab over a small layer of chopped celery with a dollop of piquant cocktail sauce dropped over the top. It's served at many fine restaurants, but the best way to eat one is at the unpretentious, stainless-steel lunch counter at **Jack's Fish Spot** (1514 Pike Place; ☎ 206-467-0514) at the Pike Place Market.

Piroshky!, Piroshky!

Russian *piroshky,* also known as pierogies in many places, are fairly basic pockets of dough filled with meats or a combination of things, but at the Pike Place Market's **Piroshky, Piroshky** (1908 Pike Place; ☎ 206-441-6068), they reach an unheard-of level that approaches an art form. The apple tarts are perfectly baked and redolent of cardamom and cinnamon, and Moscow Rolls are filled with a sweetened cream cheese. They're a must-stop treat on every single visit I've ever made to the Market.

Copper River Salmon

In Seattle, all salmon is not created equal. There is a big difference between a chum salmon and a king salmon, but the most vaunted fish of them all is the Copper River salmon, which arrives in May, fresh from the Alaskan river of its origin. This salmon is rich in oil and even darker in color than most kings, and its flavor is robust. It becomes the special at most seafood restaurants and is snapped up at grocery stores. If you see it on a menu, it's definitely worth the premium price charged.

Kerry Sears' Oysters

A platter of freshly shucked oysters on the half shell nestled on beds of cracked ice is a welcome sight at any fine restaurant, but it goes up a notch at **Cascadia** (2328 First Ave., between Bell and Battery streets; ☎ 206-448-8884), Kerry Sears' fine-dining restaurant in Seattle's Belltown. Sears picks only the tiniest, most delicate morsels of oyster from Puget Sound growers and then serves them with a rack full of test tubes that contain delicious dressings and *mignonettes* to drip onto the shellfish. It's the most exotic oyster presentation in the city and kicks off one of Sears' seven-course meals perfectly.

Kenny Giambalvo's Pasta

I'd follow Kenny Giambalvo wherever he goes in Portland. The chef and part owner of **Bluehour** (250 NW 13th Ave. near Davis Street; ☎ **503-226-3394**) first caught my attention at the helm of Pazzo, where he made a ravioli that I haven't been able to forget for five years. At Bluehour he does a dazzling selection of continental and Northwest dishes, but it's the pastas that linger in the memory. Whether it's a spaghetti dish, a penne served with venison and raisins, or a *casonsei* (homemade ravioli) pocket with a braised beef and porcini filling, it's sensational. Try anything he does that involves fresh, homemade noodles and local mushrooms, and you won't be sorry.

Huber's Spanish Coffees

Call them old-fashioned and flashy, more style than substance, but I love everything about the flaming Spanish coffees that they serve at **Huber's** (411 SW Third Ave. near Washington Street; ☎ **503-228-5686**), which has the distinction of being Portland's oldest restaurant. A guy who looks like he's been around since the place opened more than a century ago comes to the table with a heavy tray laden with liqueurs and coffee. He swirls several things together, lights it with his Zippo, and pours in coffee and whipped cream while the thing is still flaming. I tried it at home and smashed several glasses. It's easier to go to Huber's.

Halibut and Chips

I wouldn't take a chance on fish and chips at most vacation destinations (with the possible exception of London), but it's a must-try thing in Seattle. Forget about fish sticks and the cheap, oily stuff they serve as fish in other places; here, they take fresh lingcod or halibut flown in from Alaska, dip it in Panko, and fry to a golden brown. With a mound of fries, it's a delicious and cheap fast-food treat. They make a fine one at Seattle's **Little Chinook's at Salmon Bay** (Fisherman's Terminal; ☎ **206-283-HOOK**), with picnic tables that offer views of the Alaska fishing fleet tied up at long docks.

Larsen's Danish

It's pretty hard to find fault with a good Danish pastry anywhere, but how often can you buy one at an authentic Danish bakery? Seattle's Scandinavian heritage in the Ballard neighborhood is evident in the unusual food items found there (I wouldn't wish lutefisk on anyone but the staunchest Swedes, for example), including terrific Danish at the **Larsen Brothers Danish Bakery** (8000 24th Ave. NW at NW 80th Street; ☎ **206-782-8285**).

Chapter 30

Ten Words to Make You Sound Like a Northwesterner

● ●

In This Chapter

▶ Talking the talk

▶ Saying it like a local: Quirky Northwest pronunciations

● ●

*U*p to now, you probably had little reason to know what geoduck or Puyallup meant or how to pronounce other exotic Northwest words and places. Knowing them may be integral to the success of your vacation, however. Here's a rundown of the ten most commonly mispronounced words in the Northwest landscape, many of which were based on Native American derivations. Saying them right helps you avoid confusion, and spares you a lot of guff from the locals.

Willamette River

The river that runs through downtown Portland, so easily mispronounced, is the will-*am*-ette, not the will-a-*met*.

Puyallup

Most visitors simply scratch their heads in wonder at the name of this Northwest town near Tacoma that hosts a big fair every year. Your first and second guesses probably aren't even close: It's pronounced pyew-*al*-up.

Sequim

This is another place name that separates the locals from the tourists. This town on the Olympic Peninsula, the home to some awfully good oysters and crabs, by the way, makes the "e" silent: It's simply squim.

Glisan Street

This is a main drag that runs through Portland's Pearl District, so saying it wrong gives you away as a tourist in a heartbeat. It's pronounced *glee*-son, like the comedian, not *glye*-son.

Geoduck

That big, sloppy clam at the Pike Place Market that looks like it could eat you if given half a chance is something of a Northwest delicacy when stewed in a chowder. It's pronounced *goo*-ee-duck, and I dare you to take a couple home as souvenirs.

Aloha Neighborhood

This Portland neighborhood isn't a place brimming with Hawaiian goodwill, as the name may suggest, although a large population of Hawaiians does live in Portland. It's not even pronounced right: The locals call it a-*low*-a. Go figure.

Benson Bubblers

Those clovers of stainless steel drinking fountains mounted on pedestals on Portland's downtown streets aren't water fountains at all: They're Benson Bubblers, so named for the industrialist Simon Benson (namesake of the Benson Hotel), who donated the first ones to the city as a kind of stance against whiskey drinking. The fountains bubble constantly almost all year round.

U-Dub

Seattle's major university is officially known as the University of Washington, but you never hear a local call it that. You simply go to U-Dub, which is located in the U-district. The campus, by the way, is a lovely setting of redbrick buildings, tall trees, and distant views of Mount Rainier.

Pill Hill

If, God forbid, you get sick in Seattle, you'll probably get sent to a hospital or treatment center on what is officially known as First Hill, but which is widely known locally as Pill Hill thanks to its concentration of medical facilities, which include the Virginia Mason Medical Center and Swedish Hospital.

SoDo

Since the Kingdome in Seattle is no more (it was blown up in a spectacular implosion in 2000), you might not understand the acronym that is pronounced *so-dough*. It refers to the area south of the former Dome where Safeco Field now sits, as well as Starbucks' corporate headquarters. Local politicians try to claim that the "Do" part refers to "downtown," thus making SoDo still relevant, but it really refers to the late, not-nearly lamented Kingdome (from whose ashes is rising a sparkling new football stadium).

Chapter 31

Ten Ways to Look Like a Northwesterner

● ●

In This Chapter

▶ Appropriate wear for dinner out, a night on the town, or a hike

▶ How to get the "aggressively plain" look down

● ●

*O*kay, I admit it: People in Seattle and Portland are not exactly fashion plates. It's not that they don't know how to dress up; it's just that they prefer not to. You almost never see people going out in suits or fashionable dresses, and furs are absolutely nonexistent here. Casual and comfortable is the theme, and if you don't want to stand out like a sore thumb, you need to adopt some of the local fashion principles, as outlined in this chapter. "But what do I *wear*?," you wail, uncertain of what to do. As a general rule of thumb, when you go out at night in the Northwest, pretend that you're dressing to walk the dog . . . on a misty day . . . in a muddy park. You'll fit in just fine.

Flannels and Denim

Wearing a flannel shirt and a pair of blue jeans doesn't mean you're a lumberjack; it means that you weren't sure if the evening's dress code was business-casual or semi-formal. Jeans and flannels are accepted almost everywhere as the universal uniform of the Northwest. Ladies don denim skirts only if they're going to Portland's Rose Festival carnival or touring naval ships on the Seattle waterfront. If you're heading out on the town to a popular club or concert, wear the flannel shirt open over a plain T-shirt — rock and roll! Jeans in black and green are also acceptable, the former at art gallery openings and the latter at a save-the-salmon rally.

Plain Cotton Sweaters

You can't own enough lightweight cotton sweaters, preferably in plain, solid colors, unless you wish to trumpet your Scandinavian heritage (which is perfectly acceptable) by wearing a Swedish or Danish patterned sweater. Sweaters go great over a T-shirt or a turtleneck, complemented by jeans or a long skirt — but no necklaces or jewelry to clash with the plainness. A cashmere sweater is an acceptable alternative, but only in a muted color and preferably a cotton blend.

Sport Jackets and Scarves

Ooh, watch it, you're entering dangerous waters here. Wearing a sport jacket (for a man) or a fashionable jacket or scarf (for a woman) is possible, even welcome, but it must be pulled off with the utmost delicacy. Blue blazers and camel-hair should be left on the cruise ship, and black jackets over black T-shirts practically scream "I'm from L.A.!" Women look sharp in a man's sport jacket, preferably an older one (the sport jacket, not the man) that might have been a great find at the Value Village. Scarves almost never appear. Men can wear their sport jacket over an open shirt as long they make a concerted effort not to match everything (trousers, shirt, jacket, socks) too closely. When in doubt, try to dress as consistently to the ethic of Aggressively Plain as you can.

No Sweatsuits

Before you get the idea that anything casual goes here, don't even think about bringing your Fila sweatsuit to the Northwest, unless you're tall enough to pass as a member of the Utah Jazz. Sweatsuits of any kind are only to be worn in L.A. If you do decide to wear a sweatsuit and someone does look at you askance, start to run: Jogging, particularly in Oregon, allows you to wear anything.

Sturdy Shoes

Think wet here; for that matter, think flash flood. Footwear is meant to be functional, and little else. Up until a few years ago, everyone wore rubber-coated leather shoes with thick, pencil-eraser-colored rubber soles. They're due for a comeback. It's not unusual to see people at the store and otherwise in public wearing garden clogs. Smart leather shoes are the rule, preferably waterproofed, even on sunny days. Men wear Topsiders and running shoes; women like hiking shoes. It may be the West, but nobody here wears cowboy boots. If you sense crowds of people following you in the shopping mall, it's because you forgot and wore the lace-up espadrilles or Italian straps halfway to your calf, and everyone is intrigued to see if you'll fall.

Fashionable Sandals

Not allowed. Visible, painted toenails: No. Thongs and flip-flops: No, this is not Hawaii. Northwesterners are not particularly interested in looking at bare feet. Birkenstocks and sensible sandals made with some vague promise of promoting overall health are the exception. Wear socks with them.

Leather Coats, Yes

Black leather coats are the one fashionable item that people wear in the Northwest. They're a sensible garment for this climate, which is cool but not cold and frequently damp (not wearing your leather jacket because it's raining outside, or using an umbrella while wearing one instantly brands you as a tourist). Stick to motorcycle-jacket lengths and simple styles: Full-length leather works best for someone who can really pull off such a herculean fashion statement, someone like Shaquille O'Neal.

Portland Only

The flowing hippie dress or skirt done in bright, floral patterns is acceptable — nay, embraced with open arms — in Portland. You can even get away with wearing cut-off blue-jean shorts over black leggings if you're so inclined. Tie-dye is still "in" here. And if you're a man and have been mulling over growing a ponytail for your vacation to the Northwest, Portland is the place for you — but not Seattle, where hair styles are less demonstrative.

Parkas and Shells

Your choice of outerwear is where you can really express yourself. Your wind-and-rain-resistant parka in bright colors can practically scream, "I'll be hiking in the mountains this weekend!" or "a-kayaking I will go!" Stores like REI, Patagonia, and Columbia Sportswear have done quite well by shrewdly gauging the interests of the Northwest public, who want their outer layers breathable and lightweight, yet clearly visible to bears at a distance. This is where you can get away with wearing synthetic fibers. In fact, the approving nods you get at the Opera or Experience Music Project are because you look prepared for a sudden shower or an impromptu trek through the mountains.

Jewelry and Accessories

Rings are okay. Everyone wears rings, even multiple rings. A huge diamond, however, tells everyone in sight that you don't garden much. Earrings are fine, too. But necklaces, tennis bracelets, and large, ostentatious brooches? Not here in the Northwest. Every woman carries a purse, of course, but the practical-backpack ethos has crept into the collective psyche, so that purses now tend to resemble satchels. Leave the elegant Italian designer purses, and matching shoes, at home.

Quick Concierge: Seattle

Fast Facts

AAA Washington

General information: ☎ 206-448-5353. Emergency Road Service (24 hrs.): ☎ 800-222-4357.

American Express

Travel agency (6450 Southcenter Blvd.; ☎ 206-246-7661). To report lost or stolen cards: ☎ 800-992-3404. For information on traveler's checks: ☎ 800-221-7282.

ATMS

Widely available throughout downtown and on most retail strips. Ask your hotel for the location of the nearest one, or ask any storekeeper where to find one.

Baby-sitters

Ask your hotel to recommend one. Otherwise, **Best Sitters** (☎ 206-682-2556) or **The Seattle Nanny Network** (☎ 206-374-8688).

Camera Repair

Ballard Camera (1836 NW Market St.; ☎ 206-783-1121); **Ken's Camera** (1327 2nd Ave.; ☎ 206-223-5553).

Convention Centers

Washington State Convention & Trade Center (8th Ave. and Pike Street; ☎ 206-461-5840). Convention Center stop on downtown bus tunnel.

Dentists

Ask your hotel, or call **Dentist referral service** (509 Olive Way; ☎ 206-448-CARE).

Doctors

Call **911** for urgent situations. Go to a hospital emergency room for immediate care (see Hospitals), or call the **Doctor referral service** (☎ 206-448-CARE). If your child is sick and you're not sure if he or she needs care, call the **Children's Hospital Nurse Consultation** line (☎ 877-526-2500 or 206-526-2500).

Emergencies

For police, fire, and ambulance, call **911**.

Hospitals

Harborview Medical Center (325 9th Ave.; ☎ 206-731-3000) is the major trauma center. **Swedish Medical Center** (747 Broadway; ☎ 206-386-6000); **Swedish Medical Center/Ballard** (5300 Tallman Ave. NW; ☎ 206-782-2700).

Hotlines

HIV/AIDS/STD Hotline (☎ 206-205-7837). King County Children's Crisis Team (☎ 206-461-3222). Rape Relief Crisis Line (☎ 206-632-7273). Suicide-Survivors of Suicide Crisis Clinic (☎ 206-587-4010). Better Business Bureau (☎ 206-431-2222). Seattle Times Info Line (☎ 206-464-2000).

Information

Seattle-King County Convention & Visitors Bureau Visitor Information Center (Washington State Convention & Trade Center, 800 Convention Place at 8th Avenue and Pike Street; ☎ 206-461-5840). Internet: www.seattleinsider.com. Also, the **Seattle Times** Web site (www.seattletimes.com).

Internet Access

Many hotels offer Internet access in guest rooms or business centers. Otherwise, **Kinko's'** many locations are wired for high-speed access (735 Pike St.; ☎ 206-467-1767; 1335 2nd Ave., ☎ 206-292-9255; 1740 NW Market St., ☎ 206-784-0061).

Liquor Laws

The legal drinking age in Washington is 21. Beer and wine are sold at grocery stores and convenience stores. Hard liquor is only sold at state liquor stores (2105 6th Ave.; ☎ 206-464-7841; 515 1st Ave. N.; ☎ 206-298-4616), which are closed Sundays and holidays.

Maps

Available from the **Visitors Bureau** (see Information). Street maps generally available free from hotels and car-rental agencies. Great selection of local and international maps sold at **Metsker Maps of Seattle** (702 First Ave.; ☎ 206-623-8747) and **Wide World Books & Maps** (4411 Wallingford Ave. N.; ☎ 206-634-3453).

Newspapers

The **Seattle Post-Intelligencer** and the **Seattle Times** are both morning papers; they publish a joint Sunday paper. **The Seattle Weekly** and **Metropolitan Living** are free, arts-and-entertainment weekly newspapers. There is a major newsstand selling local and international newspapers and magazines at the **Pike Place Market** on the corner of First Avenue and Pike Place.

Pharmacies

Major pharmacies are **Bartell Drug Stores** (☎ 877-227-8355 for locations), **Rite Aid Pharmacies** (☎ 800-748-3243), and **Walgreens**, which operates 24-hour prescription service at its Ballard (5409 15th Ave. NW; ☎ 206-781-0056) location.

Police

Call **911** for emergencies.

Radio Stations

NPR is carried by **KUOW** at the University of Washington (**94.9** on the FM dial). **KJR-AM** (**950**) is an all-sports station, and **KIRO-AM** (**710**) is good for local news.

Restrooms

Hotels and restaurants have restrooms that are available to the public. You also find public restrooms at the **Pike Place Market** (one level below Pike Place), **Westlake Center, Pacific Place,** and **Seattle Center.**

Safety

Seattle has long enjoyed a sterling reputation for street safety, but recent events have tarnished the city's image. Avoid **Pioneer Square** late at night, particularly when the bars are letting out and during major revelry celebrations such as Mardi Gras. The area is completely safe during the day and early evening hours. Be wary of events that draw huge crowds onto the streets; these have grown increasingly violent in recent years.

Smoking

Smoking is not allowed in most restaurants, bars, or public buildings, and it is generally frowned upon in public gatherings. Look for designated smoking areas or confine it to your car or smoking-allowed hotel room if you can.

Taxes

Washington's sales tax is 8.8 percent. Hotel rooms within the Seattle city limits get hit with an additional 7 percent, and car rentals have an 18.3 percent rental surcharge and yet another 10 percent if you pick up the car at the airport.

Taxis

Can be found at most major hotels; otherwise, you need to call one (see Chapter 12 for info). Rates are $1.80 for the flag drop and $1.80 per mile.

Time Zone

Pacific Standard Time, which is three hours behind New York. Daylight Savings Time is observed in the summer.

Transit Information

Call **Metro** for 24-hour information (☎ 800-542-7876 or 206-553-3000) on buses. For ferry information and schedules, call the **Washington State Ferries** (☎ 800-84-FERRY or 206-464-6400).

Weather Updates

Seattle Times information line (☎ 206-464-2000).

Appendix B

Quick Concierge: Portland

Fast Facts

AAA Oregon/Idaho

Travel agency: ☎ 503-222-6767. Emergency Road Service (24 hr.): ☎ 800-222-4357 or 503-222-6777.

American Express

Travel agency (1100 SW 6th Ave.; ☎ 503-226-2961). To report lost or stolen cards: ☎ 800-992-3404. For information on traveler's checks: ☎ 800-221-7282.

ATMS

Available at banks and credit unions downtown and on retail corridors. Ask your hotel for the nearest one.

Baby-sitters

Ask your hotel to recommend one. **Wee-Ba-Bee Child Care** (☎ 503-786-3837).

Camera Repair

Advance Camera Repair (8124 SW Beaverton Hillsdale Hwy.; ☎ 503-292-6996). **Camera World** (400 SW 6th Ave.; ☎ 503-299-4010).

Convention Centers

Oregon Convention Center (NE Martin Luther King Jr. Blvd. and Holladay Street; ☎ 503-235-7575). The MAX stops right outside.

Dentists

Ask your hotel, or call **Multnomah Dental Society** (☎ 503-223-4731).

Doctors

Call **911** for urgent situations. Go to a hospital emergency room for immediate care (see Hospitals), or call the **Medical Society of Metropolitan Portland** (☎ 503-222-0156).

Emergencies

For police, fire, and ambulance, call **911**.

Hospitals

Centrally located hospitals are **Legacy Good Samaritan** (1015 NW 22nd Ave.; ☎ 503-413-7711); **Providence St. Vincent Medical Center** (9205 SW Barnes Rd.; ☎ 503-216-1234); and the **Oregon Health Sciences University Hospital** (3181 SW Sam Jackson Park Rd.; (☎ 503-494-8311).

Hotlines

Oregonian's Inside Line for community information (☎ 503-225-5555). Portland Center for the Performing Arts Event Information Line (☎ 503-796-9293). Poison Center (☎ 503-494-8968). Alcoholics Anonymous (☎ 503-223-8569). Counseling Services (☎ 800-THERAPIST). Legal Aid (☎ 503-224-4086).

Information

Portland Oregon Visitors Association (POVA) (Three World Trade Center, 26 SW Salmon St.; ☎ 877-678-5263 or 503-275-9750; Internet: www.pova.com). Websites for **The Oregonian** (www.oregonian.com) and **Willamette Week** (www.wweek.com) are also good sources.

Internet Access

Many hotels offer Internet access in guest rooms or business centers. Otherwise, go to a **Kinko's** copy center (221 SW Alder St.; ☎ 503-224-6550 and 950 NW 23rd Ave.; ☎ 503-222-4133). Online services also located at the **Multnomah County Library** (801 SW !0th Ave.; ☎ 503-248-5123).

Liquor Laws

The legal drinking age in Washington is 21. Beer and wine are sold at grocery stores and convenience stores. Hard liquor is sold at licensed liquor stores (925 SW 10th Ave., ☎ 503-227-3391; 4630 SE Hawthorne Blvd., ☎ 503-235-1573).

Maps

Available from **POVA** (see Information). Also available from **Powell's City of Books** (1005 W. Burnside St.; ☎ 503-228-4651) and, for members only, the **American Automobile Association** (AAA) (see AAA).

Newspapers

The **Oregonian** is the major daily paper in town. **Willamette Week** is a free arts-and-entertainment paper that is distributed at coffee shops, restaurants, and boxes around the city. Ask your hotel for copies of POVA's **Weekly Hot Sheet**, which lists major entertainment sources. A good newsstand is **Rich's Cigar Store** (820 SW Alder St.; ☎ 503-228-1700), which sells a number of out-of-town papers.

Pharmacies

Central Drug is downtown at 538 SW Fourth Ave. (☎ 503-226-2222). In the Hawthorne district, go to **Fred Meyer** (3805 SE Hawthorne Blvd; ☎ 503-872-3333).

Police

Call **911** for emergencies.

Radio Stations

KOPB (91.5 FM) is the local NPR affiliate. For news, try **KEX (1190 AM)**.

Restrooms

Hotels and restaurants have restrooms that are available to the public. You also find public restrooms at Pioneer Place and at Pioneer Courthouse Square.

Safety

Downtown Portland is generally safe for walking at any time of the day or night. One exception: Try to avoid the streets directly around W. Burnside Street in the Old Town/Skidmore and Chinatown districts late at night. Also be sure to lock your car in those areas at all times.

Smoking

Portlanders light up a bit more than their Seattle counterparts. Almost all restaurants are non-smoking, however, and some have smoking sections. Bars for the most part allow smoking.

Taxes

There is no state sales tax in Oregon on purchases. Hotel rooms are taxed 9 percent, and rental cars picked up in the city are taxed at 12.5 percent (22.5 percent when picked up at the airport).

Taxis

Generally available outside major hotels; otherwise, you have to call for a pick-up. See info in Chapter 21.

Time Zone

Pacific Standard Time, which is three hours behind New York. Daylight Savings Time is observed in the summer.

Transit Information

Call **Tri-Met** for info on buses and the MAX train: ☎ 503-238-7433.

Weather Updates

POVA's **weather information line** (☎ 503-275-9792), or **Weatherline Forecast Service** (☎ 503-243-7575).

Appendix C

Toll-Free Numbers and Web Sites

Airlines

Air Canada
☎ 800-776-3000
www.aircanada.ca

Alaska Airlines
☎ 800-426-0333
www.alaskaair.com

American Airlines
☎ 800-433-7300
www.americanair.com

Continental Airlines
☎ 800-525-0280
www.continental.com

Delta Air Lines
☎ 800-221-1212
www.delta.com

Horizon Air
☎ 800-547-9308
www.horizonair.com

Northwest Airlines
☎ 800-225-2525
www.nwa.com

Southwest
☎ 800-435-9792
www.southwest.com

Trans World Airlines (TWA)
☎ 800-221-2000
www.twa.com

United Airlines
☎ 800-241-6522
www.ual.com

U.S. Airways
☎ 800-428-4322
www.usairways.com

Car-Rental Agencies

Alamo
☎ 800-327-9633
www.goalamo.com

Avis
☎ 800-331-1212 in
Continental U.S.
☎ 800-TRY-AVIS in Canada
www.avis.com

Budget
☎ 800-527-0700
www.budgetrentacar.com

Dollar
☎ 800-800-4000
www.dollar.com

Hertz
☎ 800-654-3131
www.hertz.com

National
☎ 800-CAR-RENT
www.nationalcar.com

Thrifty
☎ 800-367-2277
www.thrifty.com

Making Dollars and Sense of It

Expense	Amount
Airfare	
Car Rental	
Lodging	
Parking	
Breakfast	
Lunch	
Dinner	
Babysitting	
Attractions	
Transportation	
Souvenirs	
Tips	
Grand Total	

Notes

Fare Game: Choosing an Airline

Travel Agency:_____ Phone:_____

Agent's Name:_____ Quoted Fare:_____

Departure Schedule & Flight Information

Airline:_____ Airport:_____

Flight #:_____ Date:_____ Time:_____ a.m./p.m.

Arrives in:_____ Time:_____ a.m./p.m.

Connecting Flight (if any)

Amount of time between flights:_____ hours/mins

Airline:_____ Airport:_____

Flight #:_____ Date:_____ Time:_____ a.m./p.m.

Arrives in:_____ Time:_____ a.m./p.m.

Return Trip Schedule & Flight Information

Airline:_____ Airport:_____

Flight #:_____ Date:_____ Time:_____ a.m./p.m.

Arrives in:_____ Time:_____ a.m./p.m.

Connecting Flight (if any)

Amount of time between flights:_____ hours/mins

Airline:_____ Airport:_____

Flight #:_____ Date:_____ Time:_____ a.m./p.m.

Arrives in:_____ Time:_____ a.m./p.m.

Notes

Sweet Dreams: Choosing Your Hotel

Enter the hotels where you'd prefer to stay based on location and price. Then use the worksheet below to plan your itinerary.

Hotel	Location	Price per night

Menus & Venues

Enter the restaurants where you'd most like to dine. Then use the worksheet below to plan your itinerary.

Name	*Address/Phone*	*Cuisine/Price*

Places to Go, People to See, Things to Do

Enter the attractions you would most like to see. Then use the worksheet below to plan your itinerary.

Attractions	Amount of time you expect to spend there	Best day and time to go

Going "My" Way

Itinerary #1

☐ _____
☐ _____
☐ _____
☐ _____

Itinerary #2

☐ _____
☐ _____
☐ _____
☐ _____

Itinerary #3

☐ _____
☐ _____
☐ _____
☐ _____

Itinerary #4

☐ _____
☐ _____
☐ _____
☐ _____

Itinerary #5

☐ _____
☐ _____
☐ _____
☐ _____

Itinerary #6

❏ _____
❏ _____
❏ _____
❏ _____

Itinerary #7

❏ _____
❏ _____
❏ _____
❏ _____

Itinerary #8

❏ _____
❏ _____
❏ _____
❏ _____

Itinerary #9

❏ _____
❏ _____
❏ _____
❏ _____

Itinerary #10

❏ _____
❏ _____
❏ _____
❏ _____

Notes

Index

● **C** ●

• *D* •

• *Restaurant Index* •

Notes

Discover Dummies Online!

The Dummies Web Site is your fun and friendly online resource for the latest information about *For Dummies* books and your favorite topics. The Web site is the place to communicate with us, exchange ideas with other *For Dummies* readers, chat with authors, and have fun!

Ten Fun and Useful Things You Can Do at www.dummies.com

1. Win free *For Dummies* books and more!
2. Register your book and be entered in a prize drawing.
3. Meet your favorite authors through the Hungry Minds Author Chat Series.
4. Exchange helpful information with other *For Dummies* readers.
5. Discover other great *For Dummies* books you must have!
6. Purchase Dummieswear exclusively from our Web site.
7. Buy *For Dummies* books online.
8. Talk to us. Make comments, ask questions, get answers!
9. Download free software.
10. Find additional useful resources from authors.

Link directly to these ten fun and useful things at **www.dummies.com/10useful**

For other titles from Hungry Minds, go to **www.hungryminds.com**

Not on the Web yet? It's easy to get started with *Dummies 101: The Internet For Windows 98* or *The Internet For Dummies* at local retailers everywhere.

Find other *For Dummies* books on these topics:
Business • Career • Databases • Food & Beverage • Games • Gardening
Graphics • Hardware • Health & Fitness • Internet and the World Wide Web
Networking • Office Suites • Operating Systems • Personal Finance • Pets
Programming • Recreation • Sports • Spreadsheets • Teacher Resources
Test Prep • Word Processing

FOR DUMMIES
BOOK REGISTRATION

Register This Book and Win!

We want to hear from you!

Visit **dummies.com** to register this book and tell us how you liked it!

- ✔ Get entered in our monthly prize giveaway.

- ✔ Give us feedback about this book — tell us what you like best, what you like least, or maybe what you'd like to ask the author and us to change!

- ✔ Let us know any other *For Dummies* topics that interest you.

Your feedback helps us determine what books to publish, tells us what coverage to add as we revise our books, and lets us know whether we're meeting your needs as a *For Dummies* reader. You're our most valuable resource, and what you have to say is important to us!

Not on the Web yet? It's easy to get started with *Dummies 101: The Internet For Windows 98* or *The Internet For Dummies* at local retailers everywhere.

Or let us know what you think by sending us a letter at the following address:

For Dummies Book Registration
Dummies Press
10475 Crosspoint Blvd.
Indianapolis, IN 46256

™

BESTSELLING BOOK SERIES